Greville Wynne's b
provided the vital
described in *The
Following the event
retired from spying,

By the same author

The Man from Moscow

GREVILLE WYNNE

The Man from Odessa

PANTHER
Granada Publishing

Panther Books
Granada Publishing Ltd
8 Grafton Street, London W1X 3LA

Published by Panther Books 1983
Reprinted 1984

First published in Great Britain by
Robert Hale Limited 1981

Copyright © Greville Wynne 1981

ISBN 0-586-05709-9

Printed and bound in Great Britain by
Cox & Wyman Ltd, Reading

Set in Times

Contents

Contents

Foreword

Recently I have learned that I am now at liberty to tell the story of the secret intelligence assignment I undertook in the colourful Black Sea port of Odessa in 1959. At this late date, the lives of certain Soviet citizens who played a role in this drama cannot be endangered by my disclosures.

In 1967, in a book called *The Man from Moscow* (published in the US as *Contact on Gorky Street*) I made brief mention of this assignment, which was a prelude to my later experiences as the agent who was sent to make contact with Colonel Oleg Penkovsky, perhaps the highest-ranking Soviet official ever to co-operate in the interests of peace with Britain and America. One or two further events which were referred to in passing in my earlier narrative (and were recounted out of their proper time-sequence) are here described in detail.

At that time, the British Foreign Office decided that their interests would be best served by disassociating themselves entirely from some of the revelations in *The Man from Moscow*. It was claimed by Whitehall that 'certain passages . . . would almost certainly have been objectionable on security grounds, had they been true.'

One learns to expect this sort of thing. Their squib, incidentally, came after I had, at the request of the 'D'-Notice Committee, agreed to delete mention of the public figures to whom Penkovsky had been introduced when he came to Britain, and episodes that do not reflect much credit on the working relations between British Intelligence and their American opposite-numbers.

Recently there has been a revival of uninformed and half-

witted speculation concerning the Penkovsky affair. I see
that Mr Chapman Pincher, in particular, has been attribut-
ing to his unnamed sources back-room gossip to the effect
that Penkovsky was nothing more than a spectacularly
successful Soviet 'plant', who took the Americans as well as
the British for a ride. The headline-begging implication is
that the Soviets used him to gull both our nations with
worthless 'disinformation'.

It is chiefly for this reason that I have decided to reveal
additional details of Penkovsky's involvement with British
Intelligence in the present book. Chapman Pincher was not
there with me in Lubyanka Prison when I saw Penkovsky
through the spy-hole of his cell, slumped and broken by his
Russian tormentors, or there would be no question in his
mind about his being a double agent. Penkovsky's life and
mine were inextricably entwined from the moment we first
met until we stood together in the dock in Moscow. The
cold and brutal result of this involvement is that I am alive
now and he is dead.

Therefore, I write this story for us both.

In this new book I also want to give some account of my
background, recruitment and war-time service as a counter-
intelligence operative in England, and of my 'normal' life as
husband and successful businessman that paralleled my
deepening involvement in the shadowy world of international espionage.

These autobiographical digressions may, I hope, give the
reader some insight in the psychological make-up of a man
who chose to lead a double life. Businessman or spy? Many
friends and colleagues (and for a time, Fleet Street as well)
have never been able to see round the conundrum or know
quite what to make of me. I should be very glad indeed if
these labels can be dispensed with before it comes time to
order an inscription for my headstone.

Once again: I write from personal experience. 'Major

Sergei Kuznov' was not the true name of the man from Odessa; it is, however, the name by which London referred to him in my presence. For obvious reasons, it was better that I should not have this information in the event that I was captured and interrogated. After more than twenty years, the Soviet authorities have doubtless long since concluded that the man in question was a defector, but his real name was one of the things that I was never told.

In writing this record I would like to express my grateful thanks to several colleagues who have encouraged me in the preparation of this book; in particular, to Robert Latona who as a professional writer has given me his generous help and advice.

Greville Wynne

Palma de Mallorca
Spain

Prologue: Exchange Point

Berlin, Checkpoint Heerstrasse.

It must be getting on towards dawn by now. There's a faint iridescence outlining the dark, looming clouds that hang over the city, just enough for me to make out their shapes. Of course it's dawn, I say to myself. The hushed hour when spies used to be marched out of their cells and shot. But this is 1964, and the rules of the spy game have been brought up to date. Instead of the traditional pay-off in front of the firing squad, governments are more inclined to make secret deals to each other's mutual advantage. One of ours for one of yours, what do you say, old fellow? A sensible and eminently civilized arrangement and one much appreciated by the captured spies who are the pawns in the exchange thus decided upon.

For obvious reasons, it is a policy which gets my wholehearted approval.

I am wedged between two Red Army guards in the back seat of a battered yellow Mercedes. All during the night it has been raining at intervals and now a thinnish drizzle starts up again, spattering heavily on the cobblestones of the deserted, tree-lined road that is bringing me closer and closer to freedom.

For now I am sure of it. They wanted to keep me guessing until the last possible minute, the bastards, enjoying their final twist of petty sadism. Twenty-four hours earlier, when I had been rushed in an armoured van from Lubyanka Prison to Moscow Airport, it had all been done without a hint of explanation. No doubt that bloody-minded KGB colonel, Chevshenko, was hoping I would think I was being taken to Hungary or another of the satellite countries for further interrogation. Something new and more brutal, perhaps. That had always been the pattern.

I wasn't altogether buying it, not even then. Usually whenever my captors had something new and nasty in mind for me, it was preceded by smirking threats or a barrage of ranting. This time not. So during the 1,500-mile journey by air I'd managed to keep track of the sun and guessed that we were heading west, not south to the Balkans. But there was no way I could be sure until I saw the signs in German at the airport when we finally landed.

Then they had taken me under heavy guard to the Red Army Barracks in the eastern zone of the divided city. The Soviet Consul was brought in to see me. There was a matter of some £30 which my wife had sent me to buy food and medicine while I was in prison. This is the first I've heard of it, needless to say. Now it is to be returned to me, he says in his amiable diplomat's English. But not in cash: currency regulations, you understand. Is there anything you might care to take back with you? For form's sake, I protest indignantly but finally agree to his suggestion of some caviar. Now there are three tins of the stuff going with me to the West. I was never particularly keen about caviar anyway, and much later, when I opened them, I was to find they were all covered with a green slimy mould.

Damn their caviar anyway. From the barracks I was whisked away to a detached house in a different section of the city surrounded by wire fencing and uniformed guards with ferocious-looking dogs. In the upstairs room where they have left me momentarily unattended there comes another man, civilian, who speaks to me in English.

'You are staying here tonight. I have to remain in the room with you at all times, but you can have a bath now if you wish and we'll have a meal up here later in this room.'

With an effort of will, I try not to let my face betray me to this flunkey and reveal the almost indescribable feeling of pure joy that his words have triggered in me. How many months since they last allowed me the luxury of hot water? And what bliss there is in simply being able to use a toilet with a proper seat to it. The stench of that lidless oildrum in my freezing cell in the prison at Vladimir is a memory I am already trying to bury. Another good omen pointing to imminent release: my suitcases are brought in, the ones they took from my hotel in Budapest on the day I was arrested. But all hopes and worries, all thought of past or future is driven from my mind when an orderly brings in a plate of hot food on a tray. The East Germans hovering by the door look on while I greedily devour the food they've put in front of me, their lips curling with contempt. I pay no attention to their muttered jibes; this miserable meal is the object of all my attention.

Afterwards, feeling marvellously fortified, I decide to have my revenge on them. As soon as the tray is fetched away, I take out the vile Russian sausages I have hidden in my pocket and peep out into the corridor. Nobody in sight. Excellent. Lifting up the chimney flue of the old cast-iron stove standing opposite the door. I thrust the sausages up the stove pipe as far as they will go. Come winter, when they tried to light a fire in there, they'd have the most awful stinking, smoking mess on their hands. Would they realize that this was one more act of despicable sabotage by the ungrateful imperialist spy? I certainly hoped so.

Childish? Yes, of course it was. But that was exactly the point, you see. It was by just such trivial acts of defiance that I'd managed to hang on to my sanity, or at the very least some elemental sense of human dignity, during my eighteen months' ordeal in two of Russia's most brutal prisons. James Bond might not have approved of such pointless mischief, but neither would he have understood how vital it was to maintain one's battered self-respect by not knuckling under to their bullying, striking back at their ludicrous regimentation in countless small and inconsequential ways. Otherwise, they broke you. It was that simple.

After a few hours of sleep I am awakened, given another meal with a steaming mug of coffee, and led off to the yellow Mercedes that has been waiting outside. A small convoy of black limousines goes ahead of us, and as we turn on to the Heerstrasse I catch a brief glimpse of the other traffic.

Now there are concrete blocks laid out in a zig-zag pattern in the middle of the road. The frontier checkpoint can't be far, as obviously these have been placed there as a slalom course to slow down vehicles trying to crash the barricades. The Mercedes pulls up in front of a blockhouse and I am unceremoniously thrust into a circle of soldiery with fixed bayonets. Someone has set up a telescope on a tripod, and two or three officers take turns at fiddling with it. On the other side of the border, in the growing half-light, I can make out a cluster of parked vehicles and huddled figures.

A short, stocky man with a chestful of ribbons showing under his open greatcoat comes up to me. He is the Commander of the Soviet Army in the German Democratic Republic. He barks something at me in a low voice and the civilian interpreter who is never far from my side says, 'You must remain absolutely silent. Make one sound and you will be shot.'

'Tell him to fuck off,' I snap back at him. Rarely do I swear, but this seems the only appropriate comment under the circumstances. As if they would dare shoot me now! My reply is translated, and the Commander's face goes bright red with fury.

A figure in the dim light seems to be coming briskly

towards us from the other side. A pair of my Russian escorts emerge from the group to meet him. I know this man. In what seems like another lifetime, we had met at a briefing in one of MI6's London safe houses. So he must be the one who is to identify me. He gives me a look, nods, and hands over a stiff, official-looking envelope to his Russian counterpart. He turns round, makes a signal with his hand to his people and steps aside.

I do not wait to be ordered. I will never have to wait for their orders again. I just start walking in the direction of the frontier. From the other side, a squatty figure in a yellow raincoat starts walking towards me. We pass each other in the eerie morning silence and for a brief moment we stop and exchange meaningless stares. I croak 'Good morning' to him; his plump, dark-complexioned face appears startled but there is no reply. He walks to his destination and I walk on to mine. I could not know it then, but the man in the yellow raincoat is Konon Trefimovich Molody, alias Gordon Lonsdale, the Soviet master-spy and given a twenty-five-year jail sentence in what the newspapers called the spy case of the century – my Insurance Policy as arranged by James.

Suddenly I am on the other side. It has taken just twelve minutes. Still half-dazed from shock and weakness, I am only vaguely aware of the roar of car engines turning over, of a gentle hand on my shoulder steering me towards a black limousine with Union Jacks stencilled beneath the headlamps, of the reassuring, almost-forgotten sound of voices speaking English. I see, hear and feel all this but some part of me still cannot seem to process the sensory data or take it all in. A part of my conscious mind refuses to believe that this is really happening.

All I know is that I am going home. I do not, dare not look back over my shoulder, now or ever again.

What happens to me in the next couple of hours flashes

by in memory as a parade of discontinuous sensations and images like a film that has jumped its sprockets. Strange that this should happen to me now, and not before. I know that I am brought straight to the home of an RAF Station Commander not very far from the checkpoint. The first thing his wife says to me is, 'Would you like a bath?' Blinking back the tears that are starting to collect at the corners of my eyes, I tell her, yes, thank you, I would very much indeed.

Towelling myself dry and feeling much better now, the gaunt reflection in the bathroom mirror catches my eye. For eighteen months I had not seen myself in a mirror. I move closer to inspect the damage. The face that stares back at me with ever-widening eyes is a face I scarcely would have recognized as my own. The sunken cheeks are easily accounted for. All told, I have lost three and a half stone of what I used to weigh. Almost fifty pounds, by God. How's that for slimming? The deep furrows scoring my forehead are the souvenir of countless interrogation sessions in Lubyanka. The stubby grey hairs sprouting from my close-cropped skull are as thin and patchy as the endless acres of stunted farmland that sweep eastward from Moscow in the direction of Vladimir, the city I will never be able to forget. Gentle pressure from my thumb is enough to set all my teeth wobbling in their sockets. Vitamin starvation, of course. My fingernails are likewise loose and brittle. The teeth would have to go. Hard to believe I was only a fit 42-year-old when the Russians picked me up, and now I've just turned 45. Whatever happened to the old, debonair me? I ask myself this question in a sudden mood of bitter levity. But at that moment freedom is too new and precious a gift to be undermined by self-pity.

The Commander and his wife couldn't have been kinder to me. Their offer of a real English breakfast I accept with more gratitude that I can easily convey to them. I can't help noticing my hostess's eyes knit together in dismay when she sees me attack the food on my plate like a famished wolf, holding the plate up with one hand and scooping forkfuls of egg into my mouth. Flustered, I catch myself and try to be unobtrusive about lowering my plate to the table.

'It's really very good,' I say, lamely.

Old habits die hard. Without wishing it, I have given these two kind people a glimpse of a state of mind which I still have not been able to shake. Noting his wife's evident concern, the Commander starts to chuckle. And all three of us are suddenly laughing uproariously.

'Well,' the Commander says at last, 'I'm sure you're anxious to be off. That is, if you're quite certain you're feeling up to it. There's an RAF Valetta waiting for you at our airbase, Galeta. Don't let that worry you though. If you'd rather rest up a bit.'

'No,' I said firmly. 'I just want to get home.'

'Good for you, Greville. Some people will be coming for you shortly.'

Not an hour after we have shaken hands and said our goodbyes, I am aboard a twin-engined military aircraft winging my way homeward to Britain. The inside has been luxuriously fitted out like an executive boardroom: pine panelling everywhere, swivel chairs and ample tables in the aft section. The VIP treatment. To be perfectly honest, I am revelling in this unaccustomed poshness.

There is one other passanger on board with me, the man from MI6 whom I glimpsed at the frontier when the exchange was carried out. His name is 'Roger', and I have a vague recollection that the couple of times we had met before I got the impression he was a fairly senior official in the service, though of course nothing was said – nothing is ever said – outright. Very considerately, he busies himself with papers from his attaché case while I occupy myself with yet another superlative breakfast of corn flakes, eggs and orange juice. Only when the steward has taken the tray away and brought me a glass of Scotch, do we begin our chat.

'What happens next depends entirely on how you feel about things,' he tells me. 'When we land at Northolt there'll be a mob of reporters waiting for you. No reason you should have to face them if you don't feel up to it. We can get you out to the country for a rest and let the doctors give you a good going-over, if that's what you'd prefer.'

I consider this for a moment. 'They're at Northolt now, you say. That means I won't be able to get back to my home until I've seen them. They'll all be hanging about the gate.'

'Quite right. It's probably just as well to get it over with. I leave it entirely up to you. Just let me know before we land and I can radio through. Remember, it's no problem getting you off to the country if you feel that's best and you can meet your wife and your son there.'

'I'll face the reporters.' With two good breakfasts in me and a few whiskies warming my belly, I feel fit for anything.

During the plane journey, I sit back in my seat with my eyes closed and try to think about what my future will be like, but find it next to impossible to consider it in any coherent way. Letting one's thoughts dwell on a future is a habit one learns to suppress after only a few weeks inside a Soviet prison, and they had kept me for eighteen long, agonizing months. A year and a half since that November evening in Budapest, the beginning of the ordeal.

It was a Friday, yes. Memories begin now to sweep over me, little quiet ripples on the pool of conscious awareness of my surroundings: the vibration from the engines, this fancied-up plane, my ultimate destination. Oddly enough, they take the form of questions.

What made them pick that particular day for my abduction and arrest? Try and figure that one if you can (I tell myself). It's the logical place to start. They must have known there would be witnesses. A very select gathering of English businessmen and officials from the Hungarian Ministry of Foreign Trade. I had invited them to my mobile exhibition caravan in Varosliget Park for drinks at five, after making sure the manager of the Hotel Duna I stayed at had spared no expense in laying out a spread of good food and abundant liquor for my very mixed bag of guests.

After all, it was what was expected of me. As a successful businessman with an established history of lucrative deals to which I had acted as a middleman between British manufacturers of heavy industrial equipment and machine tools, and the state-controlled buying agencies of the Soviet Union and its satellites, I had a reputation to keep up. It had taken me six years to build up my business to the point where I was able to arrange for informal parties such as this one.

The talks had been coming along well, I thought. But the Hungarians had left after two hours, all in a group. I had seen them to their limousines and was just about to start up the steps and rejoin my colleagues when I heard my name being called out and quickly turned round. Suddenly the cold pangs of fear gripped me; I knew something was going to happen and that I would never make it back to the caravan.

There were four of them. Heavy-set, expressionless, all dressed identically in trilby hats and belted raincoats. They came from nowhere, closing in on me, and the next thing I knew, my arm was wrenched back and up to my shoulder-blade in a vicious hammer-lock. I saw my shifty-eyed Hungarian interpreter standing impassively in the shadows, my British driver frozen with astonishment in the driveway. I managed to cry out as I was dragged and pushed towards the waiting saloon car that materialized ahead of me. Then something hard came crashing down on my skull and I could remember nothing more.

Eighteen months ago. It happened on 2 November 1962. Today is 22 April 1964. That long a time.

My hand trembles just a little as I light up another cigarette. Roger is busying himself with his papers. More memories, more questions.

How many hours from my life had been spent in their windowless interrogation rooms, filthy dens fit only for animals, confronting some slovenly, chain-smoking general or colonel, the pride of the KGB, yelping and bawling threats at me? Dozens of hours.

How many days lying on a reeking pallet, staring up at the crumbling ceiling of my cell, conscious only of the unbearable stench of body filth, faeces, and disease? Hundreds of days. Two endless Russian winters shivering under my thin blanket while the sub-zero numbed my face and limbs.

How many mugs of sour tea in the morning, how many bowls of yellow soup with fish eyes floating on a thin film of grease, a piece of stale bread to keep me alive for one more day? Thousands of meals like that.

The images blur and fade; Roger glances my way when a deep, involuntary sigh escapes my throat.

He attempts a smile. 'It won't be long now,' he tells me. 'Sorry?'

'Until we land. Don't want to change your mind? About the reporters, I mean.'

'No, not at all. It is something else.' I turn and gaze at the wispy trails of cloud through the cabin window. But his mention of reporters has set me thinking.

'What do I tell them?' I ask Roger.

'Tell them that you're glad to be home, what else?'

'I don't mean that. How do you want me to play it? I still have no idea of what my position is, officially.'

Roger gives it a moment of thought. 'I take your point. Of course, the Foreign Office came out with statements disclaiming any knowledge of you and your activities when the Soviets had you in the dock. The Fleet Street boys have had no help from us in figuring out how much truth there was in your prepared confession.'

'I suppose they're going to be after me now.'

Already I can see a glimpse of what lies ahead of me. Shall I go on pretending that I was an innocent business-man who just happened to fall into the clutches of the nasty Russians and was put through a hellish time? Or should I come out and admit that for ten years I have been working under the direct orders of the British Secret Service? How the Russians had tried to pry that admission from me! I know there will come a time in the future when disclosure of the real story can do no harm to the Russian principals with whom I was involved. I am thinking of one particular man, condemned by his own countrymen to a traitor's death, but possibly still alive. Oleg Penkovsky, my collaborator and my friend.

Not now, but someday. The British public deserved to know the truth; I would get it down on paper for the sake of my own peace of mind, if nothing else.

'It'll all die down eventually,' Roger had told me.

I do not answer but I am silently thinking to myself: no, never. Not for me, it won't. Realizing that, making up my mind in that aeroplane even before I had set foot in England, marked the beginning of my new life.

PART ONE
A Spy in the Making

1

Valley Childhood

Everything has its real beginning somewhere in the past. Fate, if you believe in it, or a given set of circumstances may thrust you into a new or unexpected situation, but something has already happened to prepare the way and determine the final outcome. I think this is particularly true in my case. How does one get to be involved in the murky world of international espionage? I've been asked this question a hundred times and always my answer is the same: you don't. It's something that just happens to you, if it happens at all. Later, thinking back on it, you realize it isn't quite as simple as all that. So many seemingly insignificant things have already tipped the balance for or against.

Whatever instinct it was that led me towards undercover work probably has its roots in the somewhat banal fact that, as a child, I suffered from dyslexia. Fifty years ago, this common educational disability went completely unrecognized as such, and the difficulties I had learning to read and write meant that I was regarded by parents and teachers alike as a boy without a future, a truly hopeless case. As a result, I had to become a precocious expert in the art of dissimulation. Learning everything from memory. Arriving at school exams with my arm in a sling and a plea that I might be allowed to dictate my answers to the teacher. Often enough, it worked. Coming up with the most ingenious excuses when it was my turn to read the lesson in Sunday School. Little tricks of winning people's sympathy, making them feel sorry for you, before they had a chance to stop and realize how strange my behaviour might otherwise appear. And all the while keeping up a 'cover' as the most accident-prone, luckless schoolboy that ever lived. These constant stratagems and role-playing were for me an early if unwitting training in the essentials of how to lead a double life.

In every other respect, I suppose the preliminaries to my future career were nothing much out of the ordinary. I was born in Shropshire in 1919. When I was about two years old, my father was offered a job in South Wales, so my three sisters, my mother and I followed him there to the mining village of Ystrad Mynach, about twelve miles from Cardiff.

Unlike many Welsh villages of the 1920s, Ystrad Mynach was neither an appalling case study in industrial blight nor yet a place that could be called unduly picturesque. It fell somewhere between the two extremes, a pleasant enough village to grow up in. Cheerless granite houses with slate roofs where the working people lived. A half-dozen chapels of as many different denominations, Salvation Army included. And in any direction you'd care to look, the slag piles standing sentinel round the outlying mines that kept the village economically on its feet. Then there was Powell Dwffryn, my father's employers, whose engineering works supplied equipment and castings to all the collieries in the area.

Dad was what you might call an extreme case of the old-fashioned homebody and working man. His life was divided between his job at Powell Dwffryn and his home; and of the two, I'm sure it was the first of these that gave him the most satisfaction.

Here was a man utterly without any sense of personal ambition, who never dreamt of questioning his lot in life. As senior foreman, his take-home pay of six pounds per week (which was always left out on the mantelpiece for my mother to pocket and disburse) was just about adequate for a family that knew how to budget tightly and look to every little domestic economy. But never was he allowed to keep even one penny for himself. On Saturdays, a truck would pull up in our drive and unload a case of beer which had to last out the week. Once in a very great while, there might be a bottle of whisky for him as a special indulgence, but that was as far as the leash of family finances could be stretched to accommodate him.

He never complained about it, though. One day, when I was perhaps thirteen or fourteen years old, I asked him, 'Why aren't you like Mr Beanland?' He was the general manager at the plant and I had got to be friendly with his son Albert. The Beanlands lived in an enormous, well-kept house, went about in a company car, and owned the first gramophone I'd ever set eyes on.

'Mr Beanland doesn't work as hard as you do,' I went on. 'And they even went on holiday for three weeks in Swansea.'

My father was not the sort of man who would be put out even by a question like that. Patiently, as if explaining something obvious to a small and none too bright child, he just said, 'I like my work.'

It's hard to imagine a greater contrast in personalities than him and my mother. Even my sisters and I thought it odd that they should have ended up married to each other. She was a stoutish lady with hard-chiselled, almost masculine features, much given to wearing flower print dresses in outlandish colours. They met, so I was told, at a carnival song contest where their rendition of 'Bluebells I gather' won some sort of prize. Father, no doubt, was hooked before he knew what was happening to him.

That they were able to get on at all was mainly due to my father's unwavering policy of accepting whatever life pitched to him. Had he dared to speak his mind, I'm sure our house would have erupted in bloody warfare. For my mother's sole purpose in life, it often seemed, was to hoodwink an indifferent world into believing we were living beyond our station.

Sometimes this would be carried to ridiculous extremes. My youngest sister, Nada, was sent to a fee-paying private school in Cardiff. No matter that we could hardly afford what it cost in train fares, school uniforms, books and tuition. It was all part of the great, never-ending show that had to be put on for the neighbours' benefit. Likewise, we always had miners' wives calling twice a week at our house to pick up and return a hamper full of laundry. My mother could not bear the thought of our wash hanging on a line in the back garden just like everyone else's. Having a woman come by our home was even better, as that way the neighbours would be sure to know that we could afford to send the laundry out.

Despite all this, I very much doubt whether any of the people she so desperately hoped to impress were taken in by my mother's pretensions. Somehow she managed to quarrel with nearly all of the women in the neighbourhood. Who made such an ungodly racket banging that gate? Isn't it shameful the way those people don't look after their front gardens? Mrs Usher from the house next door and my mother were forever shouting at each over something trivial like that. In the midst of one of these verbal brawls, I remember Mrs Usher abruptly said, 'You are either a marvel or a mystery,' and walked away, slowly shaking her head.

Because of these on-going neighbourhood squabbles, it wasn't easy for me to make friends with the other children who lived in Tredomen Villas. (This short terrace was lined with company-owned bungalows and two-storey houses for middle-echelon workers, a few minutes' walk from the engineering works.) My father, too, had his problems as a result of the feuds, but the men took care not to let this spill over into their own friendships. He would have to apologize to Mr Usher: 'Oh, there they are going at it again. But you know what it's like. It's their age, their age.'

'Don't think nothing of it, Bert,' Mr Usher replied. 'I understand.' Neither one wanted to get dragged into it.

As for me, I learned early on that it was safer and by far more pleasant simply to get out of the house the first chance I got and wander around on my own. Most of the time when Mother did not have me running errands, I would hang about with boys of my age, exploring the pleasant green countryside away from the house. We played football, climbed trees, and made friends with the signal-box man whose house was behind the railway station. Farther afield, we all enjoyed tracking foxes, hunting for snakes, or building dams in the sooty-black streams that straddled the coal seams. It took me a few years to work it out that all free-running water was not necessarily this colour. We had great fun in those days roving about the countryside. Perhaps this is one reason why I've never been able to feel really comfortable in a typical family situation, tied down to a routine of home and work. The old urge to get out and about and have a look at what's going on in the world always prevails in the end.

School was the next big item in my young life. For me, it was the council elementary school. Of recent construction, it was run by people who clung to strictly Victorian ideas of discipline and unsparing corporal punishment. Boys and girls were segregated from the moment their parents first signed them up for kindergarten.

We had to learn all the usual things, reading and maths but, apart from the regular curriculum, religion and the Welsh language were also forced down our unwilling throats. Certainly the standard of teaching I was exposed to did nothing to help my dyslexia – not to mention force-feedings of Welsh grammar on the side. Let that be a warning to parents and pedagogues.

Every time I was called to the blackboard, I'd be risking a terrible chewing-out in front of the class and quite likely three or four of the finest with the master's supple cane. Fear, I'm told, is no longer promoted as an incentive to budding scholars, and I have to say that it accomplished very little practical good in my case. The class, however, had some fine entertainment at my expense and for all I know it gave these men with the ready birch some sick kind of satisfaction. No matter how hard I struggled, I simply could not manage even to copy the letters of the alphabet in any recognizable way. So I learned what I could by repeating the master's words silently to myself, trying to review and order these snippets as I walked home from school. This went on for years, until in the end they simply gave up on me.

By the time I left school at fourteen, I had developed a passionate interest in electricity. Science and technical drawing had always been my strong suits, so I suppose it was inevitable. Electrical gadgets in particular were a source of endless wonder. There was an older friend of mine named Ambrose, a dark, curly-haired lad with a serious turn of mind who first introduced me to what would eventually be my life's work. He had put together an electric hooter for his bicycle that actually hooted. Four times out of five, at any rate. That impressed me no end.

'How could a battery make that noise?' I demanded. Patiently, Ambrose tried to explain what a circuit was and how it worked. To me, he was a boy genius in the Edison class. We spent long winter evenings together fiddling with wires, coils and simple solenoids and, guided by an assortment of twopenny wireless magazines and a borrowed set of earphones, managed to build a primitive, if perfectly functional cat's-whisker radio receiver.

The most exciting time of the year for us schoolboys was in the spring when the fair came to our village. We'd be lolling about the fields when the pitchmen and their wagons were due to arrive and offer to help in setting it up. Another annual event was the Sunday School outing on Whit Monday, when the entire class would set out for Barry Island and they'd put on a special train for us. For months we'd have been hoarding pennies to glut ourselves on toffee and sweets. Later in the summer we had the church fête. Colonel Lindsay, the incumbent village squire, used to open his magnificent house and gardens to the local people and I was happy to be among the boys recruited to hand out programmes, sell raffle tickets, and collect money at the gate.

In the mid-Thirties, when the Depression had come down on the Welsh mining country like a boot in the face, the Working Men's Hall was the scene of a much less happy venue as literally hundreds of out-of-work miners and factory hands queued up on Friday mornings for the dole. It was terrible to see these men just standing there, their shoulders stooping, an expressionless, beaten look on every face, waiting in the queue for hours on end. One by one they would doff their cloth caps and shuffle inside to draw their miserable thirty shillings from the government. Incredibly, there was never any trouble. The Salvation Army sent round horse-drawn soup kitchens to hand out bowls of gruel from the flap-down hatches at the sides and back of the wagon.

The thing I'll always remember are the stalls in the square where hucksters of every description tried to prove the eternal truth in the old adage about a fool and his money. Medicine men called out that they possessed a sure

cure for arthritis or heartburn; musicians, jugglers and
conjurers all wandering round with a hat in their hand.
Quite a lot of unofficial gambling went on there too. The
miners of the valley would lay down their money on
whippet races, cockfights, just about anything that came
their way.

When we were on holiday from school, it used to be fun
to go along to the dole queues and gape at the man with the
performing dog, the ventriloquist in a bowler hat, or the
shrivelled old man with no teeth and a stubble of white
whiskers auctioning off trinkets or cutlery. As young boys
in an otherwise sleepy, out-of-the-way Welsh village, it all
seemed terribly colourful and lively. Only when I was a bit
older did I begin to see the horror of it.

I think it was the shock of the Depression that made me
aware that side by side in our little village there existed two
vastly different ways of life. By Ystrad Mynach standards
only could my family have been called reasonably well-off,
that is, on an economic and social par with the successful
shopkeepers, garage owners, factory draughtsmen and 'that
sort' of people. You had to look quite a few more rungs up
the ladder to find Mr Beanland and his class, families where
the men all wore trilbies in the style of Anthony Eden and
met regularly to play golf on the links just outside the
village.

As time went on, however, I saw that the taproots of the
British class system extended even as deep as my little
group of friends. While I might have a simple meal of
brains or trotters for lunch, plenty of my schoolmates had
to be content with dry bread and jam. Then, too, my
mother saw to it that I was always well-dressed and
presentable. Other children were kept home from school
because their parents could not afford to have their boot
heels repaired. My friend David's father, a miner, would
come home at the end of a day's bone-breaking, grimy toil

and wash himself in a tin basin on the stone floor of the kitchen, after which every other member of the family took a turn in it.

With this awareness, there was growing within me a determination that I would not let myself be caught up in the oppressive circle of poverty and hopelessness I felt closing in on me. I had good reason to be frightened, even at that age. I'd be out of school in another few years, and then what? My parents were talking about sending me to the School of Mines. That meant the rest of my life 'down the pit'. At best, Father would be able to arrange something for me with Powell Dwffryn. I didn't want that either. Prompted, no doubt, by my mother's incessant social striving and my father's personal work ethic, the more ambitious side of my nature was starting to take shape.

Very well, I'd set my mind to making some money and see what came of it. Lying about my age, I got my first paper route when I was ten. Up and out of the house at seven every morning to pick up the papers at the station and cover a mile before school began. I was paid a penny for every half-dozen papers that reached their destination without complaint. On Saturday morning, the local baker would have two or three boys to help out pulling loaves from the ovens and stacking them on trays to cool. A shilling for a morning's work. Soon I had enough money to buy a second-hand, rather shabby and rust-worn bicycle. This purchase was in the nature of capital improvements since, with a bicycle, I was able to double my income from the paper route.

I was fourteen years old and still living at home when the first tremors started to shake my complacent adolescence. Mother had fallen ill and was in bed for about a week. My sisters took over the cooking and housework and Father went about his usual routine. Nothing seemed amiss. But one night when I came home late, long after tea, my father was waiting for me at the door. He put his hand on my shoulder and said very quietly, measuring his words with care, 'I'm afraid your mother is very seriously ill. The doctor is here and I've called the vicar because I think she is going to die. You must be a brave boy and not say anything to her.'

Reverend Williams came and gave her the last communion and the next day she was dead. Cancer or brain tumour, I never did find out exactly what it was. Not that it made any difference. It had happened with such chilling suddenness, we were all too stunned to take it in. My father's uncanny self-possession had its effect on us. He brought his children up to her bedroom for the last time. 'You must see this for yourselves so as to understand something about life.'

As is the way in small villages everywhere, all of the neighbours turned out for the burial, even the one she had been bickering with for as long as I could remember. Everyone tried to be helpful to my father. That Sunday, as the vicar intoned the funeral service, I was at the organ, pumping. It was all that I could do for her now.

2

Cloak and Dagger

No, you wouldn't call it a particularly happy home life. I suppose a certain lack of affection in early youth could be taken as a decisive factor in the grooming of any future spy. Penkovsky was another one, though certainly he had it much worse than I ever did. He never even knew his father, a White Russian officer killed in battle when he was still a baby. I've heard it argued that men who get into this line of work are secretly looking for figures of authority to tell them what to do with their lives; it may be so, I wouldn't want to make too much of it, however.

In my case, it was always my mother who had the final say in household affairs. If one of my sisters was caught doing something 'unladylike', my mother was the one to read out the riot act. Father sat still and said nothing. When he came home from work at half past five and we'd all sat down more or less together for high tea of fried faggots, potatoes, and cakes, he'd lose no time in pulling his armchair up close to the fire, tamping his pipe, unfolding the evening paper and reaching for his first bottle of beer. He went to bed at ten and was up at six the next morning and that was his life.

After my mother died, the day-to-day routine of living gradually reasserted itself, bringing a kind of peace. Father went back to his job and Nada rolled up her sleeves and took over the cooking and housekeeping part of it.

It sounds cruel to say it, but I honestly don't think we missed her all that much. My sisters were free now to invite their friends over to the house to listen to our newly-acquired gramophone, and keep company with the young men they fancied. No more of my mother's constant criticism of how they dressed, how they should wear their hair, who was too 'common' to be seen with. Father made it a point not to interfere with our lives. He stayed with his pipe and his chair by the fire, pondered the football pools, and now and then stepped out in the evening for a pint.

I was then in my last term at school, more apprehensive than ever about my immediate prospects and my long-term future. Only one hopeful sign pointed to better things to come. Realizing that my interest in electrical engineering was serious, Father paid for me to take a correspondence course in the subject. Then someone told me about the technical college at Bargoed, a town about five miles from where we lived. Just before school finished, I pedalled over there on my bicycle and had a talk with the principal. I told him how keen I was to learn, and was honest about the difficulties I'd been having with the written word. Sensibly, and happily for me, I was allowed to enrol. Getting back and forth on my bicycle took a bit of effort, especially in winter, but I wouldn't have missed these classes for anything.

School ended, and that was a relief. I started in as a day-labourer at Powell Dwffryn. As a stop-gap measure and a necessary evil, I didn't mind it so much. I knew that my father's cosy world of machinery, cutting presses, boilers and casting furnaces would never be mine. Still ambitious, still desperately anxious yet hopeful of making a life for myself a long way from Depression-ridden Wales, I decided to take the matter of my future into my own hands.

I went on my bicycle all the way to Caerphilly to the head office of Gibson Ltd, Electrical Contractors. Mr Gibson, the owner, was quite an important local figure and I had to wait several hours to see him. Every time his secretary would ask what I wanted, I repeated nervously that I wished to speak to Mr Gibson himself.

Finally the great man emerged from behind the pebble-glass doors. He was a short, wiry man well-past middle age, but with sufficient dirt on his hands to show he was not the kind of boss who ran things from behind a desk. After conferring a moment with the secretary, he turned to me with a baleful look of impatience.

'Well, and who are you?' he demanded sharply.

'My name is Wynne, sir, and I should like very much to speak with you.'

'To speak with me. I see. And what, if I may so inquire, do you wish to speak to me about?'

'I – I want a job.' I quickly explained that I'd been going to night school and what I had learned there.

He looked good and hard at me for a long minute, fingering the buttons on his vest. 'Very well. You won't earn much until you can prove yourself, but I'll give you a trial at seven and six a week. Can't promise more than that, mind you.'

I could hardly believe it had all been so easy. 'Fine by me, sir. When can I start?'

Mr Gibson was already halfway out the door. He glanced over his shoulder and said, 'Now. You can get busy loading up that lorry outside.'

When I got home that evening and explained where I had spent my day, Father just grunted and took a deep puff from his pipe. The next day, without saying anything, he went to call at Gibson's to see that the firm I'd got myself mixed up with was sound. It was the first time in all his years at Powell Dwffryn that he had taken a day off from work.

To begin with, my job was to carry tools and equipment around for the workmen and lend a hand on the loading dock when a crew was sent out. Soon, with Mr Gibson's approval, I was doing some of the simpler jobs on my own. Most of their work involved wiring up new buildings for light fixtures and power points, and making repairs to existing installations. There were also a number of villages in that part of Wales still undergoing conversion to electricity. Before the end of my eighteen months at Gibson's, he was allowing me to complete the wiring up of a couple of small, private houses entirely on my own.

In due course, I learned that my evening classes would qualify me for a new government scheme which allowed apprentices from depressed industrial areas to further their studies with the help of a small stipend and a guaranteed part-time job. Having passed the required examinations – giving my answers orally, or making drawing to explain what I couldn't put into words – I was given the choice of going to Manchester, Nottingham or Rugby for training. The year before, a friend of mine named Reg had been awarded the same kind of grant. One weekend, when he was back in Ystrad Mynach to visit his family, I asked him where he thought was the best place for me to go.

'Come on up to Nottingham,' he said without an instant's hesitation. 'Here's why. First, you've got Boots the Chemists – about seven, eight thousand there. Raleigh Cycle Company; they've got five thousand or so. Ericsson's Telephone have three thousand by day and another two thousand by night. Then the Beeston Boiler Company—'

'Wait, hold up just a minute! What d'ye mean by all this thousands business? Thousands of what?'

'Unmarried girls, you idiot!' He exploded in a fit of laughter. 'Don't you see?'

Ah, well, he did have a point worth making. British factories before the war did not take on married women. In a big industrial city like Nottingham the prospects were certainly to be reckoned with.

There was just one obstacle to be overcome: my father. I asked Reg to stop by and have a talk with the old man, stressing the career opportunities, not the girl situation.

Father agreed with surprisingly few reservations. 'The Basset boy, young Jackie, I hear he's gone for the Merchant Marine. I guess it can't be too easy for a young lad making a start these days.' With all of South Wales in the maw of the Depression, even the most senior men in the mines and factories could count on no more than three, and in many instances only a single day's work from one week to the next.

The money I needed for the train journey from Cardiff I got by selling the motorbike I'd salvaged from the scrap heap at Gibson's and lovingly rebuilt. It was one of those old belt-driven cycles where you had to put the oil and the petrol into the tank together, and it had served me well for getting around to work and back and to Bargoed in the evenings for night school. Now its last useful act would be to provide the means of my deliverance from Ystrad Mynach.

Reg was waiting for me when I at last got off the train in Nottingham Station. He and four other students had hired a leaky old houseboat which they kept moored on the River Trent; there was room for a fifth. In accordance with the terms of my grant, Ericsson's Telephone Company took me on as an apprentice; they were a big outfit in those days, specializing in all sorts of communications systems, telephone exchanges and traffic control equipment. They put me to work in the maintenance department, the idea being to give their apprentices a grounding in practical job wiring, doing repairs and installing factory extensions.

My classes at Nottingham University occupied a few hours in the evening and on Saturday mornings. The instructors I seemed to draw were all good, practical men. By this time I was finally beginning to master the maddening intricacies of reading and writing. Outgrowing the dyslexia that had always been a blight on my life gave me a tremendous boost of confidence at my studies.

The world into which I was tentatively feeling my way bore little resemblance to the tight and (as it now seemed) dismal village I'd known as a child. I was anxious to meet new people and extend my horizons. As befitting my new status I went to Burton's and had myself measured for a tailor-cut suit and invested in a respectable-looking Inger-soll watch. I had to work on and off for local contracting firms when the rest of my class was on holiday to pay for these touches of dandyism – the suit cost all of £1 10s – but in my mind I was preparing myself for great things and there was no doubt the sacrifice would be worth it in the end.

Acquiring a much-needed bit of social polish was my number-one priority. Monday evenings would find me at Halford's Dancing Academy, determined to master the foxtrot and other intricacies of ballroom technique. Four men lined up opposite four girls, we'd be shown the steps then have a tentative go at it ourselves. Overcoming my initial clumsiness, I became a regular at the Palais de Danse, Greyfriars Hall, and the Victoria Ballroom where the girls were plentiful and the shilling entrance-fee put no strain on anyone's finances. It was all 'quick, quick, slow' in those days, with an occasional tango thrown in for variety's sake. By today's standards, these would be accounted pretty tame affairs. No drunkenness, no fights, and nobody seemed to be in the least put out when the girls announced they had to be home at eleven o'clock sharp.

Living on that mad, wonderful houseboat was a kind of education in itself. The eldest of the five boys who shared quarters on board was Tony, a ginger-haired Scottish lad employed at Ericsson's as a full-time draughtsman. He naturally took charge of things and was very good about seeing that everything was running smoothly and none of us had reason to grumble. Every morning the bilge had to be pumped out by hand, and the dingy bailed out. Then we would take turns with the rest of the chores, Reg doing the cooking, someone else the cleaning and washing-up.

With five practical-minded student engineers to fall back on, we soon had the houseboat fixed up and liveable. Fresh water was a bit of a problem until we got a pump system running from the electric impeller set up at the weir, drawing water from an old zinc tank we had salvaged from somewhere. Each of us had his own narrow cabin which our various girlfriends fitted out with curtains and other pleasant homey touches. When one of the lads had occasion to entertain a young lady aboard, privacy was ensured by means of a little red warning light, which when switched on meant: This lounge is engaged, so get the bloody hell out of here.

Mostly, I grant you, we were all looking to have a good time. I had my youth and my government training grant and that was more than enough to keep us happy. Twenty at a time, my friends and I would assemble on Thursday nights at the Ritz Café, where a shilling at the door entitled one to coffee, biscuits and the amenities of a live orchestra. We called ourselves the Ritz Café Companions. One day a dozen of us decided to go down to London on the train and take in the sights. It was my first trip to the big city. After Ystrad Mynach, Nottingham had seemed the epitome of cosmopolitan living; now, lunching with my friends in a Lyon's Corner House looking out on Piccadilly Circus, I saw that as an ambitious nineteen-year-old social climber I still had a long way to go.

That was in 1938, the year of Munich. Headlines screamed about the 'crisis', sandbagging and ARP practice were introduced, gas drills with box-like respirators were solemnly announced. If we demanded a full measure of merriment from our lives, it was only because any fool could see that Europe was moving headlong into war, and none of us needed any reminding that our age-group would

be the first to get the call-up. Understandably, we were
determined to live it up for as long as the fun lasted. Our
unspoken thoughts regarding the world's future and our
own were not by any means happy ones.

My old friend Reg was the first from our little group to
enlist. He chose the Auxiliary Air Force and, before long,
another half-dozen boys had followed him. That was the
glamour service. I had no desire whatsoever to remove
myself from contact with dear Mother Earth, and accordingly put myself down for Officer Training Corps at the
university, continuing with my classes in electrical engineering.

Those first few months of OCTU we were issued
broomsticks to present and shoulder when we drilled, real
rifles being in short supply. I was pleased, however, with
the instructor they'd assigned us, an elderly colonel whose
enthusiasm for the military life and desire to be useful had
kept him off the pensioned list. Personal cleanliness and
keeping up a good appearance were his two great concerns.
'A slovenly person can never amount to much as a soldier,'
he used to tell us. 'If you keep yourselves looking
reasonably tidy, then you'll be neat and efficient in
everything you do.' That was his gospel. Still, when he got
down to the essentials, map reading, basic field tactics, that
sort of thing, it was clear to all of us that the old boy knew
his business.

Later that same year came my first brush with British
Intelligence. I was just going on twenty years old.

For the past year, as a student apprentice, apart from my
part-time university studies, I was engaged in practical
electrical work at Ericsson's factory. The money was good,
and the experience, I realized, would be a great help in the
long run. They had decided to expand their existing
facilities and build a new plant for the manufacture of red

lead, to be used as a base in paints. Work on the installation was being done by a German firm, who sent over their own engineers and technicians to supervise construction. I was put to work on the wiring gang, running cables and feed-lines to the combination office and laboratory building that was to be at the centre of the complex.

One November evening, just before the five o'clock whistle was due to go off, the supervising foreman came over and asked me if I'd mind putting in a few hours of overtime. Some machinery in another section of the plant that needed rewiring before the operators clocked on for the morning shift. I told him I'd take care of it, not to worry. As I'd already made arrangements to meet some friends for an early dinner, I decided to leave it for the time being and stop in later that night on my way back to the houseboat.

It was getting on for midnight by the time I was waved in at the factory gate. The night watchman knew I had access to the grounds.

First of all, I had to collect my tools. They had been left behind in the half-completed red lead plant. I had been working in the underground part of the building, you really couldn't call it a cellar, where concrete beams were sunk into the ground to support the raised floors of the structure.

Arriving at the site, I lifted up the rough planking that closed off the mouth of a short tunnel that served as a passageway. I had to stoop uncomfortably to keep from banging myself against the jerry-built wooden support beams; there wasn't quite enough headroom for an average-sized man to stand upright. Luckily, I knew my way around that labyrinth. Some instinct, I don't know what, made me proceed very quietly as I threaded my way through the maze of exposed pipes and conduits, the crates and workmen's litter on every side.

Then I saw it – a faint glimmer of light just up ahead round a turning. Now what's this, I thought to myself. A smouldering fire? Then I stopped short. I crept forward a few steps and peered round a concrete pillar. My eyes blinked in the sudden glare of a hand-torch, and re-focused slowly on the figure of a man, one of the heavy-set, crop-headed Germans I'd seen often enough around the plant. What the bloody hell does he think he's doing down here? Fiddling with something – looks like a radio transmitter. My mouth hanging open like any half-wit's, I stared and let it sink in. Of course it's a radio. Now the man pulled a red handkerchief from his pocket and wiped his face. He bent over the transmitter. Something went click. A string of staccato-like phrases in German broke the silence. Another click. Then he seemed to be repeating the words he'd just spoken a moment before. Click. Silence.

I took the longest, shallowest breath of my life. I wasn't at all sure what to do at this point. Better get the hell out and think this one over. So I crept away in furtive silence, all thought of my tools completely forgotten, and replaced the wooden hatch over the passageway with all the carefulness my trembling hands could muster.

Now, what to do next? This German, whoever he is, obviously is up to no good. I knew that Ericsson's was involved in some very hush-hush research connected with the military. My first impulse was to run and tell the night watchman and have the fellow hauled up. But then it struck me that this wasn't necessarily the way I'd seen it done in films. Where there was one bad apple in the barrel there might well be others. There was such a thing as being too clever, tipping one's hand too soon. I needed time to think about what I'd seen.

As I was walking back to the houseboat, doubts began to assail me. Had I done the right thing by not doing anything at all? One way or another, this matter had to be settled quickly. Before I went to sleep that night, I'd made up my mind that I would talk to the colonel I knew from OTC and put the matter in his hands.

The following day during my lunch break I caught a bus that let me off near the Derby Road Barracks. The Colonel agreed to receive me in the Officers' Mess.

The man I chose to confide in had lost nothing of his spit-and-polish brusqueness of manner. Not a word was said while I recounted my adventures of the night before. He stroked his clipped regulation moustache thoughtfully, then let loose a barrage of questions. How could I be sure the man was speaking German? I didn't know the language, did I? Was I absolutely certain it was a radio transmitter and not some other device? 'All right, Wynne,' he said when I had finished, 'I'll see that this matter is dealt with. I cannot discuss the details with you and I don't have to tell you it's best not to mention this affair to anyone else.'

There was so much more I wanted to know at that moment, but something in the Colonel's manner warned me that he was not a man to be pressed. I had no way of knowing then that by doing so I had passed an important test. I went back to my work, mystified but resigned. At any rate, I had done what I could. Probably in a few days' time the story would be splashed all over the headlines.

About a fortnight later, the Colonel beckoned me aside after class. 'I just wanted to congratulate you on the way you handled yourself,' he said. 'You were quite right in bringing the matter to my attention.'

I could only surmise that I had put them on to something important. Of course, I was brimming with questions. Was the man a Nazi, after all? Were there any others involved with him? Perhaps he was recruiting a fifth-column in Nottingham or preparing the ground with safe houses for German spies to be smuggled into the country. Eagerly I waited for the revelations I thought would come with these well-meant words of commendation.

At that time, to be sure, I knew nothing of the fundamental rule of all intelligence work, the 'no need to know' principle. If I did not come straight out and ask the Colonel, that was only because I thought it would be unseemly and tactless, like asking 'How much do I get?' at a job interview. So I kept still and waited. All to no purpose, as I soon found out. I never did learn what action was taken about the mysterious German, not then, not later and not ever.

Changing the subject entirely, the Colonel noisily cleared his throat. 'By the way, Wynne, I suppose you realize that National Service is going to be coming soon, eh? Well, I thought I might ask you if you'd be interested in taking some selective training before the call-up. A chap such as yourself could prove useful in the Army, you never can tell.'

I didn't know what he could be getting at and wasn't about to jump to any conclusions, but I said, 'Yes, of course, I'd certainly like to consider it.'

'Good. I'll arrange for you to meet a friend of mine who should be able to help.'

We shook hands. I went back to Nottingham and to my job. Whatever happens next, I thought, can only be a step in the right direction. Intelligence work, spy stuff? To be perfectly truthful about it, I'm sure the thought never crossed my mind. All I knew was that I wanted to be in the Army as an officer and was afraid my dyslexia problem might squelch any chance I had of getting a commission. Now, quite by accident, I had got my foot in the right door and made a favourable impression with the top brass – and I wasn't even in the Army yet!

A week went by. There was a typewritten note for me, sent care of the agents who were letting the houseboat to us. Would I kindly ring up the Colonel at such-and-such a number at my earliest convenience? The Colonel seemed unusually affable over the phone. We arranged to meet the following Saturday in the 'Black Boy', the poshest, most elegantly-appointed hotel in Nottingham.

As a student, I was far too careful with my money to have ever made the 'Black Boy' one of my haunts. The saloon bar was fitted out with black leather upholstery from one end to another decked out with mahogany and mirrors, and the Colonel was waiting at the far end. We both downed a quick beer. The Colonel leaned close to me and said, 'We will be going up to my friend's room and you can talk to him there.'

All these years later, I find it hard to bring a clear picture to mind of the Colonel's mysterious 'friend'. He was not very tall, in his forties wearing an expensive charcoal-grey suit, definitely a Whitehall type, I remember thinking, yet curiously nondescript as a person. He and the Colonel seemed to know each other well.

'Ah yes, Wynne,' he said, extending a pale, blue-veined hand. 'Please sit down. I've asked for some Scotch to be sent up, that'll be all right, won't it?'

I gulped and said, 'I'd prefer beer for myself, if you don't mind.' At that time, I had not yet started to drink spirits.

'Now then.' He paused to retrieve the words he had prepared for the occasion and filed away in a head that was obviously much occupied with more important matters than this one. 'I've heard about your discretion concerning this German chap and his transmitting device. I must tell you that we are very grateful – you handled it in a most exemplary fashion.' The keen grey eyes narrowed. 'Most exemplary indeed,' he repeated. 'If you don't mind telling us, we'd like to hear a little about you, your background and present interests and so on.'

For an hour or more we talked, very pleasantly too, while the Whitehall warrior sized me up. He wanted to know about my family in Wales, my hobbies and future plans, and was I a member of any political party?

I told him no, I'd always been much too busy with my
work and my studies to give any thought to politics.
Besides, I was still too young to vote. And my family? I
laughed and explained that my father invariably voted
Conservative at election time, though this was scarcely
from any personal conviction. Rather, it was still another
manifestation of my mother's constant contriving to maintain our imaginary social status by following the Tory line
that the wealthy families in our village vociferously supported.

Yes, of course, he nodded sympathetically. Then the
subject changed to world affairs. What about Hitler and
that lot? I replied that from what I picked up here and there
and heard on the radio, I was pretty sure I was dead against
what was happening in Germany. Oh, yes? Giving the Jews
a bad time, you know. How do you feel about that?

I had to think for a minute. 'Well . . . I don't exactly
know, sir. I don't believe I had any feelings one way or
another about the Jews until Hitler started picking on
them. It sounds like a load of rubbish, this claiming that
they were responsible for Germany losing the War and all
the rest of it.' I added that in Wales, where there were so
many different churches, the major religious groups and
Dissenters too, everybody seemed to get on perfectly well
together, so why shouldn't the Jews? My understanding of
European history and current events at that point could
take me no further than that.

I see. And the Communists? I replied that their system,
from what I gathered, was against individual freedom and
the right of each person to make whatever he could of his
life. This was definitely not for me. I was happy with my
own progress and nobody had told me what job I had to
take or where to live. Poverty I'd seen as a child in Wales,
but I was convinced that help could be and was being made
available to the poor without overthrowing Britain's basic
freedoms.

The Colonel and his friend glanced at each other. More questions followed, and it was with some difficulty that I succeeded in holding back a torrent of my own. What was this all about? I was dying to know, but I deliberately tried to avoid giving the impression of being an awkward customer.

My well-dressed interrogator drained his neat Scotch and took a deep breath to cool his throat. 'I wanted to have this talk with you because it occurred to us that you might be a useful chap for us to stay in touch with when you get into the service. Your age-group will be called up in a few more months, and I know you've decided to go in the Army. Splendid. What we have to know now is whether you'd care to make yourself available for some special testing and instruction before you officially go in. We can't tell you much more about it now, other than it would take about a month of your time. After that, you would still have a few weeks to put your private affairs in order before you're called up. Oh yes, we'll see to it that you're paid something for the short time you're with us; no need to worry on that account. Think it over carefully. Get in touch with the Colonel here when you've made up your mind, and let us know, eh?'

The interview – if that's what it was – was at an end. I returned to the houseboat and on Monday I let Ericsson's know that I would soon be leaving them. They were very good about it, I must say, and suggested that I be sure to use up the vacation time that was owing me before the Army swallowed me up. Not wanting to seem too headstrong about it, I waited a few days before ringing up the Colonel. 'That's fine,' he said when I told him of my decision. 'Just carry on for the moment with your job and all. We'll be in touch with you presently.'

Another month went by. It was winter in Nottingham, and after the factory shut down for the Christmas holidays

I stayed on to attend the gala New Year's Eve party at the Palais de Danse.

Finally, towards the end of January, I received a note asking me to call the Derby Road Barracks again. I was put through at once to the Colonel who told me to pack a good suit, a few changes of clothes, sports gear if I wanted it, and that he'd be waiting for me at eleven o'clock sharp the following Saturday at a place I knew near Beeston, down by the river.

'And one more thing, Wynne. These friends of yours on the houseboat. For that matter, anyone else who's likely to be missing you. You'll have to tell them that your father is ill or something. Use any excuse that sounds plausible. I take it you haven't mentioned our meetings to anyone else? Good. See that you don't.'

The meeting-place the Colonel had described for me was not too far from where we kept the houseboat moored, so when the day came, I set off on foot across the muddy wet fields, following a rutted path where the earth had been flattened by tractor treads. At the end of a narrow lane that led to a turn-off from the main highway, I caught sight of a sleek, official-looking limousine, parked and waiting, almost ludicrously out-of-place in this setting of quiet barley fields. My God, I remember thinking to myself, here I am not yet twenty years old and I'm going off to war in a chauffeur-driven car.

3

Intelligence Test

The car was a brand-new, glistening black Wolseley, a real beauty. Its coat of polish couldn't have been more than a day old, not in this winter weather. Remembering the Colonel's near-obsession with keeping up a smart appearance, I gave him high marks for practising what he preached.

'Get in, Wynne. I see you're packed and all. We're going to Woolington Park first.'

The driver was not in uniform, but I saw that he kept his cap on the seat beside him. Woolington Park was the estate where the Colonel lived, not my ultimate destination. He was going to be let off there and I'd go the rest of the way by myself. The driver had his cap on his head by the time we swerved round a bend in the road and drew up in front of a pair of wrought-iron gates, and though he didn't actually salute, he stood very much to attention as he got out and opened the door for the Colonel.

'You'll be all right, Wynne, the driver knows where to take you. My friend – the one you met in the hotel – will be there when you arrive and he'll explain what it's about.'

I eased back into the plush upholstered seat, more bemused now than worried. These people don't give anything away for free. I tried asking the man up front where we were heading, but all he said was, 'Oh, we've got a fairly long drive, a good three hours.' No use making an issue out of it. I thought it might be fun to keep an eye out for signposts and landmarks, and have a go at figuring it out for myself.

All I had managed to establish, when eventually we

slowed to turn into a long, elm-shaded drive, was that I was somewhere in Sussex and a long way from a town of any size. We braked in front of a large, elegant, Georgian red-brick country house. There were a few other cars parked out in front, most of them as brightly polished as mine. 'You're expected in there,' the driver said, motioning, and I noticed this time he did not stand to attention nor even offer to help me with my suitcase and coat.

A man in a neat brown suit was standing by the door. Eyebrows peaked above his rimless glasses and he asked me my name. 'Oh yes, Mr Wynne, you're expected. I'll show you to your room. If you'll just come this way . . .'

Up a carpeted staircase and down a hall that smelled faintly of old cedar. 'In here, please.' The bedroom was on the small side but nicely done up in chintz, with a voluminous chest of drawers and a Turkish carpet over the polished oak boards. 'You'll find the bathroom just opposite.' I put my suitcase down on the bed. 'Now you must excuse me. Please have a shower or a bath if you feel like it. You're expected to report to the main lounge at seven.'

That left me with about three hours, so I decided I'd do a bit of wandering about, just to get my bearings. I discovered that the grounds were extensive and immaculately kept up. At the back of the house was a swimming pool flanked by two reconditioned barns. Other smaller outbuildings stood out on green and brown hillocks some distance away. It would be nice here in summer, when the grass was studded with cowslips. Some men – young men like myself – were wandering about in groups of twos and threes. I nodded hullo and one of the chaps came up to me. 'What are we here for?' he asked nervously. 'I don't know, do you?'

'Haven't a clue,' I said, remembering that I had been instructed not to discuss the episode with anyone, or mention my briefing at the hotel. I noticed my questioner spoke with a public-school accent. His companions seemed a bit on their guard.

At seven o'clock, all fitted out in my best brown suit, I came down to the lounge. I had been expecting to see uniforms. There weren't any in sight. Only well-dressed, ordinary types such as you might see hovering round an executive conference room, waiting for the chairman to call the board meeting to order. Standing with his back to a glass-faced *étagère* was the man whom I had met in the 'Black Boy' in Nottingham. He immediately came over to me and thrust out a hand.

'Right, you're here. That's fine. You'll hear all about the situation in just a moment so I suggest you just grab a chair and sit down.'

There were, I saw, about a dozen other chaps who looked to be my age mingling in the lounge, and nearly that many other, older, more distinguished-looking men, chatting, trying to make them feel at ease.

As if by unspoken command, everyone in the group fell silent as a large, burly-looking man made his way to the stuffed leather chair at the head of the library table. Automatically, we all stood up for this imposing figure while he glanced through an imposing stack of papers he brought with him.

His voice was a deep parade-ground rumble. 'If you please, gentlemen.' His deep-set eyes swept round the table like a searchlight, settling for a moment on every face. 'What it is all about you'll presently learn. I can only tell you that you have been selected as potential officer material, which we hope your stay with us will confirm. We don't know as yet what special duties you are best able to render, but we intend to find out while you're here. I should make it clear that you are under no compulsion and may leave at any time, if you find things are not to your liking. Is that clear? We're not forgetting that none of you are in the Army yet.'

There was a cautious murmur round the table. One of the lads reached in his jacket pocket and brought out a cigarette lighter but kept it clenched in his hand, not sure if it was the proper thing to light up.

'Yes,' said the burly man, eyeing him. 'You may smoke and relax. If there's anything we ask you to do, you are perfectly free to refuse to do it. No explanations required. However, for as long as you're here, we would ask a few things. First, that you do not go out into any of the neighbouring villages. There is a beer canteen here but no spirits, and the food is as good as we can find it. In the evening you've got billiards, you've got table-tennis, there's a swimming pool and a library, and we hope you will look on us as a family in the course of the next month. We expect one more thing. Please do not discuss among yourselves the course of events that brought you to this establishment. You'll each be given a number to use at all times, and we put you on your honour not to inquire into each other's names and backgrounds. Wear your number on your lapel. My officers will refer to that only. We trust you to observe these rules for the whole of the period you are here. Eventually you will understand why you have been invited, and why these rules are necessary.

'Now,' he said, dropping the crisp tones. 'Let's have some dinner.'

The next day was the beginning of our routine. The man was right, it proved nothing very demanding. A good English breakfast at half past seven. The evening meal was always a three-course affair with a generous cheeseboard and coffee to follow. Additionally, there was always tea and coffee brewing in the mess room and brought to your room for the private interviews with the staff officers that occupied a fair number of our mornings.

The day after I arrived, there was a slip of paper under the door advising me that a Mr Cecil would be calling on me at ten o'clock. That gentleman, chubby, well-dressed, precise in his manner, turned up at the specified hour and, after introducing himself and asking how I'd slept, got right down to business.

'I should tell you that you'll be seeing quite a lot of people today. Many of them will probably be asking you the same questions, over and over, and I'm sorry that it has to be such a bore, but there's no getting round it. So why don't we start in with you telling me what you think we ought to know about you? You're Welsh, I take it . . .'

'No, English in fact, but I don't mind telling you I'm proud of my Welsh connections . . .' And so began our conversation. Every once in a while he'd slip in a question having to do with my political opinions – immature, I'm sure he wrote in his report – but most of the time he just listened while I did all the talking. After an hour of this, he said, 'By the way, we are all assembling in the lounge at midday. A briefing on today's programme of events.' He looked at his watch. 'I see I've made you miss most of the sports activities. We'll try to schedule the rest of these interviews so you'll be free in the mornings to take part. You'll find some of the chaps have already started in on it. They were kicking a football around when I came in.'

Someone had gone to a good deal of trouble in setting up the facilities, I soon found out. In addition to a nicely equipped gymnasium in one of the barns, they had regulation tennis courts, basketball, fencing and horseback riding. 'There's no compulsion to attend,' we were told, but most of the lads required no encouraging. I played tennis when I got the chance and, thinking to make the most of the free instruction, put myself down for fencing lessons.

The rest of the day would be given over to tests and loosely organized group discussions. In these, one of the officers would try to act as a catalyst to see what we knew, or thought we knew, about world affairs and things in general. 'Does anyone know where such and such a country is?' 'Have any of you been there? Who can tell us what it's like?' Politics occupied a large part of these informal sessions. On the second evening somebody brought up Aneurin Bevan's scheme for a nationalized health service which was getting a lot of play in the newspapers then. I was glad to take part since as a boy I had heard Bevan speak in Wales, and Ness Edwards and Ernest Bevin were also from my part of the country.

Another question that we all took turns debating was what we thought Britain should do with the forces at her disposal in case of war. Again, I took the floor on this one. I felt strongly that we weren't prepared for anything like a major engagement, and argued that we could hardly do more than undertake a holding operation unless the French, with their larger army, gave us a chance to prepare. 'Our industries are run down,' I thundered like any opposition back-bencher, 'and in case of war we're going to be in the soup.' I sat down and there was some sarcasm and a round of facetious hand-clapping. But the officer who was presiding that night said very seriously, 'Would any of you care to comment on that?'

From the second week on, our afternoons were set aside for various kinds of field tests and exercises in problem-solving. They brought us to two trees, and the idea was to try to cross from one to the other on a pair of ropes. The tricky part was that there were three sets of ropes to choose from. The top two were about thirty feet up, but stretched absolutely taut. The second pair was a good bit slacker, but only fifteen feet off the ground. The third and wobbliest were just six feet up. 'Now,' the officer said with an evil glint in his eyes, 'who wants to have a go?'

I craned my neck at the topmost ropes and caught my

breath. That really seemed a bit much, and I never liked heights anyway. I watched as two or three in the group tried the very slack bottom ropes and promptly tumbled off. So I volunteered to do the middle set, and somehow managed it with much less difficulty than I'd expected. 'Well, Number Fourteen,' the officer said, 'mind telling me why you decided to go for that pair and not the others?'

'I guess it seemed a reasonable compromise. I don't really care for heights, to tell the truth.'

'Ah,' he said, and proceeded to scribble something on the clipboard the instructors always carried around with them.

As time went on, I realized that we were constantly being kept under observation and prodded, never coerced, into any number of challenging or telling situations. Being spied on, if you will, yet we were supposed to be bright fellows and perhaps they wanted to see if we could catch on to the fact. For instance, we were told to sign a chit for the beer in the canteen, and at the end of the course we'd be billed something nominal – threepence for every half-pint, I think it was – to be settled out of our allowance. But we were particularly told that we should not buy drinks for others and I'm sure it must have been because they wanted to keep track of how much and how often we drank.

Likewise, when the officers and recruits all sat down together in the oak-panelled dining room, the officers would never sit in the same position two nights running. Thinking back on my Colonel from OTC and his mania for correct deportment, they were doubtless making notes on our table manners. And when some new activity was announced, you had to put your name down on a list if you wanted to take part. Why? Quite likely because they wanted to keep track of which students seemed to be making the most of the time available. If we just stayed in bed, I suppose we would have been written off as a dead loss. On the other hand, if we jumped around the gym or at least spent our time in the library it was safe to assume we were reasonably active types with some sense of self-initiative. For my part, I took part in just about all the activities, with two exceptions. Horses, for some reason, I've never liked. And when they brought us to a large practice hangar at a camp a few miles from the house, I firmly but respectfully declined to get involved with parachute jumping, not even the training drops.

One day it was suggested that we each go to the library and prepare notes to give an after-dinner talk to our fellow students on a subject of our own choosing. I decided to make mine about telephone exchanges and how they worked; not, I'll grant you, the most fascinating of subjects, but I saw it as a good way of calling attention to my technical expertise and scoring off one or two of the others in our little group whose public-school airs and graces were getting on my nerves.

With one exception in addition to myself, all of these boys assembled in Sussex as potential recruits for British Intelligence had been culled from the class of prewar British society known to us vaguely back in Wales as 'regular toffs'. On the whole, they seemed to me a pretty pampered and inept lot, for all their cleverness. I remember a couple of them who actually had the nerve to complain to the officers about the lack of sherry, and there was one in particular who affected a long, Bertie Woosterish cigarette holder.

I can give only my impressions and it may be that I'm being unfair, but I could not help thinking that perhaps half of these chaps would never make the grade. Even if we had wanted to break our word and confide to each other about our private lives, the officers at Sussex saw that we were never left for any length of time without supervision. In fact, though I couldn't swear to it, I wouldn't be surprised if one of the twelve boys was a 'plant', a veteran of an earlier session who was given a chance to prove himself by keeping an eye on the new boys. If we asked an awkward question about him, that would have meant he flunked the test. This is just an idea of my own, but it would have been quite consistent with the deviousness and mania for double-checking everything I encountered when I started working for MI5.

Had it been possible, I would have enjoyed getting to know the odd man out in the group, a tall, lanky Scot whom we all privately called Jock. He was a character, no doubt at all about that. A dry sort, and a cocky, hard-working perfectionist. It was irritating to see how absolutely sure of himself he seemed to be. When he was due to give a talk on Scottish history, the rest of us boned up in the library, hoping to trip him up with the date of some obscure battle. It did no good – he parried all our questions in that dry voice of his, adding, for good measure, 'Page thirty-five, I believe, will substantiate my point.' Our joint action had failed. It struck me that the Germans would have a hellish time if they ever captured this lad. He was rugged, too, and would have made a good Commando.

We also did some work, not too much, with military problems, as it was assumed that there would be plenty of time for us to pick up the essentials when we went for regular officer training. So we might have a day's practice pitching dummy grenades, or be shown how to take compass bearings from the local landmarks, nothing very difficult. Selection was the primary objective here, not training, and I believe the idea was to sort out the ones who were mechanically-minded, for example, or had a gift for languages. On the other hand, it was necessary for them to find out what we had on the debit side of the ledger, perhaps little taste for physical exertion or a fear of explosives. So from time to time we'd be given these little exercises.

Toy soldiers and a model stockade. 'If you were asked to defend this fort and only had this number of soldiers, where would you put them?' Mind you, none of us had received any previous instruction on this point. They simply wanted to see if our instincts were sharp and if we could justify our decisions logically. What should one do, anyhow? I took my time trying to figure that one. Concentrate one's forces by the gate? But nobody had said if the attack was coming from one direction. I arranged my troops at scattered lookout points with a few extra men at the vulnerable spots. 'All right, Number Fourteen. Mind telling us all what made you decide to do that?' This is the way it went. Usually we'd never be told whether our answers were right or wrong, it was just brushed off with a noncommittal grunt.

Another test involved a piece of canvas and some odd bits of wood. The officer in charge said, 'Supposing you were given command of a group of soldiers and you received a message that the general was on the way. It's raining but you've got to rig up something in the way of shelter for him. Anybody got any ideas?' I volunteered for this one. By arranging the planks and two-by-fours just right, it was possible to rig a flimsy sort of wigwam with the canvas sheet. There was a battered wooden crate nearby which I requisitioned as a table. 'There,' I said proudly. In a mood for fun, the resident humorist in our group went off and came back with a flower stuck in a tin can. Then the officer asked, 'Hey, Number Three, would you spend an hour in that?'

'Well,' he replied thoughtfully. 'There's nothing better around, is there?'

In general, I did pretty well on the mechanical tests. We were asked to try to repair a broken typewriter or find out why a car wouldn't start. Locating faults in a radio circuit was a piece of cake. I had some difficulty with the Morse code on account of my dyslexia problem, but I think that if

I had to I could have mastered it. When it came to foreign languages, I think they must have soon realized that I was hopeless.

With some of the tests, you could never be sure exactly what they were getting at. One, I remember, involved two ferocious-looking Irish wolfhounds. They'd toss a football around and the two animals would chase after it, snapping and barking savagely, and our job was to get the ball away from them. I suppose they just wanted to see how we reacted, or took it as an indication of personal courage. Of course, the dogs were trained so that if you handled them correctly and gave them a smack, they behaved perfectly all right.

In the evenings, after beer and billiards, we'd settle in beside the well-banked-up fire, reading, talking or listening to the radio. We were shown feature films and shorts on army manoeuvres, warships, or the air displays at last year's Hendon Air Show. Afterwards we'd be given question-naires to fill in, testing our recall and comprehension. What was the name of the ship in the film? How many funnels did it have? How many lifeboats did you see? Almost like Christmas party games. My main piece of luck, though, was that there were no long written examination questions during my time at Sussex. I still hadn't told anyone about my dyslexia; I wasn't sure if I should or not. My reasoning was that I had always been successful in talking my way out of these situations, so I thought I'd just keep quiet and fake a broken arm or something similar. I was afraid that they wouldn't let me get through the course. Besides, we were supposed to be crafty sorts, weren't we? Good. Leave it at that.

There was, finally, one essay which we were supposed to do, and I decided simply to ignore it. When they asked me why, I said, 'Frankly, I'm not all that interested in the subject. I've been thinking very carefully about yesterday's discussion. I understand we're going to continue with that today, and my mind's been set on that. I'm still working on the answer.' They bought my story. Apart from some written work at the end of the course, that, fortunately, was the only big hurdle. There were other exams where we had to put a tick against the correct answer, but that presented no problem.

After the first week or so, the military training began to be stepped up. We had an explosives expert in to demonstrate his skills and were shown film on how vehicles and buildings could be blown up. Later, in the lecture room, the staff put up pictures of buildings and factories and asked, 'If you were going to blow this, where would you put the explosives?' Quite a lot of the less mechanically-inclined students had trouble with this part. We were shown a new model portable radio transmitter that could be dropped by parachute behind enemy lines – it was a complicated gadget, unlike any of the radio equipment I'd ever seen before, and I know I was fascinated by it.

Intelligence-gathering techniques were phased in a bit at a time with our regular programme of coursework and sports. It was never billed as such, and the way they put it across to you made it sound as if they were just giving you common-sense advice.

Along with this, we had lectures in international affairs in general, with special sessions devoted to Russian and German history. I think I've made it clear that for a nineteen-year-old my awareness of the world situation was pretty vague and muddled, so I naturally got interested in these. With slides, newsreel film-clips and charts we started with Lenin and the Revolution and went on to analyse the activities and programme of the Communist Party since that time. Questions and comments were always welcomed at the end. We went over much the same ground with Hitler and the Nazis. This led us into counter-espionage and we were given a rough idea of what MI5 had been doing to counteract it. I remembered the German in the cellar and smiled. We talked about the political changes that were taking place in Britain, the proposals for a national health scheme, the growth of trade unions, the shadow factories being built for armaments production. Then, less formally, we were given a lot of useful advice on how to cope with being in the armed forces.

The interviews with the individual staff officers in rotation continued. I was having a chat with one of their senior men about three weeks into the course. All the recruits had been on a cross-country run and I had managed not too badly – a lot of rowing and tennis in Nottingham had seen to that. 'I think you'll come through this course, somehow,' he said. 'But, you know, you've got a terribly young-looking face. Why don't you grow a moustache on it? Then you might frighten the enemy a little bit more.'

Young-looking? A careful examination in the dressing-table mirror led me to conclude, sadly, that there just might be something in what he said. So from that moment on, I let the hairs on my upper lip grow to profusion, cultivating them as proudly as if it had been a bed of prize roses. Then when I finally started to serve in the Army, we had a session with the brigade psychiatrist as a part of the medical boards. He took one look at me and asked, 'For God's sake, man, what do you think you're doing, wearing a moustache?'

A bit taken aback, I muttered something about how I wanted to give the enemy a proper fright. That seemed to satisfy him. He jerked his thumb in the direction of the door and said 'Out!'

There was a last examination. We were supposed to write a few paragraphs giving our impressions of the course and indicate which service we were planning to join. Since they still hadn't tumbled to the fact that my spelling capabilities were only barely up to minimal standards, I went into my sprained wrist act, which by this time I had polished to perfection. Three of the officers agreed to hear my replies.

'You ask me why I think I've been brought here.' Better play it on the cautious side. 'It obviously has some bearing on the German with the radio back in Nottingham and from that I would assume – I hope I'm correct – that you have in mind that I've got the makings of an officer. As for the service I'd choose, from what I've seen so far, I prefer to keep my feet firmly on the ground. I like the sea, but I wouldn't be much as a sailor. Nor do I want to fly. As for the parachute corps – you'd never get me into that.'

It put a smile on their faces. I decided to make it short. 'So obviously, I would prefer the Army. Hopefully you would give me something connected with engineering or communications work. You know by now that's what I'm good at doing, but of course I'll take anything that comes my way.'

'Thank you, we appreciate your being forthright.'

Then at the evening meeting the burly man who had spoken to us on our arrival spoke to us all: 'You know you're going to be called up in the ranks and do your basic military training very soon now. After that, depending on your performance, you could be sent to an officer training unit. As we look upon you as gentlemen, we therefore ask that you do not discuss where you have been this past month with anyone. Not even your family. Believe me, it is as much in your interest to do so, as ours. Later, perhaps, you'll understand exactly what I mean by that. Life will take its course and none of you will regret your stay with us here, though some will gain more from it than others. That's all.'

They put on a very big dinner for us in the evening and once again we were ceremoniously thanked for our attendance.

The beer flowed freely, and we all – officers included – made merry, singing rugger songs and telling each other outrageously filthy stories.

The next morning we collected the £25 gratuity we'd been promised and train tickets to our choice of destinations. Still not taking any chances, each student was taken separately to the railway station in an ordinary saloon car – no more chauffeured limousines. To the very last moment, I realized with some astonishment, they had kept the show going without once actually giving us more than hints as to what it was all about. That is, never saying it outright. But it had been obvious, I think, to everyone there. But what exactly would they have us doing when the time came? Parachuting behind enemy lines, robbing an ambassador's safe? Seducing a dark-eyed, dusky-skinned countess – now that would be fun. I didn't think I could count too much on that sort of thing, however. From what I experienced in Sussex, I had an idea that the spying business would prove not all that much removed from ordinary Army duties. In any case, I was pleased with myself for having made it this far.

4

Under Cover

The £25 we'd been given to cover expenses in Sussex along with two weeks' extra pay from Ericsson's – unexpected, but a nice gesture on their part – saw me through the next couple of months in Nottingham, waiting for the call-up. I had neither the means nor the inclination to live lavishly on my borrowed time, so I did what I could to keep busy, spending my mornings in the public library, where I read up on engineering and technical handbooks. Later in the day, I'd either take in a film or likely as not visit some of the larger factories whose managers were extremely good about showing a young engineering student around the works. Every so often I stopped by the Derby Road Barracks to talk to one or two junior officers I'd met, and picked up a lot of useful hints on how to cope with the military life.

At the end of the second month, my National Service papers finally came through so I packed my bags and set off for Hereford and the Army.

With all the time they'd had to draw up the plans, you would have thought that mobilization should have been an orderly, sensible affair. Far from it. The training camp was at Hereford Racecourse, an immense city under canvas, and each day's intake of raw recruits seemed to push the operation closer and closer to complete anarchy. The small core of regular officers and experienced NCOs who were running the show seemed quite overwhelmed by this tideswell of unfledged, bewildered humanity, most of whom had never spent a night away from home in their entire lives. These boys had the worst of it, suddenly finding themselves roused from their beds before dawn and out in the pouring rain to shave from a cold tap over a galvanized trough. The rain hammered down on our six-man tents day and night during those first few weeks; and none of the instructors thought to show us the proper way to dig a ditch and avoid a soaking while we slept.

Even to look at, nobody could have possibly mistaken us for soldiers. The new lads would be sent to the stores and emerge in hopelessly ill-fitting uniforms. We laughed to think that we were the clowns in this ghastly circus, and certainly dressed for the part. Some of us were issued riding breeches and ridiculous puttees. There was nobody to tell us how to strap the damn things on, adding to the mood of grim hilarity. If you were lucky, the company quarter-master-sergeant might spare you a quick glance to estimate your shoe size, and if your luck was really exceptional, you'd be given a pair of boots no more than one to two sizes off the mark. Otherwise, three days of parade drill and you risked being crippled for life.

It went on like that for about a month, until they finally brought things under control by bringing in veteran soldiers from the Guards and other crack units and posting them as corporals or lance-corporals in each company. Then we got down to the serious training. We had all the usual marksmanship and weapons practice, including Lewis machine-gun drill. With plenty of cross-country marches and keep-busy work, a semblance of proper military discipline was gradually established. It was a good many weeks, though, before they decided it was safe to allow us to run loose in the pubs of a sleepy market town like Hereford.

Chamberlain declared war while I was still in basic training at Hereford. A group of us were sitting around the canteen listening to his speech over the loudspeakers. When he ended with 'We are now at war with Germany', everyone burst out in a tremendous cheer. I don't think there were many – and I'm certainly not including myself – who fully understood what a long, dirty and dangerous business it was going to be.

Immediately after that, the bugle sounded and we were called out on parade. The rain was pouring down as usual as we stood to attention, rivulets trickling from our caps and into our eyes. The CO ordered us to break camp at once. Five hundred newly-painted white tents arranged in a neat rectangle in the centre of a level racecourse was an open-ended invitation for an air-raid. So we had to move all our kit and reassemble our tents at scattered parts round the perimeter of the course, with the result that some units ended up by having nearly a mile's walk just to get to mess. A week later, we were given paint to camouflage our tents.

We were in our second month of basic training when the adjutant came into our tent in the middle of the night, and told us to pack up our kits and rifles. Parade in half an hour in front of the main administration tent. Two sections were called out, twenty-four men in all, and before we knew what was happening to us we were bundled into a pair of transport lorries and went off into the night. Groggy with sleep, it took a while before we realized that nobody had the slightest clue as to where we were headed.

'I just hope it's not another bleeding exercise,' said one of the men. 'They've got no call to wake us up like that.'

After we had travelled for miles, though, it seemed a sure bet that finally we were going off to war, to France at the very least.

But when the canvas flaps were drawn back and we scrambled down to stretch our legs, I thought there was something pretty damn familiar about the contours of the countryside. Blinking my eyes in the brilliant daylight. I saw that the trucks had pulled up in front of the Crumlin railway viaduct. I was back in Wales.

'Make up your beds in that hut over there,' the sergeant

barked. It appeared that we had been posted to guard this particular railhead, apparently a vital link to some armaments factories down the road. It was rumoured that the IRA had threatened some mischief. For the first time we were issued live ammunition and took turns patrolling the bridge, day and night. Before the sergeant left, he had given me two stripes and promoted me on the spot. 'You take charge of this bunch and see that they stay out of trouble.'

I wouldn't be at all surprised if, to this day, down in the tiny village of Crummock, the people are still talking about what happened to this detachment, my first command. It turned out that I was to be responsible for bringing a taste of the Second World War to this tucked-away corner of Wales.

Three nights after we had settled into our billets, the man I had posted on sentry duty heard a rustling in the bushes by the tracks and sang out, 'Come forward and be recognized!' just as he'd been taught to do. A sudden, startled movement in the undergrowth was the answer. A shot rang out, followed by a horrifying shrill scream that echoed down the length of the valley. When I got there with my men, with the rest of the village in nightshirts hard at our heels, I saw the sentry prodding the crumpled form of an extremely dead goat.

We were ordered back to Hereford. A week or so later, I was told to report to the CO's office in two days' time, boots polished and buttons twinkling. What can it be now, I wondered. The District CO had called a Court of Inquiry over that damned goat and I thought that was the end of it. But when I presented myself and gave my sharpest salute, the CO told me to stand easy. 'Congratulations,' he said. 'You've been selected for officer training.' We chatted for a few minutes. He offered me a cigarette and wished me the best of luck.

Shrivenham Artillery School specialized in the training

of anti-aircraft regimental leaders under the Defence of Great Britain Act. We learned about mine-laying, searchlights and ground-to-air artillery. Night patrol exercises and frequent cross-country marches. We had live grenade practice, too.

One morning, about three weeks before the course was due to end, one of the older men came up to me in the orderly room and said, 'Post-corporal's been looking for you, did you know? There's a letter.' It had a London postmark and the handwriting didn't seem familiar. I tore it open and scanned the single sheet of flimsy paper. Dear Greville . . . How are you getting on. It went on like that, all very chummy in tone, saying that the writer had heard of my posting and thought he might like to drive up from London to see me. I glanced down at the bottom of the page. Hope to see you soon, it said. Signed Alec.

Trouble was, I didn't know any Alecs. And most of what he went on about in the short letter seemed gibberish to me, mentioning people I'd never heard of and escapades I seem to have been involved with. Then my eyes were drawn to something about 'the good times we had down in Sussex' and immediately I knew what it was all about. Pretty clever job, in fact. This was their way of getting in touch with me.

The letter concluded by saying that he would be glad to see me for a pint at the 'Goddard Arms' in Swindon Old Town next Saturday.

So that was the way it was done. I turned up at the pub and there had no difficulty in spotting one of the junior officers known as Robbie who had met me at the house in Sussex.

'Come over here with us, Greville. What will you have? I want you to meet a friend of mine.' An immaculately dressed – and obviously military – man stepped forward. 'Captain James.' We shook hands. 'Now, let's go over to that table in the corner where we can talk.'

Captain James showed me an identification card with his picture on it. He was a good ten years older than I, and slightly taller. His sandy-brown hair was parted down the middle with a slight wave, in the style of Ronald Colman. Even in his civilian finest there was an intangible something about his bearing that marked him unquestionably as a Sandhurst man. Later I heard he had been to Trinity College, Cambridge.

'Here's the score, Greville,' Robbie said. 'From here on in, you're officially under MI5 orders and James will be your contact man. In a few more weeks you'll be leaving Shrivenham, and we've got things to keep you busy. I'll let James fill you in on the next moves.'

James spoke in a quiet, crisp tone, trying not to sound like a superior giving orders. 'Neither of your commanding officers at Hereford or Shrivenham know that you've been recruited for counter-espionage activities,' he explained. 'So outwardly, you must carry on behaving exactly like a normal officer cadet. You're due for a couple of weeks' leave after finishing up the course. What would you ordinarily do on leave?'

'Probably, I'd go to Wales to stay with my father until my next posting.'

'Fine,' said Robbie. 'Do that. We'll intercept your posting papers from Shrivenham and issue you with new ones. Incidentally, don't mention this to your CO or to anyone. During the second week of your leave we want you to come up to London and stay at the Royal Overseas League in St James's.'

'You'll like it there,' James put in. 'It's a popular spot for young officers on leave, with a very nice social life and plenty of activities. I can give you my personal assurance the young ladies who attend the tea dances are all stunners.'

'Sounds like my sort of place, sir.'

'Don't "sir" me in public. We're just friends talking.

Now, the Monday after you get to London' – he scribbled on a piece of notepaper – 'we want you to give us a ring at this number. I shall probably be in London myself, but if I'm not there, Robbie will be in touch. We'll have plenty of time then to explain your assignment to you.'

'One more thing,' added Robbie. 'We'll fix you up with an official pass giving a War Office number that's easy enough to confirm in case you get stopped by the Military Police checking for deserters. You may have to show it on occasion when you are working out of uniform.'

That was how it started. I could hardly wait for the course to finish so I could get to London, and after that the real action would begin. In Cardiff, I stopped to have the military outfitters make up my spanking-new officer's uniform. My father couldn't have been prouder or happier when he saw me come through the door with a shiny brass pip on my shoulder straps.

When I got off the train in London, I went directly to the Overseas League as I'd been ordered, and was glad to see that it looked to be every bit as pleasant as promised. As soon as I'd plonked down my seven-and-six for a room, I dialled the number James had given me from the telephone in the lobby.

A familiar voice at the other end said, 'James here.'

'This is Greville.'

'Oh yes, Greville. We've been expecting your call. Everything all right? Why don't you just stay where you are. Robbie and I will meet you for lunch and we can talk then.'

This time the two officers turned up in full uniform, maybe because they thought I needed some reassurance. We had a drink at the bar and James said, 'Robbie has to leave soon, but I'll explain your mission to you over lunch.'

We were shown to a table in the downstairs restaurant. I noticed that James seemed to be on first-name terms with most of the staff, but it would be wrong to assume that the Overseas League was a cover organization for MI5 activities. In fact, I'm sure it wasn't. The Nuffield Foundation very generously subsidized it as a club for officers from all branches of the service, which is what made it the logical place for James to frequent, if anyone was keeping him under observation.

'So now you're about to start work for us.' James smiled mysteriously, and looked down at his soup, like a fortune-teller peering at my future in a crystal ball. 'You might even find some parts of it amusing. Hope you've got a sense of humour; it might come in handy for starters. It's going to be uncomfortable to begin with, I'm afraid. We're reducing you to the ranks for this one.'

I tried not to let my disappointment be too obvious. No bright new lieutenant's uniform for me, no whisky in the officers' mess, no chance for the girls to eye me in my brand-new Sam Browne.

'We're sending you to the Command Workshop in Aldershot. You have all the right qualifications, so we've arranged for you to join the electrical division, which handles the modification of armoured combat vehicles. Lately they've been having considerable leakage. A lot of the blueprints are being photographed and sent abroad.

'Now, here's where you come in. We'd like you to get on friendly terms with two of the men who work there. We want to know everything there is to know about them, right? They're both civilians. In fact, the permanent staff there is almost entirely civilian, we just send our boys down to get the technical experience. Just make their acquaintance as naturally as possible and see what develops.'

He took an envelope from a bulging briefcase and fanned out on the tablecloth a half-dozen cards with names, personal data and photographs. 'This man,' his finger stabbed one of the cards, 'he's our chief suspect, but we have an idea the circle may stretch a lot wider than that. You're the one who's going to tell us. Get to know him, see if he's living within his income. You know what to look for. Also, find out about his political leanings, and what he thinks about the war. Don't ask questions, just let it all come from him.'

I stared and tried to fix the man's face in my mind. After a moment, I lifted my head and asked, 'Is there, you know, a special procedure I should follow when I have something to report?'

James chuckled. 'Do it just as you've done today. Every four weeks you'll have a forty-eight-hour pass. Just come to London and ring me up at the same number. If there's anything doing, say "I'd like to get together" and I'll tell you where we'll meet.'

I was asked to wait ten minutes after James got up and left before I went out of the room myself. This, I later learned, was another rule.

Aldershot, when I got there, quickly shattered any lingering penny-paper illusions about the glamorous life of a secret agent. Marched from the cramped, stinking and horribly overcrowded barracks at seven in the morning, toiling in the workshops all day, queueing behind fifty other men for a tin plate of sausage and mash, then herded back to barracks at five. The black-out screens were so ineffective it was forbidden to strike a light in the early winter darkness, but they did serve to prevent the slightest whiff of fresh air from entering our quarters. The complete lack of privacy was what annoyed me most of all.

The workshops were quite extensive, and in the main one where I was posted, they had a good five hundred people employed. My target, the presumed enemy agent, was in charge of the electrical section and a very busy man, so it was a matter of weeks before I was able to strike up an acquaintance with him. Playing it casual at first, I would nod to him in the pub, play darts with some of his friends. James had made it clear that this sort of surveillance work never has a time limit. Eventually we were buying each other drinks and exchanging gripes about military life on a Christian-name basis.

Before too long, just as hoped for, the man invited me to his home, a detached three-bedroom house in a nice residential area about two miles outside of Aldershot. As for worming out secrets from him, I had it easy on this first assignment: once he accepted me in his confidence, the man made no secret of his pro-Nazi sympathies. His line was the old Mosley one about how Hitler had pulled his country together, and that the war was a terrible fraud engineered by the Bolsheviks. Fine, but more than that was required if MI5 was to pin him down as a collaborator. So I put my eyes and my common sense to work, just as I'd been told. The inside of the house was just a little too fancy; he had a brand-new Ultra radio console and fitted carpets in every room; all the furnishings were smart and new-looking, without being ostentatious. I had especially been told to check for fitted carpets and lined curtains. Both were expensive items in those days.

The other man who was under suspicion I never managed to make contact with, so I suppose my first assignment could only be called a partial success. He was working in another section of the plant, and the opportunity for meeting him just never presented itself. My instructions were clear. Leave it, don't force it. An agent should never risk his cover to force a situation that was anything other than natural.

When I booked in at the Overseas League, I could hardly wait to put my call through to James and hope that this would be the end of it.

'I'll see you at the bar on Sunday evening,' James said as soon as he got on the line. The procedure for making contact was to act casual, make it look like a chance encounter with an old friend.

A drink together, then James suggested, 'Let's try the reading room.' I made my report. No notes were taken and James had very few questions to ask me. I'm sure what I was able to supply him was only a fraction of the input they were getting from other sources.

'Why don't you keep on seeing this fellow for a while longer, in any case,' James suggested. 'Don't worry about collecting information, you've given us more than enough. But it might be wise not to break it off all at once and arouse suspicions. In a few weeks, we'll pull you out of there.'

The thought of spending more time at that dreadful place must have put a crease in my mouth. 'Now, cheer up, Greville,' James said quickly. 'You'll be posted on another mission soon enough, but as it's been a come-down in the world for you, I'll arrange for you to have a month off before you go. How's that sound? Better? That's the stuff.'

My next few assignments were pretty much along the same lines as Aldershot; all involving people both in and out of the service who for some reason needed vetting. I was put in as an officer cadet in camps all over Britain where soldiers from German-occupied nations, the Free French, the Polish Government in exile, and other shadow governments were receiving officer training. Of course, it would have been easy for the Nazis to have planted one of their own boys in the group, or to be using hostages to pry information from a genuine resistance fighter. My job was to see to it that all of the officers were what they appeared.

To do this, I became possibly one of the most over-trained officers in the British Army. Three separate three-month courses of Pre-OCTU work, and then on to four other fairly rigorous officer training courses. I trained with the Artillery all over again, dragging 25-pounder guns up and down Ilkley Moor through the snow, as well as attending cadet courses for the Royal Army Supply Corps, the Royal Engineers and the Royal Electrical and Mechanical Engineers. By the time I'd sweated my way through these, I felt more than qualified for an immediate promotion to brigadier, with enough left-over training for a dozen warrant officers. All of these postings involved a great deal of specialized study and strenuous effort, though possibly the North Wales course remembered by all participants for its twenty-five-mile mountain marches with full pack gets the prize in the latter category. I had to do it twice in the same year.

At least there were my weekends in London to break the drudgery. On completion of longer assignments, anything from ten to thirty days' leave. MI5 looked after all expenses. The procedure was roughly as follows: I'd get off the train at Waterloo or Paddington station and immediately hop into a taxi that let me off in the neighbourhood of any of the three London safe houses the Department had set up. One was a smart Queen Anne house on the Chelsea Embankment, the others were flats in the Holborn and Regent's Park areas. The first thing was for me to change to civilian clothes; there were suitcases in each of these places for that purpose. It wouldn't do to have a chap who knew me, say, as a corporal at Aldershot spot me going around London in my officer's uniform.

Then I'd give James a ring. It wasn't always James, of course, more likely one of his subalterns. After I made my report the contact man would count off crisp pound notes from a thick wad, and hand them over to me. This represented the difference between the enlisted man's pay I collected under my assumed rank, and my officer's pay. They were good about seeing to that.

James himself opened the door for me one spring day in 1942 when I turned up at the Chelsea house on my regular weekend leave. 'Come right on in, captain,' he said with a smile.

'Are you serious?'

'Certainly I am. Why, don't you think you deserve it by now?'

There's no denying I was pleased at the news: it went a long way to making up for all the nights I'd spent in freezing cold, corrugated-metal huts, lying awake listening to men grind their teeth in their sleep, or hear them clamber in and out of the three-tiered iron bunks to relieve their beer-swollen bladders.

'I should tell you, though,' James said as he led the way through the hall and held the door to the sitting room open for me. 'We have a rule. I'm afraid this promotion won't be gazetted. It's one of these things the service insists on. They've made me a lieutenant-colonel, did you know?'

An orderly brought in some tea and disappeared. 'Planning on staying at the Overseas League tonight?' James asked pleasantly.

'I thought so, yes. They usually manage to find a room for me in the annexe. It's quiet and out of the way.'

'Well, we'll have to change all that. I thought you might enjoy a breather from the kind of work you've been doing for us these last few months. You're a good socializer, aren't you? You know your officer's card will get you into a number of service clubs that our Allies have set up.'

'I know that. In fact, I've spent some time in the Maple Leaf Club in the Mall. I like these Canadians . . .'

'Excellent.' James broke in. 'Do you know the Polish Officers' Club? It's in St James's Square, near what used to be Disraeli's house. Good bar there, too. Take a look at these photographs.'

It was a Polish captain that time, in the months that followed it could just as easily be one of de Gaulle's Free French or an American bomber pilot. In the months following Dunkirk, some 150,000 refugees from Denmark, Norway, Holland and other countries had poured into Britain, and it was logical to assume that an undetermined number of questionable types had slipped through the initial screening.

An unpleasant business, but one that was simply done and soon over with. To get a line on a certain young Czechoslovak lieutenant, I got myself invited to a party at his girlfriend's flat. All I had to do was keep track of the guests, and look for extra telephones. Thankfully, it wasn't often that I had to put myself in the position of checking up on my target in his own home. It was generally a matter of staying a few nights at the service club, having a couple of drinks with my target, and that was it.

The RAC Club and Grosvenor House were the scene for quite a few of these encounters. Also, the English Speaking Union, though I can't say that I enjoyed the time I spent there. To me, the place was just a little too formal and toffee-nosed. You had mostly elderly types in there, ex-colonials from the far-flung outposts of empire, ladies with wide-brimmed hats who spent their afternoons sipping tea and nibbling at their biscuits. There was a certain type of junior officer to be seen there hunting for rich, slightly dotty widows, and this I adopted as my protective camouflage.

Were any German agents brought to bay as a result of my efforts? I only wish I knew. If it happened, they never told me. Most of the men I came across seemed perfectly ordinary and above-board. But there was no way I could ever be sure. The full picture would emerge from the reports of perhaps a dozen other men, a mosaic of patterns, habits, personal trivia. And what it showed was simply none of my business.

Sometimes I remembered the recruiting posters that seemed to have sprouted overnight on every wall and street corner of Nottingham during that long-ago, nervous week of Munich. An accusing finger. 'Your country expects *you*.'

Is this what they meant? Thinking of Nottingham brought to mind a kaleidoscope of memories from my all-too-carefree student days. One face haunted me. Reg, who had been almost an older brother. A born pilot, high-spirited and reckless, just like a cinema Flyboy. I had been with him that day when he was presented with his silver tankard to hang in the RAF officers' mess. Reg, from the village where I grew up. He was in the cockpit of his Spitfire when the Battle of Britain erupted in the skies in August, 1940. A month later, he went down in flames over the Channel. His country had expected a lot from him.

A hero's death. I could almost hear Reverend Williams back in Ystrad Mynach intoning the eulogy, groping for the right words to comfort his mother and father. I wasn't particularly looking for that or any other kind of death, but I did want to feel that I was being of some use to my country. No matter how hard I tried, I could not square that idea with this life of drinking, going to dances, and spying on the men who were supposed to be my comrades. There was only the bitter consolation of knowing that, if not me, someone else would have to do it.

Not that it made me feel any better about it.

5

Cornwall to Brussels

Nineteen forty-three was a good year for the Allied war effort. Ever since Montgomery's troops had given the supposedly invincible Rommel a good knocking at El Alamein, the victories, large and small, seemed to follow one another in quick succession. The mood in London was almost cheerful, I noticed. Newspapers told of successful landings by Allied troops in North Africa and Sicily, while Churchill puffed his cigar and solemnly announced the turning of the tide.

And I was in a cosy village pub in Cornwall, drinking the excellent local cider and feeling not at all happy about my part in it.

My presence there in this quiet corner of Britain was due to a man whom I shall call Flintham. The Department had very good reasons for taking an interest in this fellow.

'What do you think, Greville?'

James had contrived with the staff to guarantee a half-hour of privacy in the Indian Room of the Overseas League, and he had just handed me a blown-up photograph of a tall man standing proudly with his hand on the long bonnet of a Continental Bentley. He would be about thirty years old, I guessed, and had cold-looking eyes with longish fair hair brushed flat across his forehead.

'German?'

'No. Scottish. In fact, his father's a lord.'

'And probably doesn't mind letting you know it.' I passed the glossy print back to him. 'Looks sort of a cruel fish if you ask me.'

'You're going to have plenty of chances to find out for

yourself. As for being a Nazi, well, we know he was a
student at Heidelberg back in '34, and got quite caught up
in the Hitler Youth thing. Never made a secret about it,
either. For all we know, it could be like that Mitford girl
with the pash on Hitler.

'Where is he now?'

James named the village. 'That's in Cornwall, just over
the county boundary some thirty-odd miles west of Exeter.
He's just recently purchased a farm there, and we'd very
much like to know exactly what he plans to do with it. He's
not the gentleman-farmer type.'

That part of the West Country was pretty backward and
isolated, James went on to tell me. Perhaps a little too
conveniently so. This Flintham had bought enough land to
make it a perfect landing-spot for German spies dropped in
by parachute. For that matter, it would have served equally
well as a clandestine radio base.

'I don't think it likely he would take to a civilian turning
up casually in the area where he lives,' James said. 'There's
not more than a hundred inhabitants for miles around.
Luckily for us, the Army had a twelve-man searchlight base
nearby. That's where you're being posted. During the
daytime, these units have got nothing much to keep them
busy apart from cleaning the equipment, so there shouldn't
be any problem making contact. You hold the rank of
private for the duration, because there's already a corporal
in charge there.'

Before the week was out, I was unpacking my kitbag in
Cornwall, trying to decide on how I was going to handle it.
Best not make any direct overtures, I reasoned. Instead, I
would make it my business to find out exactly who the
man's friends were, and make my approaches through
them.

That was the easy part, as it turned out. There was a
private at the base, George, a former wine-and-spirits

merchant from a town in the Midlands, who was by the way of being a clever sort. It was he who introduced me to Flintham one evening in the pub. The fact that we two were reasonably educated soldiers who could hold up our own end in a conversation obviously meant a lot to Flintham. Clearly, he felt the locals were quite beneath him.

A few days later he invited us both over to his place for an after-hours drink. It was a short walk from the pub through a field of daffodils to a slightly larger than usual Cornish stone farmhouse, nicely renovated, from what I could see. There must have been over 200 acres or so of good farmland overrun with weeds attached to the property.

Inside, I saw that Flintham had assembled quite a nice collection of antique furniture. Rough-hewn country style, nothing Frenchified or fancy. The dining room had a fireplace that extended the entire length of one wall, with seats arranged under the overhanging canopy so that you could roast chestnuts or grill potatoes in the pan beneath the enormous log fire. I didn't have to pretend to be impressed.

It soon became clear that impressing people and spending money were Flintham's major ambitions in life. He took us around the rooms, pointing out pieces and telling their age and history, trying to sound modest about it, and not succeeding.

In the vast downstairs library, I wandered over to the ceiling-high shelves, running my eyes along the rows of elegant, calf-bound volumes, trying to remember names and titles. This, James always said, was a most important item. Tell me the books a man keeps in his home and I'll tell you all you'll ever need to know about his character.

And how right you were, James, I thought to myself. The names on the gold-tooled spines were only names to me, but I had a fair idea of what they represented. Krafft-Ebing. Havelock Ellis. Titles in German which I couldn't make out. So my man's got his twisty side, I thought.

'Find something?' Flintham had come up from behind me, put a bony hand on my shoulder that brought an involuntary shudder, and with the other proffered a drink.

'Yes. You seem to have some pretty interesting stuff here.'

He plucked a tall volume in red morocco from the shelf nearest to him and began to turn the pages, showing me the plates to see my reaction, if any. 'You aren't, I suppose, an admirer of the divine Marquis?' he asked pleasantly.

'I really don't know a thing about it,' I answered, lamely.

'No. Of course not. You wouldn't.' He paused for a long moment, as if in thought. 'Wait here,' he said. 'I'd like to show you a few things from my collection.'

Two minutes later he was back with an assortment of whips under one arm, and a polished wooden case. Real whips, with ugly leather thongs on them. The velvet-lined box revealed a collection of handcuffs and other implements whose purpose he proceeded to explain to me.

I was twenty-two years old then, and I'll admit had to choke back my revulsion. Looking back on it now, it's easy to see that shocking people was for him a way of getting the attention he must have been deprived of as a child. The stagey larger-than-life farmhouse was part of it too. Like all egomaniacs, he needed an audience. The more staid and conventional – wet behind the ears, in my case – the deeper the impression he so desperately was trying to make. And that's why, I'm sure, he took to me.

Then, too, once he had a few drinks in him, Flintham made no secret of the fact that he was betting on Hitler to win the war and that, so far as he was concerned, this was all to the good. 'Believe me, my friend,' he said imperiously, 'I was there when Hitler came to power and it was simply magnificent. You couldn't possibly understand the dreadful shape the country was in. And how he put it all back together.'

I wondered whether he was hoping that a Nazi victory would give him a chance to prowl around Exeter in a shiny leather uniform and act out his fantasies with the whip.

When I reported back to London and told all this to James, he listened intently, nodding from time to time, but gave no sign of surprise. 'Really,' I spluttered, 'Boris Karloff couldn't have played this fellow, he'd have been too frightened.'

James considered this. 'It certainly sounds like we've got a case on our hands, yes.'

I started to tell James about the blood-curdling poems of his own composition that Flintham had read to us; somewhat florid and overblown imitations of the French decadents as I now remember them, but James waved it aside.

'Very well, Greville. I think you had better stick to this chap for a while longer.'

Back in Cornwall, I took James's advice and paid particularly close attention to Flintham's comings and goings. There was an interesting pattern. He would go on the train to London almost every Friday morning, and not be seen in the village for two or three days after that. I immediately got in touch with the Department so that James could have a tail put on him.

One time he and I happened to find ourselves together at the Okehampton railway station. I was ostensibly on my way to Exeter on my forty-eight-hour pass – it wouldn't look good to have me going back and forth to London all the time – which meant I would get off at that station, wait a few hours in the buffet, and catch the branch-line express to London. When I walked out on to the platform with my kitbag, there was Flintham in the midst of a noisy row with one of the porters, something about having missed his connection. I went up to say hello, and at the sound of my voice he turned round clicked his heels together, shot up his

hand in the Nazi salute and shouted, 'Heil democracy!'
Another interesting little titbit for James.

Mind you, this was after he had come to trust in me
pretty completely. Luckily, I never had to pass myself off as
a potential fifth-columnist to gain his confidence. It was
easy enough to make out that I was fed up with Army life, a
natural leadswinger. Just an occasional remark that I'd be
glad to see the bloody war over, wasting my time and my
life, and who cares whether Herr Hitler and the Russians
had it in for each other in the first place.

A particularly vivid memory connected with my surveillance of Flintham is of the New Year's Eve I spent at his
farmhouse; one of his more glittering productions, but
absolutely in character for him. Dozens of people from the
village were brought in to help out with the decorations,
and Flintham arranged with the local vicar for a troupe of
village maidens to give a display of Cornish folk dances.

It was a strange affair in many ways. He invited down a
very attractive Scottish woman to serve as hostess, and
though he introduced her round the village as his wife, I
checked and saw that they kept to separate bedrooms.
Together they made the preparations for a very expensive
affair, and on the night of the party about twenty guests
turned up. As I was introduced to each one, I made a
mental list of their names, and where they came from.

We sat down at the huge single-plank oak table to a
sumptuous meal of pheasant and haggis, served to us by
elderly waiters recruited from nearby Devonshire. Laughter,
gaiety and the popping of champagne corks heralded the
arrival of each course. After dinner we all sang songs
around the table.

As the evening wore on, Flintham regaled us with a show
of his virtuosity, first playing the bagpipes – he played very
well, too – then on to a reading of his own poetry, though
these were pretty tame compared with the stuff I'd had to

listen to before. When all the guests were occupied dancing to the gramophone or tapping the inexhaustible supply of Flintham's good liquor, I slipped outside to where the cars were parked and wrote down the registration numbers. Though it certainly didn't look much like a reunion of Nazi conspirators and, in fact, I couldn't swear but that some of the names on the guest list weren't vaguely familiar to me from the pages of *Lilliput* and *Picture Post*, James would have to run a check on every one of them.

'First rate,' was James's only comment when I reported all this back to London. High praise it was, too, coming from him. I was more accustomed by now to a curt nod of acknowledgment. Otherwise, he would just mutter, 'That seems about satisfactory', or words to that effect to indicate completion of an assignment. For the hundredth time, I felt like giving in to the constant temptation to come straight out and ask him what action was going to be taken in this case, but I knew better than to pull something like that. Much later, however, I did hear that Flintham was shipped off to an internment camp for the duration of the war. Whether or not they put his own handcuffs on him when they led him off, I couldn't say.

When I had time to myself in London between postings, I started going around with a girl named Vicki, a regular like myself at the Overseas League dances. She had spent a good part of her childhood in France, I learned. Her mother was French and there was the slightest trace of an accent when Vicki spoke. You could tell, too, from the way her Army lieutenant's uniform clung enticingly to her petite figure – give a French girl an off-the-peg dress any day and she'll take it home and alter it until it fits her to perfection.

Vicki told me she was an instructor in radio communication, Morse code and teleprinting, doing double duty teaching languages to Free French liaison personnel stationed in London. I'd always phone her office in

Whitehall every time I got to London, just as soon as I reported in to James, and we'd meet in the Studio Club in Swallow Street which was the social headquarters of the Free French in London. Arnold was a genial secretary and host.

With her high cheekbones, lustrous ash-brown hair and an ineffable air of chic, so charmingly French and to me exotic, I'll admit it was the first and only time I was in love in my whole life. Yet there was definitely a mysterious side to the lovely Vicki. A matter of moods and movements. When we were together she'd be completely relaxed and happy, playfully coquettish; the next time I saw her it could all be changed. A different person altogether: moody, nervous and on edge. I couldn't work it out at first.

Then it would happen that during the months that we were seeing each other regularly, a voice on the telephone would say that the lady I asked for was unavailable at present. Weeks later, when we got together, Vicki would say that she'd been to the north of England training the boys for wireless work. I saw no reason to disbelieve her. A few questions had clearly established that she did know her way around radios.

The second or third time that she failed to turn up for a long-standing date, I started to worry. Whitehall was characteristically unhelpful. Weeks went by, and I asked around Soho where the Free French did their drinking and a few places we both knew in Mayfair if anyone had seen her. Nobody had seen her.

This time I decided to bring my problem to James. It was the first time I'd ever had to ask him for a personal favour.

'Look,' I argued, 'I've become very much in love with this young lady, and I know it's against regulations. It's only a feeling, but I think she may be one of your people. Now she's gone missing. I want you to find out what's happened to her.'

'Is it important?'

'It's important.'

James was reluctant at first, but he realized I would not let up on it until I had some kind of answer. 'All right, Greville,' he said slowly. 'I suppose it can be looked into. If your guess is right, though, just don't expect too much from me in the way of hard information. But you'll have to give me something more to go on.'

I was able to tell James her military service number. This I knew as a result of some off-the-book spying of my own. Troubled by her sudden shifts of mood, I had at one point wondered if it were possible that Vicki could be an enemy plant. Perhaps I was flattering myself to think that the Abwehr could possibly have taken an interest in me, or just as possibly it was no more than my own crude self-justification. So one evening, when she was out of the room, I made a quick search of her handbag and found her service ID card. All is supposed to be fair in love and war, and this was an exceedingly volatile mixture of both.

James wrote the number on the back of a paper serviette and said, 'I'll take care of it personally.'

At our next meeting, however, James seemed to be in need of reminding. Finally he said, 'Look, I can tell you this. The lady you asked me about is a very brave person, a person we should respect and admire. Why don't we leave it at that?'

Don't ask questions. That was the attitude of mind that had been drilled into us. Follow orders. If you don't know it's because you don't need to know. The elementary rules of the game.

To hell with the rules.

I asked James to tell me the truth. He sighed, and his pale grey eyes evaded mine. 'All right, Greville.' His voice was absolutely level. 'Vicki has, we think, been captured by the Nazis in France. She's a radio instructor who was teaching the French *maquis* – we had dropped her in and pulled her out several times before, but now we think they must have got on to her, because she didn't turn up at the last rendezvous we arranged. I'm sorry, Greville. I wish you hadn't asked me.'

There was a light rain falling that evening in London. For some reason, I remember that. I went away from James, too shocked and humbled to feel my grief. Disgusted with myself for playing around in grubby barracks or rich men's houses, a retriever dog sniffing out trivia about nut-cases like Flintham or, worse, decent men, messmates whose friendship I cultivated solely for the purpose of sneaking a look at their dirty linen. Far in the distance, the air-raid sirens began their hollow whine. Now the one brave person I met had probably given her life in the real war. That was it. The real war. Not this sham business.

The next day was a Sunday. I got up early after a sleepless night and rang the contact number I had always used with James. I told the voice at the other end that I wanted to see James again, and would wait for him that evening in the safe house down by the Chelsea Embankment.

'. . . I'm asking you to do this thing for me. I'm fed up with all this sneaky business. How do you think I feel reading about men who are in prison camps in Burma . . .'

James let me go on like that, without trying to interrupt, knowing that it was something bottled up inside and had to come out.

'I understand what you're trying to say,' James said finally. 'Believe me, I appreciate your feelings. It may seem like a rum business to you, and I won't argue that. We gave you this job, remember, because we thought you'd be good at it. In wartime, there aren't many pleasant jobs to be handed out.'

'I know all that. Listen, all I'm asking is a chance to do something in the real war. I'm not saying I want to be a hero; I just want to be able to look at myself in the mirror when I shave and feel good about it. Let me prove that I can serve as a real soldier.'

James flicked ash from the slim cheroot in his hand. 'Prove it to me, here and now. What a real soldier does is follow orders.'

There was a long silence. James said, 'At the moment, we've come up with another assignment that's your sort of thing. Once that's completed, I'll see about getting you posted overseas.'

I let that roll around my mind for yet another minute. 'Tell me about the mission, sir,' I said finally, with heavy emphasis on the last word.

I was sent to an Army Holding Unit in Wiltshire. This camp was a collection centre for service misfits of all types: conscientious objectors who didn't quite make the Board, nancy-boys, barrack-room lawyers, men who couldn't accept the military life for one reason or another. All were, in one way or another, most definitely unsuitable Army material, hand-picked from ITC camps all over Britain, over a thousand men in all. A good number were professional Communist agitators: and a setting like that could easily turn into a breeding-ground for trouble.

Andy Logan was the name of the man I was supposed to keep under surveillance. Once he had been branch secretary of the Party in Bournemouth, never made any secret about his connections, hawking the *Daily Worker* on street corners. When not making busy with the *agitprop*, he worked for the Carreras Cigarettes people, putting up displays in tobacconists' shops. Well-read and intelligent, he was obviously officer candidate material, but he had managed it so that he stayed in the ranks to recruit for the Party.

MI5 seemed to know all there was to know about Andy Logan and made sure that I received a full briefing when I collected my rail-warrant and a new set of documents and went off to Devizes. They were also well aware that the Communist Party had set up a special committee at their Covent Garden headquarters to co-ordinate recruitment within the services. It would be interesting to know who was on that committee and what success, if any, our Bolshevik friends were having.

Getting friendly with 'Red Andy', as everyone at the camp called him, was the first and easiest part of the assignment. My assumed rank of corporal was the same as his, so it was natural for me to put my tray down at his table in the NAAFI canteen and start a conversation. Andy had thinning, fair hair, was more than a few pounds overweight and about five years my senior. I told him that I'd been to a university, put in for a commission, failed the War Office Selection Board test and been returned, unsuitable, to Devizes for more training. The Communists always checked up, we knew, so it was necessary to stick as close as possible to the truth.

The object of the camp at Devizes was to keep everyone occupied and out of trouble, so there was plenty of leisure time for Andy and me to get on close terms. We only had to supervise work crews assigned to routine keep-busy tasks, tidying up the perimeter of the barracks, weeding lawns, digging vegetable gardens, painting and washing vehicles or working on cookhouse fatigues.

Andy introduced me to several other Party members at the camp, and before too long I was invited out for drinks with them. Around the base, Andy would be handing out pamphlets and asked if I'd care to sit in at one of the informal 'discussion groups' the local Communists held in the nearby pubs. The first two times I said no, I didn't think I'd be interested, and Andy was all smiles and understanding. The impression I was trying to give was being a little on the naïve side, and easily flattered by his attention. A few days later, I'd get to talking about some item in the papers about Russia or the war, and he always had an answer ready. 'Why not join us just for one evening, Greville? I'm sure you'll meet people much better-informed than me who can give you some straight answers – not the bull the Army is handing out.' I said, well, why not, and Andy clapped his arm on my shoulder in a friendly way, excited that the bait had finally been swallowed. They didn't go in for the hard sell, these Communists.

In the pub, I listened attentively to the five men who were doing all the talking and must have asked the right questions; the atmosphere was very relaxed and friendly. Most of the session was given over to elucidating fine points of Communist theory – I found all that a bit above me – and these small-time commissars seemed pretty much a woolly-headed, incompetent lot, but that would be for James to decide on. Andy, incidentally, was an excellent public speaker who made sure he really knew his facts and figures before he opened his mouth. His wife, a pleasant, well-dressed woman, would sometimes stay at the local hotel and help to organize these meetings, never in the same pub two times running, and pass out leaflets on the streets. They were a likeable, unpretentious couple.

Maybe the Party had given him a recruiting quota, something to do with their local Five-Year Plans, I don't know. Despite my tepid show of interest, Andy stepped up the overtures, telling me that if I had a chance to meet the right people, I'd surely be convinced that the progressive forces in the world were working to a common goal of peace. 'You look like you might prove a useful chap,' he winked, repeating almost to the word what the man from MI5 had told me in Nottingham several years earlier.

I said I was always willing to listen, and so, on our next

weekend leave to London, I let him take me round to Party
HQ at No. 16 King Street.

We went up several flights of rickety wooden stairs,
pungent with the smell of spoiling cabbage. We were shown
into a dreary suite of offices, where the furniture had soiled
upholstery and the ashtrays were filled to overflowing. An
older man in shirtsleeves and a brocade waistcoat came
over and, speaking with a slight Geordie accent, introduced
himself as 'Frank'. We had a friendly half-hour chat,
mostly about me, my background, how I was getting on in
the Army, things like that. 'Frank' pressed a handful of
pamphlets on me before I left, saying he hoped that these
would give me a clear idea of the Party's aims. They were
all in question and answer form, like a child's catechism.
'Reminds me of all these bloody training manuals we're
supposed to swot up,' I remarked, but promised to read
them carefully and stay in touch with Andy.

'Well, what did you think?' asked Andy as we negotiated
our way down the stairs and emerged into the bustle of
Covent Garden.

There was no reason for me to act out of character about
it, so I just said, 'It all looks a bit shabby to me, your set-
up.'

'Oh, I know,' Andy replied glumly. 'We haven't had an
easy time of it. You wait a few years, though, things are
going to change in this country.' It seemed to me he said it a
little wistfully, as if he really believed that, come the
Revolution and they'd be holding their discussion groups in
Lambeth Palace.

I never did get to meet Harry Pollit or return to King
Street after that first meeting, for James had other things in
mind. I was pulled out of Devizes and given to understand
that MI5 would continue its monitoring of Communist
recruiting activities using other agents.

Though I never ran into 'Red Andy' or any of his

comrades after that, this episode had its sequel years later when I was arrested in Hungary and bundled off to the Soviet Union to face trial on charges of espionage, in connection with the Penkovsky affair. Seeing my name splashed all over the headlines, Andy Logan wrote to my wife, assuring her that it must be some dreadful mistake. He had got to know me well, he declared, and was convinced that I was either a fellow-traveller or in any case sympathetic enough to have bought a platform ticket. Andy even offered to intercede on my behalf with the Soviet Ambassador. Which was not only extremely well-meant of him, but an accolade to one of my better MI5 performances, coming almost twenty years after the curtain had rung down.

I was not sent overseas straight away. There was a job in Cornwall that James wanted me to tackle. Counter-intelligence, this time, was only a fractional part of the assignment. The rest was straight public-relations work, driving round in my jeep to talk to the local farmers. Was the presence of the Army causing them any special problems? If so, I gave them a number to call and assured them that I would deal with the matter. But I was also under orders to keep a sharp eye out for any of the locals who seemed unusually hostile to the Army or less than forthcoming about their activities when I spoke to them. James's people would investigate and try to find out what was behind it. Again, it was not explained to me why the Department was so concerned with what was going on in this pleasant, tucked-away corner of the West Country. My job was simply to observe and report.

The longer I stayed on in Cornwall, eating salmon, going to dances in Exeter with the lovely blonde daughter of one of the farmers I met, the more my conscience troubled me. I didn't exactly grumble, but reminded James that he had promised I would see some action. Finally, he gave in. Ten days after D Day I was sent to the Normandy beach-head with a vehicle repair unit.

Our job was to carry out emergency repairs on the fleet of transport lorries that rushed fresh troops, ammunition and supplies to the tip of the Allied spearhead thrusting down the centre of France. Neither the feeling of satisfaction nor my term of combat duty was fated to last for very long, however. Although our unit did get to witness the thousand-bomber raid on Cannes from high on a ridge overlooking the blazing city, we only came under enemy fire once, and that was the result of having been given the wrong map co-ordinates. We lost a truck to German mortars, but fortunately suffered no casualties.

After three months, we had made it as far as the outskirts of Brussels, when a messenger from Divisional HQ caught up with me drinking cider with a group of Canadians. I was being sent back to London, effective immediately.

'Sorry to have to spoil your fun,' James said, 'but we need somebody here with your experience. You're being promoted to major, if that helps any. And then we are going to arrange for you to be discharged from the service.

The explanation for this was that somebody high up in the Department had decided that a soldier engaged in questionable activities might have his guard down when talking to a civilian, so a civilian I would be from now until the end of the war, though continuing under James's orders. He showed me a long list of names with question marks pencilled after them. I was to be given a card identifying me as a War Office employee (so that I could continue to frequent service clubs and other social functions open to military personnel) and a ration book.

This new arrangement suited me. Surveillance work took up relatively little of my time; I felt like a civilian in fact as well as in name. I got together with a friend of mine from the Navy and put my accumulated savings into the purchase of a bomb-damaged house in South Kensington, which we proceeded to fix up ourselves. It would give me just enough income to see me through the transition period to civilian life looming just ahead.

A week or so after the German capitulation, I had one last meeting with James. 'We would be delighted to have you stay on with us, Greville. There's an opening for you on the Allied War Commission in Germany, if you're at all interested.'

I'd been giving the matter of what to do with myself a good deal of painful deliberation, so my answer was immediate and definite: 'I don't think so, but thanks anyway for the offer. I'm happy now fiddling with my house, doing all the rewiring myself and helping out with the construction work.'

Actually, I was glad to make it a clean break with the Department and anxious to get off to a new start in life. Looking back on my intelligence career to date produced very mixed feelings indeed. It was a job I hadn't asked for and didn't much like, but I had stuck it out to the end. Nothing in the least bit heroic in what I did. The feelings of guilt I experienced didn't easily go away. Possibly sensing this, James bent the rules slightly and let me know that as a result of information provided by me, ten men had been dismissed from sensitive positions as potential security risks and another five interned during one eighteen-month period. And so many others whose names had been quietly and discreetly cleared without blackening their service records. Necessary? Well, perhaps it was.

There remained, however, a vague feeling of regret, an idea that I still owed something to my country for having given me such a cushy war while so many others had to suffer. Ten years would go by until the opportunity would come for that debt to be paid in full.

PART TWO
Odessa

6

Back in the Fold

What would you do if you were invited to give up a successful career, comfortable family life and security – in short, everything a perfectly ordinary man like myself could hope to achieve in life, to take daft risks spying behind the Iron Curtain?

If someone had asked me that any time before the summer of 1955, I honestly couldn't tell you how I might have answered. Nor could I tell you why I almost immediately said yes when the question was put to me. But here is what led up to it.

Nine months before the war in Europe guttered to an end, I had been demobbed a few jumps ahead of half a million hopeful young men looking to resume a way of life that we all took for granted before September 1939, and was now just a dim memory so far as most of us were concerned. Like the majority of my contemporaries, it took some time after shedding the uniform, about a year in my case, to find a foothold in the profession I had trained for. Then I heard of a medium-sized electrical supply and service outfit, the Jeary Engineering Company, that had been forced to shut down for the duration of the war on account of the shortage of skilled personnel. They had a good relationship with a number of firms in the south of England, supplying them with switchgear, motors and other electrical equipment for industry. Mr Eastick, who had run the company with his brother before the war, now had his hands full trying to keep up with the demand from factories and contractors who were desperate for equipment after so many years of restrictions.

My new job gave me entry to a great number of renascent manufacturing firms, and I felt it was perfect training for the day when I would start a company of my own. To succeed as a technical sales representative in those early days was no great problem. All you had to do was find the suppliers to keep up with the orders that kept rolling in as British industry slowly got back on its feet. Basically it was a matter of customers looking for suppliers, rather than the other way round. So once I had oriented myself to this topsy-turvy situation, it was really just a problem of working backwards to discover who might be producing what, and how soon could it be delivered.

As time went on, I became more and more interested in the international export side of my job. Postwar reconstruction on the Continent was off to a sluggish start, and the demand there for all sorts of light and heavy equipment was even more acute than in Britain. I persuaded Jeary to exhibit at the first British Industries Fair held at Olympia after the war, and there I met the representative of a French company who told me that he was very interested in some new fluorescent lighting that had just come on the market. I let him know that we could supply the lamps and I would do my best to locate a firm to furnish the control gear and fittings. After a frantic search, I found a small shop tucked away under the arches of one of the main railway lines running out of London where they did the job for me. Then I organized the delivery of the order privately, crating up the lots myself, and found that I'd made one hundred per cent profit on the deal.

Immediately after that, I decided to spend my upcoming 'holiday' in France, paying a casual visit to the same company just to see what else they might be in the market for. I daresay they were overjoyed to see me. The firm was urgently shopping around for an up-to-date office intercom system and, as it happened, I knew exactly where to obtain the product they wanted. This was the beginning of the small private export business I built up as a sideline to my work at Jeary. Through other contacts I'd made at trade fairs, subsequent 'holiday' trips to Belgium, Holland and Germany were not long forthcoming. As my work for Jeary had never kept me fully occupied, I still had sufficient time and energy to devote to my own business, and it was fast becoming one of my principal and most profitable activities.

About the same time, I sank some of the money from these deals into the purchase of the Trojan Club in Kensington. I had already been a member of some years' standing, and when the club came on to the market at a very reasonable price, I thought I might have a go at running the place myself. As a means of impressing my clients and business contacts, it seemed a pretty wise investment, too, so I arranged for an ex-RAF friend to become the secretary/manager, and took over the lease. The members were happy with the way it was run, and I had a lot of fun personally, going in on Sundays to work behind the bar and help organize the evening's entertainment. We had two waiters, a barman, a small orchestra and three people working in the kitchen. We were the only club outside the West End to have a licence to serve drinks until midnight, six days a week, a fact much appreciated by our regulars. Frank Sinatra, as a guest of one of the local residents, visited the club a few times. Even the head of the local CID, Arthur Phillips, was on our membership books. Altogether I kept it on for seven years, eventually bringing an ex-Naval commander and his wife in as partners. Towards the end, I had less to do with the day-to-day business running of the club, but it was great fun while it lasted.

By the time I was involved with the club, I had already been married for some years. Sheila and I had met at a

Saturday night dance at the Overseas League shortly before
the end of the war. She told me that she worked as a secretary
for a hospital finance department, organizing fund-raising
schemes and activities. Here, I thought to myself, was a very
attractive young lady indeed, and before too long I was
asking her over to my house in Kensington. Our relationship
flowered and led to the inevitable proposal. Her parents
were a little Victorian for my taste, but we got on reasonably
well. Her father came from a little village in Scotland and
owned a chain of chemists' shops in the centre of London.
The thing I remember about him was how carefully he
managed to keep his drinks cabinet locked up. He kept the
key in his waistcoat pocket and could take his sweet time
fumbling to get it out and put some liquor in his future son-
in-law's glass. Even then he'd generally offer me sherry,
knowing, I'm sure, that I couldn't stand the stuff. For my
part, I was only too painfully aware of the perfectly good
bottle of Scotch tucked away in the corner.

Our wedding took place in a church in Wandsworth, as
my parents-in-law lived in Spencer Park. It was quite an
impressive do˙ – even my father came up for the day from
Ystrad Mynach. Afterwards all sorts of people whom I had
never seen before or since turned up for the reception. We
had decided on a honeymoon in Switzerland. It got off to a
dreadful start when our car broke down en route to the
station and we had to hitch-hike the rest of the way with all
our luggage; but Switzerland, when we finally got there,
seemed glorious to both of us. All the shop windows were
filled with consumer goods, food and merchandise of all
kinds, and at night the city blazed with light. It was a
welcome change from the dreary reality of Britain, where
wartime rationing and restrictions were still in effect, and a
perfect start to our marriage.

Our early years together were pleasant enough in many
ways. Our son, Andrew, was born eighteen months later and

I was delighted when the 'old firm' sent James as their representative to the christening. Needless to say, I introduced him to my wife as just another old friend from the war. It was a good life we were living in those days. The money coming from my various business interests was more than adequate. The club was not making a fortune, but it provided us with all the free food, drink and entertainment we could hope for. I had a successful career, an attractive wife, a son, and a large comfortable home.

Still, there was the feeling that something was missing in my life. A touch of excitement, perhaps. Not, mind you, if you take the word in its James Bondian sense; that of course, had never been in my line. Rather, I suppose you could say it was the sense of being involved with what was going on in the world, the very personal satisfaction of being useful to one's country.

In large measure, it's true, it was simply a question of temperament. Sheila was a superb housewife and mother. I cannot fault her in any way for the growing restlessness which manifested itself as my business trips abroad became more and more frequent. To be perfectly honest, I looked forward to getting away from home and being on my own. Sheila must have sensed this and was annoyed and more than a little hurt. She couldn't understand why I didn't stay with my family like any ordinary husband.

In those days Paris was the hub for almost all of my business activities. I used to stay at the Hôtel Royal, just behind the Arc de Triomphe. The Bal Tabarin was putting on the best shows in Paris, much better than anything the Lido or Moulin Rouge could manage today. They had everything from chorus girls to conjurers, and the dancing was superb. From the business aspect too, things could hardly have been better. My clients were all very pleased to have an Englishman call at their factory gates and I often found myself invited out for an evening on the town with the manager of some firm or another picking up the bill, which is not the usual way these things are done.

Using Paris as my base, I started venturing further afield, sometimes taking a month at a time to make a swing through several countries. I didn't speak very much in the way of foreign languages, just enough to get the basic idea across to a taxi-driver or waiter, but somehow I made out all right. Usually there was at least one person on the other side of the conference table who spoke English, and that was all I needed.

In a few years' time I was able to give up my job with Jeary Electrics and set up my own export agency, Greville Wynne Ltd. My family and I moved into a large Georgian house on Upper Cheyne Row, Chelsea, and I carried on my business from an office extension I built on to the back. Sheila helped out on the secretarial side. Trade exhibitions were once again being held all over Europe, and I made a point of attending as many of these as I could to build up my contacts and add to my knowledge of overseas selling.

I worked hard promoting British exports. Anything I knew where to lay hands on could sell in those early days. Again, this was less a testimonial to my skills as a salesman than to the widespread hunger for industrial equipment in nearly every European country. Then, gradually, as business on the Continent picked up again, manufacturers in the UK were becoming more competitive. Now the practice was to appoint permanent agents in each branch of industry, by-passing the freelancers. Accordingly, the emphasis of my work had to change. By the mid-1950s I was specializing in the organization and training of sales representatives for other companies on a fixed-fee basis, and this was working out pretty well for all parties concerned.

Looking back on it all after twenty-five years, I have to stop and ask myself if I really was as happy and successful as I remember it. I had money in the bank and property of my own, not to mention the club. Plenty of experience behind me and a good future. Of course, I'm not trying to say that life was altogether a bed of roses. When is it ever? There were any number of business deals that fell through at the last minute, and all-too-frequent rows at home. The predictable, almost inevitable clash between the demands of career and family. Not to mention a hundred minor grievances against life that you or I or anyone else could tick off if we suddenly had to sit down and draw up a list.

But it would be equally wrong to imagine me as an unhappy man trying to keep up appearances, or anything of that sort. And this is what makes me wonder: was there, could there have been some tell-tale sign of the discontentment that was gnawing away at a far corner of my mind, so imperceptibly that I did not realize it myself? Was there something I said or did that raised an eyebrow somewhere and triggered a sequence of events that led to some clerk in Whitehall digging out the dusty, wartime file which had my name on it?

Consider, as I have often done, what was happening at exactly the same time, half a world away in Turkey. A man who is paid to notice things notices a high-ranking Soviet military attaché at the Ankara Embassy having a drink by himself in an open-air café. He is a successful career officer with an attractive wife, a much-adored baby daughter, a busy and enjoyable social life. A man on his way to the top. Not just once but several times, he is observed sitting by himself in the café sipping at his drink, with a faraway, almost wistful look suggesting a vague . . . restlessness. Or vexation of spirit. Or something.

Just a man sitting alone and sipping at his drink. There is nothing in the least bit sinister or even necessarily significant in what this particular Russian officer was doing. The point is that he was noticed, a report must have been handed in and in due time passed on to the anonymous men who direct the silent manoeuvrings that are carried out behind the backdrop on the stage where peace and war and every gradation between the two are acted out in public. Like the starlet who is discovered sipping an ice-cream soda in a Hollywood drugstore, you never know until somebody comes along, taps you on the shoulder and tells you that you're 'right' for the part.

That man in Ankara was Oleg Penkovsky. It was the summer of 1955. And I was alone in my office in Chelsea early one morning when I picked up the phone and a brisk but warmly cordial voice which I immediately recognized asked me how I was getting on.

'It's good of you to ring me up, James,' I said, thinking that if he bloody well knows my phone number he knows better than I do myself about how I've been doing. That's the James I remembered all too well. I was neither surprised nor put on guard by this unexpected development. It is simply the feeling of genuine pleasure that you experience when an old friend has taken the trouble to get in touch with you.

After we agreed to meet for lunch at the Ivy in St Martin's Lane that same afternoon, I remember leaning back in my swivel chair with my eyes closed and a self-satisfied smile. Second-guessing a superior officer was never a practice that made for efficient counter-intelligence agents during the war, and I was not about to start indulging in it at that late date. Still, the old boy's up to something. Now, wait a moment, why on earth should he be? I knew from old habit that it's no use thinking this or thinking that, not where people like James are concerned. Perhaps we'll have a good time over a few drinks exchanging wartime reminiscences. Yet the possibility that there might be a chance to work for British Intelligence again left me feeling as excited as any schoolboy looking ahead to end-of-term holidays.

James was already seated at a corner table when I got to the restaurant a little after one o'clock. As he got up to shake hands, the first thing I noticed was that the intervening years had changed him very little. 'By God, you're looking fit,' I told him, perhaps with a bit of envy in my voice. Still the same almost too-formal military carriage. It would have been a dead give-away if he ever had to work the field.

Then I noticed that although the restaurant was starting to fill up with well-heeled businessmen impressing their clients with some of the best food available in that part of London, James had arranged for a table set off in the corner and the service laid so that he and I would have an unobstructed view of anyone who entered the place. Well, well, so it's to be standard procedure for making contact after all. I took it as a good sign that, in one way or another, this wasn't going to be entirely a social engagement.

We both sat down to a lavish and well-prepared meal, complemented perfectly by several bottles of wine which James had chosen from the Ivy's excellent cellar, and plenty of friendly chatter. As the waiter brought us each steaming course it struck me that the relative opulence of the mid-afternoon feast could also have a special meaning. One thing I remembered from the war is that the Department never stints in its overtures when it wants something from you.

Behind this there is, I believe, an unspoken covenant. Spying is a dirty, dangerous, lonely trade. If you're no good at it you get tossed into a cell, subjected to what they primly called 'reinforced interrogation' and quite possibly shot for your trouble. Even if you're successful, what is there to expect? No public recognition, not even the chance to confide in your wife or closest friend. A choice between ignominy and obscurity, not to put too fine a point on it. Then what is left to set on the other side of the ledger? Knowing that patriotism has no price, British Intelligence does what it can to see that you live well. An almost unlimited expense account is the spy's cold comfort.

'More wine, Greville?'

'I will, thanks.' Wine, food and service were all first rate.

We talked mostly about the war, as old army friends will, awarding ourselves full credit for turning the tide of battle in Europe. We played the obligatory game of whatever happened to so-and-so, dredging up names from memory. James was in a reminiscent mood and started to tell me about what he had been up to during his absences from London in 1943 and 1944. I learned that he had been parachuted into Yugoslavia to make contact with Tito's partisans, who were, he said, damned tough and effective as an anti-Nazi guerrilla force. From there we went on to discuss the current state of the world (a bloody mess, in our considered opinion), the pros and cons of the Cold War and what was likely to happen in Russia now with this chap Khrushchev evidently running the show. I couldn't help but get the feeling that I was gently being sounded out. But to what purpose? That was still the big question.

I told James about business activities, how life in general was treating me, and spoke of my family life. He listened attentively, running a thoughtful thumbnail along his regulation moustache and nodding at intervals. What could I say that he probably didn't know already? He volunteered no information about his current activities and I certainly knew better than to embarrass him with a leading question. Had I done so, I'm sure he would have written me off right then and there.

Finally, it was time to be on our way. James put down the bubble-glass of brandy cupped in his hand and beckoned to the waiter. Then, as he was getting up and pushing back his chair, he said, 'I understand business is fairly bristling in Eastern Europe these days.'

I just looked at him and said nothing. By saying nothing I was, in effect, acknowledging that I understood fully the significance of the remark. He was offering me an assignment. An invitation to get back in harness working for

British Intelligence. We shook hands without another word and James walked briskly to the cloakroom for his hat.

My mind was racing as I waved for a cab and hurried back to Chelsea. I knew I couldn't have misread the signal. James had been talking about Yugoslavia. That, and the comment about Eastern Europe seemed to indicate that he was in some way involved with operations in that part of the world. In that case, I could only assume that he must now be under the control of MI6, rather than MI5, which was the domestic counter-intelligence service. Not that the administrative distinction mattered in the least. The important thing was that I would be doing whatever it was I had to do under the direct control of James, as my 'case officer'. For me, that was a critical consideration. I trusted the man totally. Whatever you read about intelligence work in fact or fiction, never minimize the human factor involved. A spy would have to be an utter fool to risk his life for a faceless organization, but when a situation of total confidence has been built up over a period of years – that's a very different story.

Then what was making me hesitate? Purely selfish considerations, if you want to know the truth. Business was going well for me and I would not have liked to sacrifice that. But why should there be a sacrifice involved? James had suggested that I look into prospects in the Soviet bloc countries; very well, there couldn't be any harm in doing just that. If it came to the point where I had to curtail more profitable activities, I'd think again about it.

There was something else, too. A feeling I can't properly describe or put a label on. Call it a deep-rooted psychological need or fixation. It affects just about everybody who becomes drawn into intelligence work, regardless of personal motives. After a time, espionage is like a drug. You become to a greater or lesser extent addicted to the cliché situations of third-rate fiction, all the paraphernalia of dead letter drops, secret rendezvous and the ever-present element of danger. Once you've had a taste of that, you can never be entirely happy living a safe, complacent and prosperous normal life.

For all these reasons, my unspoken answer to James's proposal was bound to be yes.

I knew if I accepted, it would be entirely up to me to establish myself in the specified field of operation. That was the first challenge. If I was successful, I'd be told at some future point what the next move would be. If for any reason I was unwilling or unable to get my foot in the door, that would be the end of it. I remembered a chap I'd met who had been to East Berlin a year earlier, hoping to smoke out some business. It was grim, very grim, he said. The authorities over there were suspicious, if not overtly hostile. He concluded, finally, that it simply wasn't worth that much unpleasantness. So I knew from the beginning that it wasn't going to be easy and it wasn't going to enjoyable. I would have to get myself into a position where I could move about relatively unhindered in the unknown lands east of the Elbe.

Yes, but how? The best approach, I decided, would be to do it with the backing of large, well-known public firm. Preferably one offering a wide range of engineering products and heavy industrial equipment.

My chance came when the Thomas Locker group of companies advertised for an export manager. This Warring-ton-based firm seemed a good bet for a number of reasons. They were certainly big enough to impress the Communists and some their products had a quasi-military application that was bound to stir up an interest over there. I applied for the post and got it without difficulty.

Lockers had never had any dealings with Eastern Europe before – few British firms in the mid-1950s had even begun to consider the possibility. I had a job talking them round to my view. My argument was that the market potential on the far side of the Iron Curtain was comparable to the situation in Western Europe immediately after the war, and for very much the same reasons. Permission was given for me to make overtures in the company's name if the opportunity ever presented itself, but their support was no warmer than that. I decided it would be enough to get me started.

Unknown to my bosses at Lockers, I continued to operate out of the office extension in my Chelsea home, developing private contacts with other companies, trying to interest them in the possibilities of East–West trade. Again, the reaction was tepid at best, but my track record in the international sales field must have convinced them it was not wholly a pipe-dream.

I had to make sure that all the companies I handled were in different fields of industry so as to avoid conflicts of interest between firms who might end up in competition with each other. I was then representing such well-established firms as John Thompson (the late Airey Neave, one of the firm's directors at the time, approved my appointment), Edgar Allen & Company, manufacturers of special steel and cement-making plants, Plesseys, and several others. In two years' time I had lined up a hard core of eight firms who could supply everything from a complete electric-power generating station to high-capacity bottle-washing plants. Thus armed with the best of commercial credentials, I felt prepared to search out the cracks in the monolith of Communist bureaucracy and try to wriggle my way though.

This flurry of activities had its repercussions on the home front. My wife was not at all pleased that I would be involving myself with still more frequent business trips abroad. For some time she had been encouraging me to settle down and look for a fixed job in London, or consider different arrangements if I continued to work for myself.

There was no use in making her understand that this was the way I liked to live, going to new places and seeing new things. Telling her the real purpose behind all this was simply out of the question. The Department was adamant on this point: wives were not to know about our activities.

Obviously, Sheila was far from pleased with all this. I understood her point of view perfectly, but the idea of taking a nine-to-five job was simply appalling to me. So I argued the economic facts of life: it was becoming increasingly difficult to work freelance in Western Europe, business was falling off, etc. Truthfully, it was high time for me to branch out in another direction if we were to continue to prosper.

So right from the beginning, I had to do two things at once: prove that my instincts as a businessman were right, and that there was money to be made in trading with the Soviets and their satellites, while at the same time using these activities to build up my 'cover' for a mission that British Intelligence would let me know about at some unspecified point in the future.

Why, then, was I doing all this on the strength of a vaguely cryptical utterance? You must not forget, I knew from the war how these things were handled. You were never given much to go on at the beginning of a mission and, often enough, its real objective would never be made clear to you. I didn't mind that so much. What excited me more than anything else was the opportunity I was going to have to work closely with the 'Establishment' and be one of the select individuals who are trusted with their country's secrets. Call it vanity, if you like. It was something akin to knowing that the most exclusive club in the world had accepted me for membership.

7

Moscow at Last

Poland was the first of the Soviet bloc countries to grant me a visa. I went to their London embassy with an armful of catalogues and when the commercial attaché had a chance to leaf through half-a-dozen of these I told him I hoped to make an exploratory trip only, with a view to attending the Poznań Trade Fair later in the year. They were very helpful with the paperwork and went out of their way to draw up a list of government agencies it was necessary to visit before a purchase order could be authorized. Decision making in the East, I was beginning to understand, is a slow, laborious process where every proposal has to be filtered through a chain of committees before being passed upwards to that distant level where final approval is given.

In Warsaw, I managed to see all the right people in the ministries, and came away with a pretty clear idea of what they were shopping around for to fulfil the requirements of their current one-, two- and five-year plans. With this knowledge, it was simply a matter of getting in touch with the firms in Britain specializing in products appropriate for the industries the Polish authorities had singled out for development.

This, the first of my journeys to the East, provided me with some lasting impressions of what life under a communist régime could be like. Warsaw looked as if the Germans had marched out only the day before yesterday. Bombed-out rubble and the skeletons of centuries-old structures leered at the visitor from every major street. Housing for the people was low on their list of reconstruction priorities, yet the Russians had seen to it that the vast tottering ruin of what had once been Warsaw's main cathedral was pulled down and replaced with a Stalinesque parody of a neo-classical 'Palace of Culture'. I heard that the indignant Poles shunned the place, refusing to attend the concerts and exhibitions put on for their benefit at the site of this humiliating desecration.

Ten years after the war had ended, the Polish capital still looked like a suburb of Armageddon. Electricity being in short supply, voltages were kept low, making for dim, ochre lighting that only added to the general feeling of gloom and depression. Black-outs were frequent. People in the street, recognizing me as a foreigner, would scurry round the nearest corner lest they be hauled in by the police and accused of sharing the same pavement with a probable imperialist agent. My visit was taking place shortly after the insurrection in Hungary, and they must have had the clamps on good and tight.

On my way back from Poland, I had a further piece of good luck when my plane had to be diverted to Czechoslovakia for emergency repairs. As a result of this lay-over, I obtained a twenty-four-hour emergency visa at the airport which enabled me to make a quick sortie into Prague.

I asked the taxi-driver first to let me off at the British Consulate, hoping that they could give me advice on the commercial prospects at hand. Much to my dismay and astonishment they really seemed to know nothing at all about the Czechoslovak state trading-agencies and gave the impression that they couldn't have cared less about it. The lack of competence was so striking that I wondered, wouldn't it be funny if it turned out they were spies? I'd have to complain to James and see.

My luck took a turn for the better in the form of the English-speaking porter at the hotel where I had booked for the night. I explained my problem to him, put a carton of cigarettes suggestively on the table, and in half a minute he was on the phone fixing up appointments for the next day. The meetings proved even more successful than I had dared to hope. My visa was immediately extended so that I could have further talks with their middle-level officials.

Yes, I thought, everyone should be pretty pleased by the way things were working out. Especially James, who was probably following these events at a safe distance. It was a cheering thought, much needed by me, for Prague was gloomy in a way that not even Warsaw had been. The whole atmosphere reeked of the classic police state: walking along one of the shadowy, twining side-street, suddenly, in a doorway, I would glimpse a movement which, on approaching, was revealed as a couple of heavy-set guards in leather coats with turned-up fur collars, hefting their rifles, their eyes tracking me as I made my way along the street. I imagine the buildings with their peeling façades and cracked-plaster entranceways were government ministries, but I wasn't about to ask questions.

Conditions at my hotel were not much better. All Western visitors to Prague had to stay at the Hotel Arkon, just off Wenceslas Square. The place was crawling with stubble-chinned, shifty-eyed security men who looked as if they'd applied for the job through Hollywood's central casting. They made no pretence of concealing their activities, so the least bothersome alternative was simply to keep to one's room and re-read the copies of *The Electrical Review*, *Ideal Home* and *Modern Gardens* I had brought along for exactly such a contingency. These journals, I discovered, had a habit of disappearing if left out on a chair or table. On the other hand, the gift of a few shirts made the friendly hotel porter an ally for life. He reported to me on the other representatives of Western firms staying at the hotel, and gradually saw to it that I knew what was worth my attention during my Prague stopover. If not for his guiding hand, I would have missed seeing what was left of old Prague, its castles, rococo palaces, twisting cobbled alleys and grinning gargoyles. Yes, he said, he was instructed to keep a close watch on all foreign guests there. Also any female visitors the guests should have.

'Oh, really,' I said. 'You don't mean to say that ladies of easy socialist virtue are available for the repose of the weary businessmen and diplomats.'

He made a gesture of helplessness. 'Mr Veen,' he said indignantly, 'I want you to understand that I am not a . . . a . . .'

'A pimp.'

'A pimp. Yes, exactly. But you must understand, this is a part of my duties. These women, you see,' he shook his head slowly, 'they are all informers to the police. They are given cards for identification which they must show to me before I allow them to go to a client's room. Sometimes, in addition to their salary from the state security organization, they also have been known to demand money from the men they are entertaining.'

When later on I told James about this conversation he laughed and said, 'Perhaps we should have given you a briefing to cover situations like that. You wouldn't believe it, but it has been known to happen. In any case, Greville, the only safe thing to do is abstain. If you can't manage it, and you should suddenly find yourself with a popsy under the sheets and flashbulbs exploding all around you, the only thing to do is brazen it out. Look them in the eye, order a couple of eight-by-ten glossies and a few wallet-sized snapshots to hand out to your friends.'

Other than that, James had no further instructions for me. 'Keep it up,' he said, 'and we'll get back to you.' The companies I represented were delighted with the show of interest my visit had elicited, and the preliminary inquiries I'd brought back. Only Sheila had good reason to be annoyed when she found out that follow-up visits and

xploratory trips to other Communist countries were in the
ffing. The tensions growing between us were even further
xacerbated by my first journey to Eastern Europe, but I
vas too far in now to have changed the scenario, even if I
ad wanted to.

My next step after returning to London was getting in
ouch with the other Communist embassies. Being able to
oint to the favourable reception I'd had in Prague and
Warsaw made the preliminaries a good deal easier.
Bulgaria was the first to reply, so I arranged a short
expedition to Sofia along the same lines as my other visits.
The catalogues and specification papers I brought along
again were received with enthusiasm and promises that they
would receive most careful study.

So it went for a period of about a year. My chief regret
was that I still hadn't managed to crack the Soviet Union
tself, the biggest potential market of them all.

The looked-for opportunity came in the autumn of 1957,
through my job with Lockers. I was attending the Helsinki
Trade Fair on their behalf, when the Soviet trade attaché
stationed in the Finnish capital stopped at our exhibition
stand. I explained who I was and rattled off the companies I
was in a position to represent. That functionary was
sufficiently impressed to arrange for a forty-eight-hour visa
to enter the Soviet Union as soon as the fair had ended.

The Intourist representative in Helsinki booked me into
the Hotel Metropole, and told me that I would have to pay
for everything by voucher. At that time, the Metropole was
the only hotel in Moscow authorized to receive foreign
visitors. The voucher system had a double purpose: it made
it easy for Russian security agents to monitor the client's
comings and goings, and the fact that they could only be
redeemed in selected restaurants effectively served to limit
one's contact with the ordinary man in the street. Also
included were the services of a chauffeur-driven Zim

limousine, whose driver had orders to report on the subject's movements. The price for all this worked out to eleven pounds a day; pretty steep, when you considered it. I hardly thought it fair to make foreigners pay the salaries of an army of secret policemen to watch over them.

My first view of Moscow, through the curtained window of the limousine that brought me in from Moscow Airport, was of flat fields dusted with patches of white from the year's first snowfall. These gave way to zones of huge apartment blocks, rectangular, barrack-like concrete slabs. It was a sunless day, dull, misty and depressing, though not particularly chilly. As we approached the city via the Ring Road, I noticed that almost all the traffic consisted of mammoth diesel lorries belching foul black smoke.

It was the fat hotel administrator at the Metropole – they don't have receptionists, as we know them – who lumbered out of his office to confirm my reservations. He had already been forwarded a copy of the projected itinerary of my visits and was able to confirm the appointment times. 'We hope you feel entirely comfortable, Mr Veeny,' he said. I looked around uneasily at the colonnades of marble pillars and the huge coloured glass roof. It was built, I found out, by the last czar as a swimming pool.

Yet the Metropole, with its elegance of a bygone aristocracy, had a certain fusty charm to it. I cannot say the same about the other glimpses of Moscow I had on this first visit of mine. In all the main streets converging on Red Square there were sentry boxes at five-hundred-yard intervals and, at every pedestrian bridge over the Moskva River, at least four soldiers at either end standing to attention with fixed bayonets. The people in the streets walked along with shoulders hunched, eyes on the ground. Middle-aged women in heavy cloth coats with black shawls and woollen scarves wrapped tight over their stinging ears.

No coloured lights or neon signs, no flowers or leaves on the trees. Moscow was preparing for the annual siege older than its history, the onslaught of the terrible Russian winter.

The interiors of the government buildings I had to visit were remarkable, too, for their unabashed decrepitude. If not for the guards at the entrance, their reception rooms could have passed as the cluttered chambers of a Victorian solicitor. Both days I went back and forth between the offices of Mashino Import and Techno Import, twin buying agencies in adjacent buildings on Smolenskaya Street, the lift was out of order and I had to be escorted up the stairs by a detachment of office girls. The bare wooden floors were scored with black heelmarks.

The meetings were held in a formal atmosphere that bordered on ceremonial solemnity. One of the principals would make the introductions in halting English, and from there the interpreter, invariably young and female, would take over. We sat at a conference table covered with green baize cloth; ashtrays, glasses and bottles of chilled mineral water arranged down the middle. The green baize, I later understood, was a staple of Russian interior decorating. I had Lenin and Stalin gazing sceptically down at me from garishly-coloured chromolitho prints on the wall opposite to where I was sitting.

I started by explaining that I had been in Helsinki and wanted to take advantage of my proximity to Moscow in the hopes of establishing a working basis for future relations. I told them I needed to know exactly what kind of equipment they were looking for, and I'd do my best to locate a supplier. I made it clear that I would be most happy to schedule a return visit, bringing all the technical literature and, if required, qualified specialists to provide any additional information.

The burly chairman gave me a smile of tolerant forbearance, exposing twin rows of steel-capped molars. They were used to receiving twenty-man government delegations, but what were they to make of Greville Wynne, lone capitalist entrepreneur from the decadent West? I suddenly felt uncomfortably like a very small mouse who had blundered his way into a den of hungry and extremely self-assured cats.

'Very well, Mr Veeny,' the chief man said, 'I promise you that we shall give this material our most careful study. And if our response is favourable, representatives of this department in London will certainly be in touch with you.'

Meaning, to be sure, we're going to have our men run a check on you first thing, and then we'll know exactly what your game is. Or something to that effect. If I was living up to MI6's good opinion of my business acumen, I hoped the answer would be self-evident. Making money. Making lots of money. Nevertheless, I got the impression that they had been intrigued by the range of products and services offered by my client companies, and interested enough to want to find out more.

That was a start, if nothing else. I knew that it would take them months to reach a decision but the purchase order, when it came, could be a pleasantly hefty one. Flying back via Helsinki, I thought I really hadn't done too badly. In recruiting me for his own devious ends, James had actually given me some excellent commercial advice.

Forty-eight hours after I was back in London, my wife came into the office and handed me a telegram that had just been delivered. 'Meet me for lunch Savoy Grill Wednesday next James.' Well, whatever was going to happen next, at least it would wait until after the Christmas holidays. I read the telegram a second time and tore it into illegible shreds.

8

Toughening Up

James was a man who knew how to listen. While we enjoyed another excellent lunch at the Department's expense, I summarized the progress made on my three trips to the East so far. He was attentive throughout, coaxing details and impressions from me by knowing just when to ask the right questions. As we sipped our port, he loosed one of these oblique remarks so characteristic of the man when he was leading up to something but didn't want to come out and say it directly.

'You know,' he remarked, 'I've noticed lately you're not looking quite as fit as you did during the war.'

I smiled, or maybe it was a grimace. 'You're probably right. Getting a bit paunchy as I approach middle age, eh? Well, I attribute that to the side-effects of success, self-indulgence, and inspired contentment.'

He poured a bit more from the decanter and said, 'Well, I think I know just the remedy for that. We have a little job in mind for you, as you've probably guessed. But first, I think a few visits to our places in the country might be called for.'

'Sussex, you mean?' It seemed like that had been ages ago, in another lifetime.

'Sussex, yes. And at the special operations base not too far from there, you may remember it.'

'Of course,' I said, then it hit me. 'They brought us there for PT selection – to that big hangar thing where they asked us to make practice jumps in parachute harness.'

James caught the look on my face and laughed. 'Absolutely right, Greville. But you needn't worry. I wasn't thinking of any parachute jumping for you. Just an elementary brush-up course, a few simple tumbles to put all that dissipation at bay.'

I don't think the visible manifestations of my unease could have changed, for James continued by saying, 'Look, Greville, I know you don't like the idea much. I remember it was one of the few tests we gave you before the war that you flunked out on.'

'So, what exactly do you have in mind for me now?' Rarely did I ever ask James a direct question in that way, but I was beginning to worry. The answer I received, however, was hardly as straightforward as I would have wanted it.

'I can promise you there won't be any jumps from aeroplanes asked of you, if that helps put your mind at ease. Why don't you at least give it a try? If you don't like it, we'll just drop the whole thing.'

I forced myself to grin. 'Well,' I said, 'I suppose I could do with a bit of exercise. All right, you're on.'

'Let's go then,' said James. 'I had a feeling you hadn't changed all that much since the war.'

He was probably right, I thought. Psychologically speaking, he had me by the horns.

We took a taxi to Kensington after the meal, where the Department had leased an empty flat in a large block to be used as a safe house for its briefings. 'Workmen' on the roof opposite gave a pre-arranged signal that we had not been followed and it was safe to enter. Inside the sparsely furnished flat, it quickly became apparent that the little job James had mentioned would be a very complex and dangerous one.

'We are trying to help a Soviet officer make his escape from the Soviet Union,' James said. 'He's provided us with a great deal of secret information. And we need your help to get him out.'

'Tell me what I'm supposed to do.'

'First, we have to get a trip to Moscow scheduled in advance so that you'll be in the country a few days before Easter. It will be of help if you could add further credibility by arranging as many business trips as you can to that part of the world between now and then, so that your cover will be in tip-top shape. Can it be done?'

'Certainly it can. I was planning on visiting Romania in any case, to test out the waters there.'

'Then that's easy. In Moscow, you're going to explain to the Intourist people that you are interested in seeing a bit more of the country while you're there. You've heard of a tour – these are all regular, scheduled itineraries, by the way – that takes you to Kiev and Odessa. From there you'll go to Varna in Bulgaria on a cruise ship. Since you will want to make Bucharest your next stop, it's logical that you should want to take your time getting there and see some of the sights. These are all resort areas, you understand. Beaches for the workers, hotels, that sort of thing.

'Odessa is the critical bit. Here you'll rendezvous with our man. He comes from Odessa and his parents still live there, so he has permission to travel back and forth.'

James reached for a thick folder and handed me a photograph from it. Major Sergei Kuznov, he went on to explain, Soviet Military Intelligence – the GRU. He had been a member of the Soviet Commission in Vienna after the war, which is where he first made contact with MI6. Since that time, he had passed on much valuable information to the West. Now, it appeared, the security clearance that enabled him to travel abroad had been withdrawn. Any Soviet citizen whose job exposed him to contacts with foreigners automatically comes under suspicion. 'He's anxious to make a run for it,' James said. 'And he devised his own plan for getting out and asked for our help in implementing it.'

I waited for James to tell me the rest – or, in any case, the parts that concerned me directly. One thing I had noticed immediately. When we were working together during the war, I had never been given a briefing as detailed as the one I was listening to now. That in itself should have told me that there was an element of personal danger in the assignment. In spite of what you may have read in the better class of erudite thrillers, British Intelligence would never send an agent out in the field without making sure he fully understood the risks.

'When you get to Odessa we expect they'll put you up at the Savoy Hotel – don't laugh, that's really what they call it. You probably won't run into too many tourists, it's a little early in the season. Possibly a party under KGB escort from one of the cruise ships. There's only one restaurant in the hotel, no bar or cocktail lounge. Have your meals at regular times, preferably at the same table near the entrance. If you go out in the evenings, always return to the restaurant for a last drink. Major Kuznov will make contact with you there.'

James explained that a countersign would be necessary to confirm identification. A casual query when we introduced ourselves about my uncommon Christian name.

'And after that . . . ?'

'After that, you just follow his instructions. He'll arrange the most inconspicuous way for you to give him this—' and here James took a small object from his pocket and handed it to me. It was a sealed packet of Russian cigarettes, but when I took it in my hand it felt like a lump of lead.

'Solid gold,' James said. 'It's a bit heavy, as you can see. You've got to make sure that Major Kuznov receives that packet. He's going to need it to pay off the people at his end who are helping him arrange for his escape.' There was a pause, and James continued in his most level tones: 'You may not be aware of it, but it happens that the penalty for smuggling gold in or out of the Soviet Union is death in front of a Red Army firing squad.'

'I'm aware of it now,' I said.

'He'll tell you the method you'll have to use to pass this to him. Probably the standard urinal exchange – I'll explain that later. But you've got to help out when the Major is making his escape. He's going to come out by sea, and we need you to provide a distraction for the dock guards at the critical moment.'

'And I gather this has something to do with this refresher course in Sussex you've got me lined up for.'

'Quite. But we'll leave all that for later. Let's see how the training goes, then we'll talk about it. Do you need time to think it over? We can give you a few days.'

I thought it over for a couple of seconds and said, 'No, that won't be necessary. From the way you've explained the set-up, I ought to be able to handle it. All right, I'll do it. But then you knew I was going to say yes, didn't you?'

James's lips tightened in a thin sort of smile. 'Let's just say I was pretty sure. We've known each other a long time.' He scooped the twenty-four-carat cigarette package into his pocket and pushed back the chair. One of the subalterns keeping watch at the window gave the all-clear signal. James and his aides left, one at a time, and I gave myself five minutes before I followed them out and took a taxi home.

Now came the tricky part. Arranging to be out of the house at weekends for the jump training. I managed to convince my wife that I had been seized with an over-whelming passion for golf. I invested in a set of clubs and, after promising to be home in time for dinner, I set off for Sussex and found the rutted turn-off James had sketched for me on an impromptu map, arrived at the training base I'd last seen in the early months of 1939, as a raw recruit to the Intelligence game.

As a new arrival, I was given a pair of zip-up canvas duck overalls with large red numbers painted on the front and back. There were eighteen or twenty men in the beginners' group assembled by the yawning mouth of the three-sided hangar. I suppose most were junior officers in training, though there seemed to be three or four civilians in the group like myself, very possibly from another branch of the service.

The instructors were hard-boiled old commando types who punctuated their orders with cheerful profanity and in general treated us all like a bunch of clumsy schoolkids. I buoyed up my self-confidence seeing that I was being taken in hand by professional instructors, men who unquestionably knew their business.

First there were demonstrations. Then they made us do Army physical jerks on the floor mats. A short break. Now the real fun started. Each trainee was harnessed to a line and winched up to a platform about ten feet off the ground. The fall is controlled by a ratchet mechanism and they start you off very gently at first. I had my turn and found that it wasn't half as bad as I imagined. It would have been better if I hadn't been tempted to follow the progress of an advanced group at the far end of the hangar out of the corner of my eye, watching those chaps leaping out into space from the 200-foot platform with a blood-curdling Red Indian war-whoop. The routine included plenty of limber-up exercises, knee-bends, and cross-country runs to get us in shape. We finished a little after four o'clock, and I was back at nine the following morning, a Sunday. After the first two days I was feeling pretty stiff in the limbs, but fortunately had not taken too many bruises.

The next time I saw James it was a mid-week meeting in the London safe house.

'How's the training going?' was the first thing he asked.

'No problem so far. I expect I'll come out of it in one piece.'

'Good. Perhaps it'll help if you know what you're practising for. Remember, you're going to be in Odessa to meet the cruise ship that's taking you on to Varna in Bulgaria. Well, not long after you board her, while she's still tied up at the dock, you're going to have an accident. A side rail on one of the decks is going to give way and you're going to fall over on to the quayside below.'

I couldn't have been all that successful in disguising the reaction this piece of news produced, for James quickly went on to say, 'There's no real reason to be concerned, Greville. The drop won't be more than twenty feet and you're going to land on a pile of sand that cushions your fall. Cry out loudly when you hit the ground. We expect the searchlights will swing over to give you assistance. That's the whole point of the operation. While everybody's attending to you, the Major is going to slip out in a small boat from another part of the harbour and transfer to a foreign merchantman that's just getting underway at the moment you make your fall. Timing, of course, is the essential thing.'

Naturally, I asked James for more details about the jump.

'You'll be trained to make a twenty-foot jump,' he said. 'The safety margin is more than ample in view of the fact that you'll be landing on sand. Our specialists have it worked out: the sand will more than compensate for a drop from that height without paratroopers' boots. Providing you fall in the correct way and don't lose your nerve at the last minute, you'll experience less of an impact than you would in making an ordinary parachute drop from a plane.'

Was he sure that pile of sand was going to be in place?

'Don't you worry,' I was told. 'We'll take care of that

end. The sand will be there, I can promise you.'

Another point of the scenario that frankly worried me was the behaviour of the armed guards prowling about the decks. No chance of them opening fire first and asking questions later – or was there?

'Most improbable,' was the word on that. 'Don't forget, this is a civilian cruise ship. There will be guards with machine guns on board, though. Possibly stationed around the perimeter of the promenade deck. But we think it's more likely they'll stay on the boat deck, above you, where they have a better view of the passengers boarding the ship.'

I nodded and said that I understood. James then gave me two photographs. 'Keep these with you and study them carefully in your spare moments, when you're alone. We're arranging for Major Kuznov to receive similar photographs of you. That way there'll be no question of mistaken identities when you make contact. The password I was telling you about the other day will confirm it.'

The photos showed front and side views of a man in his late forties with strong Slavic features and deep creases in his forehead. I gave the photographs a few moments of quick study and pocketed them.

The weekend training sessions continued. After the fourth lesson, I was given the chance to make my first jump into the sandbox from a height of twelve feet. They had taught me to fall in a crouch, positioning myself as I dropped, heels together and roll. Concentrating intently, I whispered a prayer to my Maker and leaped off the platform. Arms flailing weakly, I nearly tumbled head over heels – the balance was all wrong. My shins took the impact when I hit, and I heard the instructor's voice saying, 'No bloody good, that time. Get up and make way for the next fellow.'

My fear of heights wasn't bothering me so much after

that first try. I knew that eventually I was going to master it; and the Department would not be disappointed in me.

As the weeks passed, I would return to Coleherne Court for occasional briefings. Bit by bit, they were feeding me the information I needed. One time, I was shown a photograph of the cruise ship and had its layout explained to me. At another of these meetings, James had a suggestion.

'It's just an idea,' he said. 'We've been thinking that in case you run into trouble over there, it might make a big difference if you were fully prepared for even the worst eventuality. Unfortunately, it's not the sort of thing you can be trained for. But we can give you a sampling of what you'd most likely have to face if you were captured and interrogated by our Russian friends.'

'I'll try anything if it will help me prepare for the mission.'

'You'd better take some time and think about this one,' he cautioned. 'I should perhaps make it clear: it's not an official request. And you may not find the experience too pleasant.'

'I can't say that taking a running jump into space is my idea of pleasant, either. But I told you I'd do it.'

'Yes,' James sighed, 'but this is different.'

He instructed me to take a cab from my home and rendezvous with him at the entrance to Battersea Park. I should expect to be gone for a few days. He wasn't giving out any hints as to exactly what he had in mind for me.

I let Sheila know that I might be called away on business for a couple of days, packed a zip bag, and caught a taxi the following morning that dropped me by the Albert Bridge entrance to the park. James's familar blue Rover was idling by the kerbside, and I quickly walked over to it and peered at the tall, lean man with a thatch of unkempt, sandy brown hair sitting behind the wheel. One of James's younger assistants; I'd met him before. But the character in the rear seat who now swung the door open for me was a complete stranger.

'Where's James?' I demanded.

'Couldn't make it. Let's go.' I hesitated just a moment and climbed in.

We drove in circles round the park, it seemed, finally taking a sharp left by the tennis courts and coming out on a spur of the North Drive. The traffic light on the Queenstown Road was still a good hundred yards in the distance when the driver braked sharply and pulled over alongside a delivery van painted gunmetal grey, unmarked except for some indecipherable registration numbers on the driving door.

'This is where we change,' said the man in the back seat.

Simultaneous with my getting out of the Rover, two men emerged from the rear of the van and started to stride towards me. I didn't get much of a look at them because all at once they closed in on me. A beefy hand clamped down hard on the back of my neck. A wrenching armlock. Stumbling, I was propelled a few steps nearer the van. Twisting my head away, I saw the MI6 man in the Rover give a quick glance over one shoulder, then the other. He didn't look at me, seemed to have forgotten I existed. No approaching traffic in either direction, not even a little old lady out walking her dog.

A cough as the ignition was switched on, and out of the corner of my eye I was just able to catch a last sight of the Rover speeding away. Then I was pitched forward, grabbed by my heels and thrust headlong into the van's gaping interior. Noise of a door slammed and latched. Seconds later, we were moving.

I groped in the darkness and crawled on to some sort of wooden bench. I buried my face in my hands. The compartment had been sealed off with a blind wall of reinforced sheet metal. Twenty minutes of stops and starts, then another twenty at what appeared to be cruising speed on an open highway. That was as much as I could tell as to where they were taking me.

When the van came to a sudden, screaming halt and rocked on its springs, I was ready to step down without a show of resistance. My willingness to co-operate didn't win me any friends. They hauled me out and bundled me through what looked like the rear door of a detached suburban house. I was prodded along a corridor until we came to a door with twin sliding bolts at the top and bottom. The muscle boys gave me a shove. I tumbled down half-a-dozen wooden steps and landed sprawling on a cold cement floor.

I raised my head cautiously, felt blood trickling into one eye. The two guards were now flanking a third figure, a barrel-chested giant with carrot-coloured hair clipped close to a chunky skull. Jowl-cheeked, florid in the face, he must have weighed near to sixteen stone. Small black pinpoints for eyes set deep into cavernous sockets. Bulging biceps like a cartoon character. Solid and mean.

I thought I recognized the type. Glass-house keepers I remembered from my Army days. Professional bully-boys. This one was a real frightener.

He barked an order to the guards. 'Strip him!' They fell on me like hungry jackals on a carcass and tore at my clothes, knocking me flat to pull off my shoes. I was stark naked on the cold floor, huddling and gasping for breath.

For hours I must have squatted there on my haunches, nursing my bruises and my outrage. High overhead a yellow bulb under wire mesh showed that I was in a cellar space, surrounded by four windowless cement walls. Nothing else, not a stick of furniture.

Very realistic these people were. Maybe I should be impressed. I *had* volunteered for it and been warned that it wasn't going to be pleasant, right? I kept telling myself that it was only a dress rehearsal and they wouldn't let me come to any real harm.

Needing to urinate, I dragged myself up the creaking steps and pounded with my fists on the door. Nobody heard me. Furious now, I chose a corner and afterwards huddled on the opposite side of my cell, disgusted and ashamed. I had to lie down after a time. Short intervals of sleep thereafter from which I'd awaken sore and aching. No matter where my body made contact with the raspy stone surface, my chin face down and body spread-eagled, my hips or ankles, the pain was sufficient to keep me on the edge of consciousness. Finally I sat with my back to the wall until my head sagged down on my knees with exhaustion.

Eventually, they came for me.

Shaken out of my semi-daze, all I could do was mumble hoarsely for a glass of water. Instead they smirked, pushed me up the stairs and brought me to a room.

The glass-house keeper leered from behind a bare wooden table. Traces of daylight behind the heavy black-out curtains at his back. I was shoved into a straight-backed chair, still pleading for water. One of the guards dragged over a floorlamp fitted with an oversize bulb and polished metal reflector. He switched it on and carefully angled the beam so that it stabbed at my eyes. They began to water almost immediately.

'Now we're going to have our little chat,' the orange-haired gorilla said, and his nostrils were actually flaring.

'I think this—' but the words were scarcely out of my parched mouth when the chair was kicked out from under me. I twisted as I went down and folded like a jack-knife. A booted heel dug into my spine between the shoulder-blades, pinning me, while the other guard kicked me in the ribs.

Choking and doubled up with pain, I was dragged up by my armpits and positioned in the chair.

'He thinks he's a clever sort,' the heavy man behind the table remarked to nobody in particular. Then he started in with the questions. It was known that I had been to Moscow, not once but several times. Who were my contacts with Soviet Intelligence? How much information had I given them?

'You're crazy—' I blurted and didn't jerk my head back quickly enough to avoid the palm that crashed against the side of my face like a tennis racket.

With the blood rushing in my ears, I could only partly understand the rest of his bellowed questions. Every time I began my denials, the two guards went to work on me. One pinioned my arms while the other slammed his balled fist into my stomach. It seemed they had done this sort of thing before. Teamwork and practice.

It went on like that for almost an hour. Supported by the guards, I was taken back to the cell and left to myself.

Pain, hunger and exhaustion now bred a fear that was hardly rational. Not of the beatings. Not of the blinding light. What if this isn't just a pantomime? What if James believed I've really sold out? Those animals in the interrogation room are not putting on an act. I was terrified by just one thing: that my people believed I had in some way betrayed them.

Probably any man can stand up to pressure of this or any other kind, as long as he knows at some point it's going to end. When you doubt that, you're lost. I wavered, I'll admit that. That was what almost broke my nerve.

They came back for me and hauled me off for another session in the interrogation room. Almost a repeat performance. The threats, my indignant denials, the beatings. Then back to my cell. I was given a bowl of mushy gruel and a mug of strong tea. A few hours later, I was once again taken to face the snarling gorilla.

Four days it lasted. The routine was never varied. In a way, it gave me additional strength to resist them, knowing what was in store for me each time, knowing that the punishment would not go beyond a careful tolerance. I gave up protesting my innocence and cursed them. They would not see me grovel, the bastards. It was a contest of snarls between me and my tormentors that had nothing at all to do with proving a point to James.

I was lying half-conscious in my cell when I heard the squeak of the bolts and muttered voices on the other side of the door. A full minute went by before it tentatively creaked open.

There was James standing at the threshold, holding a hat in his hand and squinting to see in the bad light.

'How's tricks, Greville?' he boomed, and when he said that I was a split-second away from failing the most important part of the test.

I was ready to throw myself at him and claw his throat out for his damned attempt at levity, but stopped myself just in time.

He waited. I glared at him and clenched my teeth, felt the rush of adrenalin subside. There was nothing I could say to him.

James gave an almost imperceptible nod and quietly said, 'I'll wait for you in the car.' Then he disappeared.

Someone helped me to my feet and I went up the stairs, still not saying a word. I was shown to the bathroom. Inside, a clean set of clothes had been laid out for me and the suit I had worn on the day the ordeal began was on a clothes hanger, neatly pressed. I had a scalding shower and thought to myself that I'll play this game through to the end.

When I stepped outside the house into the coolness of

early evening, I saw that James was waiting beside a sleek new Bentley. 'Take a look, Greville, isn't she beautiful? My new toy,' and he started to tell me about the wonderful acceleration and handling of the car.

We drove to a country inn about five miles from the house and ordered dinner. James and his assistant chatted about cars, cricket and politics. Not one word was said about what had happened in the house.

The main course, whatever it was, lay untouched on my plate when I pushed my chair back, rushed out into the parking lot, and was violently sick. James and his friend glanced up at me when I came back in with a white, drawn face, and went on eating. Nothing was said, nothing would ever be said about it.

And I would not understand why it had to be that way until a terrifying moment three years in the future when I would find myself face to face with a bloated general from the KGB's special interrogation section in Lubyanka Prison. I was still new enough to the game to feel hurt and resentful over what my own people had put me through.

9

Kuznov Briefing

'We'll still be friends no matter what happens,' James had promised. It was his way of letting me know that if at any point I felt I couldn't go through with it, the Department would be understanding. I realized all too well, however, that if I backed out of the mission they'd have no alternative but to call off the whole show. It would take months, years perhaps, to place another agent on the scene with a cover as credible as mine. The Soviet authorities might not trust me, but at least they knew who I was. So there was no other choice, really. And time was running out for Major Kuznov.

I had a lot to keep me busy in the months that led up to the target date. James and I met several times and discussed every conceivable thing that could possibly go wrong, mapped out alternative plans of action for every contingency. At the same time, I made short trips to the Soviet satellite countries to build up my cover. Brief visits to Romania and Hungary and again to Czechoslovakia and Poland, just long enough to meet their trade officials and let them outline their requirements. Two more visits to Moscow followed. Orders had already started coming in as a result of my previous contacts, so between the retaining fees and expenses I was paid by my eight manufacturers and the percentage of the sale price due to me on capital equipment, I was doing quite handsomely on the business side and making a name for myself as something of an expert on the East European market.

Whenever possible, on these trips, I'd take my Humber Snipe down to Vienna, avoiding the autobahn then under construction from the Hook of Holland and stick to the back roads in hope of seeing a little of the towns and villages along the way. Frankfurt-am-Main is a city that many people don't particularly care for, but I always enjoyed my stops there, making the most of the superb service at the Frankfurterhof Hotel and taking the time to nose around the small, old-world villages tucked away in the rolling green hills that surround the city. Then it would be on to Vienna by way of Munich, Salzburg and Kitzbühel, as leisurely as my appointments diary would permit it.

Vienna was a welcome prelude to the tense and nerve-racking visits I made to Poland, Hungary and other Communist countries. The Vienna Woods were irresistible in the autumn, and the Austrian people I've always thought the most well-mannered in Europe.

Once you crossed the border, it was altogether a different feeling. Repression was something that hung in the air like fog; even if it caused no personal hindrance you knew it was there. Tangible, all-pervading and ultimately very disquieting, because you knew what you could see happening to others could so easily happen to you, if you weren't careful.

I remember the chambermaid at my hotel in Prague, for instance. I'd made her a present of some cigarettes and a few harmless English magazines. To show a gratitude beyond what she could express in her ten words of English, she insisted on taking my shirts away with her to launder them personally.

When I returned to the hotel after meeting the Czech trade representatives, there came a knock at the door revealing my dumpy maid standing there with tears streaming down her cheeks. Beside her was a tall, heavily built woman who could have been a matron in a women's gaol.

'Sir,' the large woman announced. 'Your chambermaid is

to be dismissed and I offer you my apologies for her negligence.'

She then held up one of my white nylon shirts of Bond Street pedigree, its tail now bisected by a wedge-shaped hole charred brown at the edges, the imprint of an iron.

'Look,' I said impatiently. 'I've got twelve more shirts hanging in the wardrobe, so why not just forget it.' It didn't seem to make much of an impression on the boss lady. She was determined to see the culprit suffer. I persisted, though. 'Please, you mustn't sack her because she has been very kind and helpful. If anyone's at fault, I'm sure it's me.' That only seemed to make her more indignant. Finally, I had to insist on it. 'You must promise me that she will be here tomorrow morning to continue looking after me.' I dropped my voice and used the stern tones I was accustomed to uttering when my son, Andrew, was being obstreperous. 'Otherwise, I shall have to register a formal complaint with the authorities.'

The matron's cheeks were flushed with red, but she duly translated this for the benefit of her underling and stomped off down the corridor. At that, the little chambermaid flung herself at me, burbling and sniffling to give me a hug of tearful gratitude.

My having to make excuses to be away at weekends, on top of this constant shuffling back and forth to the Continent, added to the strain on my marriage. Sheila certainly must have sensed that something peculiar was going on, for I was under a continuous barrage of angry questions. Why were these trips necessary? Why didn't I want to stay with her and our son? All perfectly reasonable demands. It would have been easy to shrug off the blame for this on to the Department, and maybe if she had known the truth things might have taken a different turn with us, but I couldn't deceive myself on this point, the incompatibility went far deeper than that.

There was work to be done at the London end, too, bolstering my image as an aggressive businessman in the Russians' eyes. This made it necessary for me to call on the Soviety Trade Mission in Highgate.

I parked my Humber in front of a huge red house on the crest of the hill, with walled-off grounds containing a gymnasium, tennis courts, schools and a canteen for a staff of, I'd say, a hundred officials and their dependants. All self-contained, to minimize contact with the temptations of the decadent West lying in wait for them just beyond their doorstep.

It is also, I learned from James, the operations centre for Soviet intelligence activity in the United Kingdom. A man called Pavlov, senior commercial attaché at their London embassy, was a high-ranking officer in the KGB. A reasonable estimate at that time was to assume that at least half the Soviet combined diplomatic corps, trade representatives and commercial delegations were active, trained agents. The full extent of these activities became clear with the defections of Burgess and MacLean, and Philby.

The first time I went there I had to hammer for a few minutes on the door until a middle-aged woman answered and icily demanded to know what my business was. Explaining that I'd arranged an appointment over the phone didn't ruffle her chilly reserve any, but she turned and motioned for me to follow her into a room nicely fitted out with armchairs, decorative copper samovars, hammered metal bowls and the green baize I had come across in Moscow. 'Please wait here,' she said.

The official who came to see me had dark, Mongolian features and a stand-offish manner. After some brusque questions, he left the room and returned with a colleague, and a few minutes later we were joined by another man with wavy grey hair and glasses. This made it difficult as I had to start again with each one, explaining the work I'd done in Eastern Europe and giving a quick idea of the equipment I was in a position to offer. They listened carefully, prodding for details in impeccable English, but I noticed their suspicious hostility and sidelong glances to each other as I made my pitch.

What I did was to invite them to come and see me at my office for further discussions. The offer must have taken them by surprise, but we agreed on a mutually convenient date. Four of them turned up on the day appointed, and I watched from my upstairs window as they got out of their official car and stood and stared by the gate for a good five minutes, eyes wandering from my wife's curtains in the front windows, the garden, the other houses on this obviously residential Chelsea street. Once or twice they pulled out my card to double-check the address on it. I had not said anything about my business office being in my home, and this was the first thing that took them completely by surprise.

After they had mustered up enough courage to ring the bell, I welcomed them at the door and took them through the short entrance hall into my private office. My Russian visitors were still totally bewildered by it all. After I had piled technical drawings and catalogues on their laps and started to talk business with them, it slowly began to sink in that this actually was an office, with filing cabinets, a secretary, desk, telephone, telex machine and all.

We stayed there talking for a half-hour or so, and when one of the Russians expressed an interest in some electric brakes and clutches, I said, 'Well, I'm sure the managing director of Westool would be delighted to see you in person and show you his firm's range of products. It's always best to go directly to the man at the top, you see.'

Startled, the Soviet representative said, 'Would you be in a position to arrange such a visit?'

'Of course. I'll do it right now if you'll excuse me for just a minute,' and I picked up the phone and began to dial while all four of them leaned forward with their eyes bulging from their sockets.

They listened to my every word while I talked to the managing director, noting that I was put through to him immediately and called him by his Christian name. 'There,' I said, putting down the receiver, 'it's all set up for a week from Wednesday. Where else would you like to go?'

That produced a few minutes of animated Russian chatter. I sat back in my chair feeling rather pleased with myself, for I had not only succeeded in absolutely convincing them that I was a genuine businessman, but also something of a big-time operator and therefore a valuable intermediary.

'Mr Wynne,' the group leader said finally, 'our superiors must be informed of your most kind offer, as you will understand. Perhaps early next week, if you are free, I am sure that the commercial attaché would like to discuss this with you. We can have a limousine sent to pick you up at your home . . .'

Now I knew I had passed the test. I was in with the Russians. Formalities out of the way, I showed them through the sliding door that opened on to the adjacent lounge of the house, where I had a very nice cocktail bar set up, complete with sink unit, refrigerator, and shelves full of bottles. After I introduced them to my wife, they sat down on the leather armchairs, buried the toe-caps of their shoes in the deep pile of the fitted carpet and we all had a few drinks. The final touch must have been the air-conditioner. I knew that when they reported back, they would have quite a story to tell about Greville Wynne, the unabashed capitalist.

The critical day was fast approaching and I hadn't seen James for some time, so it was no surprise when, not long after the Russians and I had exchanged visits, I received a message through an MI6 intermediary indicating a meeting in Hyde Park. I drove there and waited by the barracks in my car. James arrived a few minutes later by taxi, got into my Humber and we cruised round the park as we talked. As usual, there were a couple of Special Branch operatives in the vicinity to make sure neither one of us had picked up a tail.

'So tell me,' James began. 'How did you make out with our people down in Sussex?'

Obviously, he'd been reading the reports but wanted to hear it first-hand from me.

'You know, towards the end, I was actually looking forward to it. Truth is, I feel better and fitter now than I have been for years.'

James chuckled. 'Your instructor says you've got a way to go yet before you'll make a combat-ready paratrooper, but he's satisfied with your progress.' He paused, seeming to gather his thoughts. 'We must have a final decision from you now as to whether you feel you can go ahead with the mission. We no longer have much time.'

I reviewed the situation as I saw it then. I was not being asked to take any foolish risks. Planning had been meticulous. What's the worst thing that could happen to me? A few bruised bones for Queen and country. I knew the drill and felt more than prepared for the consequences. 'I'm ready. I'll do it,' was the answer I gave him in the car.

There was just one question that had lodged itself in the back of my mind and wouldn't go away. 'James, supposing something goes wrong. What if they won't let me back into Eastern Europe after that. That's an end to my business, and at this point, you know, it's all I have. I've put everything into working that part of the world, and my family's welfare depends on it.'

James gave me a sharp look and bristled under his moustache. 'We'll see to it that you'll be taken care of,' he snapped. The idea that the Department might not look after me in case of trouble had really upset him. It was the first time I'd ever seen him really angry with me and I immediately regretted my tactlessness in bringing the matter up.

A final briefing, ten days before I was due to leave. Same procedure, a different safe house, in Chelsea this time. James brought in several of his aides and there weren't quite enough chairs in the flat to go around. Standing (at his own insistence) and pacing up and down, he stressed that I should be prepared to follow Major Kuznov's orders to the letter as soon as I made contact.

'It's the only reasonable way to operate when you're in the other fellow's territory. The Major is an experienced man, and a very resourceful one. He knows the language, the people, and knows his way around. If the situation were reversed, and you had to take charge of Russian agents over here, they'd be taking orders from you for the same reason.'

I said I had no difficulty in understanding that. James then handed me the curiously heavy packet of Russian cigarettes he had shown me at the first briefing.

'I don't have to tell you that you must be very careful with Major Kuznov's gold. Expect that your luggage will be searched at some point, so it's best if you simply keep it with you at all times. Best behaviour while you're out in the field. Drinking and socializing kept to an absolute minimum, so if you were planning any wild Moscow parties you'd best start making your excuses now. We'll do it strictly by the rulebook. Stay off the main streets in case of traffic accidents. We'd have a hell of a time getting you back again if the gold were found on your person.'

I played with the gold in my hand for a moment then slipped it into my back pocket.

'All right,' I said.

'And one more thing, Greville. Here's a Moscow number

for you to contact if something goes drastically wrong. I don't know whether we'd be in a position to help you, but we'll rack our brains until we come up with something.'

'I know. And I appreciate it.' James wished me luck and departed with his aides, and I did not see him again in the days remaining until I was off to Moscow.

Greville Wynne in the 1980s.

In the Scouts, aged twelve.

At Ericsson's telephone works at Beeston early in 1939. Here occurred his first contact with Intelligence.

Students' Union gathering at the Ritz Café, Nottingham, in 1938 (Greville Wynne extreme left).

Houseboat group during student days at Nottingham.

At University OTC camp, pre World War II (author front right).

Pre-Officer Training Course, 1939-40 (author extreme right, front row).

Family snapshots: *left,* with Father; *right,* with sister Christy.

Wynne's club in Kensington: inside the Trojan Club.

Greville Wynne with the Intourist guide in Odessa. This was taken on the morning of the day when Wynne created the diversion under cover of which Kuznov escaped from Russia to the West.

Greville Wynne beside the Karl Marx memorial at Highgate Cemetery, 1961.
This photograph was taken by Penkovsky.

Greville Wynne speaking at the welcoming reception for the Russian Trade
Delegation to London in 1961. Penkovsky is fourth from the left.

Greville Wynne in Prague, 1960.

Wynne's Mobile Exhibition for European Trade Fairs in which he hoped to smuggle Penkovsky out of Russia, pictured in Bucharest prior to Wynne's arrest.

Wynne (standing) on trial in Moscow. Penkovsky is seated on his left.

Verdict and sentence.

Above: Wynne hears the verdict of eight years in gaol (his translator stands on the left, his defence counsel, Borovik, on the right).

Left: Penkovsky grips the rails when he is sentenced to death.

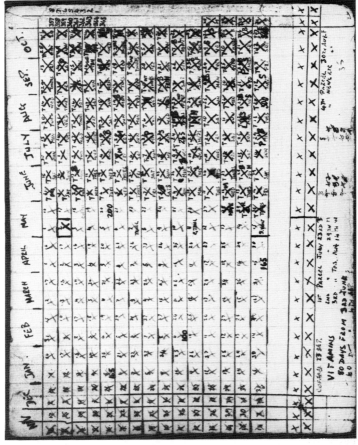

Wynne's calendar: the sheet of paper on which he kept track of the passing days when he was in the Lubyanka and other prisons.

To while away the hours Wynne often designed interiors on scraps of paper.
This is a sketch of a kitchen and a dining-room.

Home at last. Greville Wynne leaving Northolt airport under police escort,
April 1964.

Pressures of a different kind: Wynne meets the media after his return to Chelsea.

36 Maxim Gorky Embankment, Penkovsky's home.

11 Gorky Street, the Scientific Research Establishment.

(The last two photographs by Andrew Carr, 1981.)

10

Contact

I flew to Helsinki on a regular BEA flight out of Heathrow with the cigarette packet cached in the back pocket of my trousers. It would have made an awkward start to the mission if British Customs had searched me going out of the country and found that little item. The Department was standing by in case of such an eventuality, but even so, it would have been one complication I obviously didn't need.

Everything was in readiness. The Soviet Embassy in London had come through with a visa in record time. It helped simplify matters when I showed them a sheaf of accumulated correspondence from their own Ministry of Foreign Trade, and some of these letters were now placed conspicuously in my suitcase as a kind of talisman against KGB searches.

From Helsinki I went to Moscow in one of Finnair's twin-engined Metropolitans. No more than half-a-dozen of the thirty-odd seats were filled on the afternoon flight I took. As the plane banked and circled for its approach to Sheremetyevo airport, I was sweating as I thought about clearing the first dangerous hurdle: making it through Soviet Customs. Assuming I ran into no problems there, I'd still have my package with me for two days more in Moscow as I went in and out of government buildings. Literally, I was going to be sitting on the damn stuff.

In the end, nothing happened, of course. Moscow Airport is too chaotically inefficient a place for them to make proper Customs searches. Since Aeroflot has the habit of cancelling or suspending flights without any notice, the airport – just one building in those days – was jammed to the rafters with people, workers and peasants in their greatcoats, scarf-covered ladies carrying their belongings in bundles tied with string, filling every seat and sprawling over the cement floor. Maybe they would get to wherever it was they thought they were going, but in Russia, I knew, the ingrained sense of fatalism and overwhelming hopelessness rules.

In my Western business suit I stood out a mile, yet when I put my suitcase on the bench, the young policeman, with an eye to the vast traffic jam queueing behind me – 'our foreign guests always go first' – took a quick look at the complicated currency declarations, compared my face with the photo in my passport and waved me through without a second glance.

For some reason having to do with the dignity of man under socialism, there are no porters in Moscow Airport, so I struggled with my gear until I found the pudding-faced escort Intourist had sent for me. 'Mr Vinny?' she said. 'Welcome to Moscow. We take you now to your hotel, the Metropole.'

Her name, she told me, was Irina. Like most of the girls from Intourist, she was just a little tidier than average. She laid claim to a bit of a hairdo and the white blouse she wore with her jacket was spotlessly clean but unironed. Intourist girls were easy to recognize by the eye-shadow and pancake make-up they used; the ordinary Soviet women had none of these cosmetic frills. Why weren't they given deodorants while they were at it? It would have made all the difference in the world.

Vouchers checked and paperwork verified, I was shown to the waiting Zim limousine. As soon as we arrived at the familiar marble portals of the Metropole and had been greeted by the administrator, I stopped at the Intourist office in the lobby to make the necessary arrangements for my trip to Kiev, Odessa and to Bulgaria. No questions were asked as to why I was travelling alone. I booked the tour to begin in three days' time. A ship called the *Uzbekistan* would have a first-class cabin ready for me when I joined the cruise in Odessa. It was hoped I would enjoy my excursion to the Black Sea.

I was tired after my plane journey and didn't much fancy sauntering around the streets of Moscow with that gold bar in the seat of my trousers, so I made it an early night. Business talks the following morning in the familiar conference rooms of Mashino Import headquarters were going as smoothly as could be expected. We discussed wire and tube drawing machinery, haggled a bit over credit terms, and drank vodka. When I stepped out into the sunlight and started walking up the hill to Red Square, the miniature ingot was still in my pocket. It was hard to believe I hadn't been pulled aside and searched. Maybe, if they were watching me now and waiting until I was alone . . .

Careful. You're being silly. Nobody knows about the gold, nobody is going to come after you. You're just getting edgy, that's all.

It wouldn't do for me to appear too much the recluse, so I decided to try and arrange something in the way of a diversion. I went back to the Intourist office and found the lovely Irina busy with some paperwork. I asked if it would be possible for me to see a performance of the Bolshoi Ballet on my last evening in Moscow. She made a quick telephone call. Yes, there were tickets available. (All Western visitors have priority for getting into the Bolshoi, regardless of their professional or social status. High officials and model workers come next, but the ordinary Moscow resident may have to wait years to obtain a coveted ticket.) *Swan Lake* was the programme. Be in your seat by eight sharp, she cautioned, late arrivals are not admitted until intermission time.

'That's fine,' I said with one of my most charming smiles. 'And perhaps – well, if you would be free to accompany me that evening, I'd be most grateful and delighted to have you along. It would be a great pleasure.'

At this she gave a start, looked at me with widening eyes like I'd just taken leave of my senses, then flushed deep crimson. In her most brusquely official voice she said flatly, 'I'm sorry, Mr Veeny. It is not possible for me to accompany you. Regulations forbid it.' And she turned away and began to shuffle some more papers.

But I've always enjoyed a challenge. Intourist girls were famous in embassy circles as frigid untouchables, the snow-maidens of the Russian steppes. I was determined to press the point and see where it got me.

'Please excuse me if I've spoken out of turn,' I said, not letting up the attack. 'You see, I've never been to a ballet performance up to now, not even in my own country. I've heard so much about the excellence of your wonderful Bolshoi troupe. I would really like your help in explaining it to me.'

Her look, if anything, had dropped several degrees below zero. 'Regulations forbid it,' she repeated. 'It is not possible.'

We'll have to see about that, thought I. One thing I'd learned in dealing with the Soviets over the bargaining table was that in case of stalemate, the thing to do was to threaten to go to the next man higher up. It's a method seldom known to fail and it didn't this time, either. I carefully explained to the balding, harassed-looking Intourist director how keen I was to have this young lady accompany me, so I could give my friends back home a much more informed picture of one of the glories of Soviet culture.

That was all it wanted. Mention the word 'culture' to a Russian and he draws himself up, proud as a peacock.

None of them can resist the opportunity for showing off. The director spoke a few sharp sentences to Irina. Her dimpled chin bobbed assent. She didn't look terribly pleased at this development in her life, but in that country, nobody even dreams of questioning or protesting the decision of a superior.

Accordingly, I found her waiting outside the Intourist office when I came down the following evening to collect her. She was wearing a plain brown dress, the hemline well below the knees, and flat-heeled shoes of a matching colour. I caught the whiff of lavender perfume. No earrings or jewellery, however – I've no doubt there was some regulation forbidding that while on 'duty'. Though the Bolshoi was just a three-minute walk across Revolution Square, she insisted that we go in the Intourist limousine.

The outside of the famous Bolshoi Theatre can only give you a rough idea of its scale – *bolshoi* is the Russian word that means 'big' – but you have to go in to see and understand the truly larger-than-life part of the Bolshoi experience. Lavishness run riot, opulence, instant fairyland – it lifts you out of the sunken drabness of Soviet reality the minute you step into its marble-tiled foyer and glance up at the crystal chandeliers. Then you go up the white staircase that takes you to the crescent-shaped interior promenade. It's all red plush and ornate gold ornamentation, seven tiers of seats. Lenin's face, pointed beard jutting forever leftward, beams from a red banner above the heavy gold curtain as if he wanted to take credit for the baroque extravaganza all to himself but the Bolshoi was not built by the Soviets nor was the ballet created by them.

I had brought a box of chocolates along with me, purchased at the Embassy Club that same afternoon. When I offered them to Irina she stiffened with a look of genuine alarm. 'Oh, no,' she said. 'It is not permitted for me to accept gifts from visitors.'

'Now, wait a minute,' I countered. 'It is an English custom for a gentleman to present a lady with a box of chocolates when they go to the theatre. There's not the slightest thing improper about it. I hope you won't offend my English culture by refusing,' and I placed the box on her lap and peeled away the gilt paper wrapping. But they remained there untouched all throughout the magnificent first half of the performance.

During the intermission, Irina led me off to the little museum they had set up in another wing of the building. We strolled past rows of glass cases displaying beautiful and expensive trifles – diamond-studded watches, gold cigarette cases – which the dancers had collected from admirers all over the world. Any presents received by the troupe, no matter how small, had to be handed over to the authorities. Ulanova, the principal ballerina, had a case to herself that held a small fortune in jewels.

The rest of the ballet was in every way memorable. But it was the behaviour of the audience which most impressed me, during the endless curtain calls. From all parts of the theatre people rushed forward bearing huge cellophane-wrapped bouquets which were stacked in a heap in the centre of the stage. After half an hour of thunderous applause, we went outside and I saw the Zim was waiting for us. Clearly, Intourist was taking no chances on getting their little Irina back. To my surprise, she agreed to return to the Metropole with me, but once inside the lobby, she shook my hand, stuttered a few words of thanks and disappeared into the Intourist office, where the lights, I saw, were still burning. I hid behind one of the marble pillars just to see how long it would take for her to make her report on whether or not Veeny behaved like a gentleman. Ten minutes later she came out without the box of chocolates and disappeared. Did the KGB have a museum, too, I wondered, to display affectionate tributes to its members? If so, I hoped my box of chocolates would be given pride of place in the trophy room.

My night on the town with Irina was one of the things that helped keep my mind off the bar of gold in my back pocket. If I had nothing else to occupy my thoughts, it's possible I might have done something to give myself away. But I was conscious of its unnerving presence next morning when I went up the steep gangplank to claim my seat in the old Ilyushin 14 that was taking me on to Kiev.

A curious thing happened. I was passing the time by glancing at the scenery from my window seat, when on the other side of the aisle a fat lady in a quilted black coat got up and started to jabber at me, reaching across my seat to pull the curtain shut. The hostess came hurrying over and, when she saw what had happened, beamed approval. This good Soviet lady had taken it upon herself to show vigilance in defence of the motherland by making sure this obviously foreign type did not have a chance to get a look at the landscape. This attitude, I think, has less to do with patriotism (or paranoia as a national trait, for that matter) than with the fact that the Russian people by nature are the world's worst busybodies.

The sun was just a faint sliver of orange on the horizon when the rubber-wheeled Ilyushin bounced and jostled on touch-down and taxied to a halt in front of the terminal at Kiev Airport. Again, I was taken in hand by a starchy woman guide, whisked off to my hotel, and summoned the next morning for a tour of the city. I can't say I was much impressed by what I saw of Kiev. I remember mostly the horrendously ugly eleven-storey housing units of pre-poured concrete. The Intourist guide pointed out each one of these eyesores with evident pride as we drove through the city. A closer look at their chipping and flaking exteriors suggested to me an unfavourable comparison with the bleakest council blocks that ever blighted the landscape of postwar Britain. I couldn't understand why she would want to make such a fuss over these until I heard her describe for me what had happened to Kiev during the Second World War. Then I saw the point. All this had almost literally been built up from the ashes of a huge, thriving city almost wiped off the map by the German artillery and air bombardment. Recalling how the face of London had been forever changed during the Blitz and multiplying by a factor of twenty or thirty, I began to grasp what these hideous rabbit-warrens meant to the Russian people in purely human terms.

Next, Odessa.

I arrived a little before noon on the following day. The weather was mild and breezy – a better tag-end of March than we'd been having in England. And Odessa itself was a big surprise coming after Moscow and Kiev.

This port city had a picturesque charm I had never thought to encounter in any of the countries under Soviet domination, much less in the heart of Russia itself. With its quiet, tree-shaded streets and rickety wooden houses, all, unfortunately, having been left without a fresh coat of paint for many years, Odessa curiously brought to mind an unlikely amalgam of Brighton and Italy. What was missing were the crowds and the spirited gaiety of people enjoying themselves.

The Savoy Hotel had been built when Queen Victoria was still sending birthday greetings to her grand-nephews and nieces in the Winter Palace, and at one time had figured in the Baedekers as the Hotel London, the Hotel Berlin and Hotel Odessa. Certainly its better days were long in the past; but it still retained the antique dignity of a British railway hotel left over from the preceding century.

At half past seven on my first evening in Odessa, I sat down at a little round table, the first one you came to through the door of the Savoy Hotel's small restaurant, and waited for whatever was going to happen next. London had been explicit on this point: the Major would contact me. I took my time over a meal of boiled sturgeon with potatoes with a Georgian white wine Number 2, trying not to let my nervousness show. I'd been carrying the gold bar around with me for five days, slept with it under my pillow, and now that the moment for making the exchange neared ominously, its uncomfortable presence was never out of my thoughts. I would be glad to be rid of the damn thing.

My ears pricked up as I was sipping my coffee and caught the unmistakable intonations of English from a table over by the chintz-curtained windows. Two very young-looking men sitting there, not Russians by the cut of their clothes. I went over and introduced myself. It turned out that they were under contract to a British firm exporting rubber to the Soviets, and had been sent over to check the cargo as it was off-loaded from their ships. 'There's not a bloody thing to do in this place,' one of the boys grumbled. 'Sibera with central heating, that's what it is.' He was a good-looking chap in his late twenties with black, curly hair and obviously was used to having a lively time. I clucked my sympathy and both of them were full of questions about what was happening in Britain.

We were into our second or third round of drinks when a tall man in a blue gabardine suit entered the dining room. No trouble making the identification. Major Kuznov was slimmer than he seemed in the photographs they had of him in London, and a bit older. He pulled up a chair in the middle of the room, unfolded a newspaper and buried his head in it. Had he recognized me? He must have. After about twenty minutes he paid for his drink and walked out again.

That night, as I prepared for bed, I prayed that nothing had been jeopardized by this encounter. Sleep was not made easier by a massive electric clock high up on the wall of my room that gave out a loud, sharp tick with every passing minute. I pulled the pillow over my ears but the noise was still there. Finally, I couldn't take it any more. I dragged a table over to the wall and put a chair on top of that and it still wasn't high enough with me standing precariously on the chair to reach that wretched clock. I tried again with a battered but solid chest of drawers and made it. Using nail clippers from my toilet kit, I cut one of the heavy wires that ran from the grimy wall and was rewarded with blessed silence. The upshot of it was in the morning, when I came down to have breakfast, I saw that every single clock in the hotel – in the restaurant, behind the reception desk, literally every one of them – had stopped at five minutes past two. I sometimes wonder if they ever found out who it was that fused the master mechanism.

My new Intourist guide came for me at nine o'clock, a young girl of nineteen or twenty, not much over five feet tall, pigeon-breasted, with a cute dimpled face. Playing it up with her to avert suspicion, I had a lot of fun twitting this poor little blonde thing as we toured the city. 'I don't want to hear about so many tons of increased cement production per annum,' I kept interrupting. 'Tell me about yourself. Do you live with your mother and father still? What's your boyfriend like?'

'Ohhh . . . !' she'd say each time, and hastily return to the official script.

When we passed a pavement café I urged her to come in and let me buy her a drink.

'No, no! Only in the 'otel, in the 'otel!' she protested. The KGB would get a very unequivocal idea of what was on my mind when this little muffin turned in her report.

There was a church with an interesting façade and dome on the route we took back to the hotel, and I asked if we might stop and have a look. It was Good Friday, a day of solemn holiness in the old Russian Orthodox liturgy. My guide hastily and not very convincingly said there wasn't time, we had to return to the hotel.

'You return to the hotel then. I'll walk the rest of the way back after I've seen the inside of that church.'

As the car slowed for a crossing, I jerked the door open and started to get out. She ordered the driver to pull over. I walked determinedly back in the direction of the church while she scurried to catch up. There were some loutish young men in windcheaters on the front steps of the sanctuary, and as I came near they began to shout and make angry gestures of derision. The guide had to stop to shout something back at them, so I was able to enter without having to make a scene.

In the dim, musty-damp interior I let my eyes settle on beautiful stone sculptures, wood carvings, gilt icons and dust-streaked stained-glass windows. Five elderly women and one man were kneeling in the front pews before the white-bearded priest, who read to them in a low sing-song chant. I stepped aside and watched the service, until there was a tug at my sleeve and I turned to see my guide jabbing her thumb nervously in the direction of the portal.

The sad-eyed priest came over to me and said something. The girl refused to translate. If I stayed, I might get him in trouble, so I made the sign of the Cross to show him that I came from a Christian country, and followed her without a protest.

I'd arranged to meet my two English friends for dinner again. Eating together and lingering over drinks and conversation made my presence in the dining room more plausible, and I hoped that Kuznov would catch on to the fact that the two Englishmen were no obstacle to the business at hand.

We were halfway through dinner when Kuznov walked in. He had two companions of his own with him this time.

And one of the men accompanying him immediately came over and greeted the two English lads, before they sat down at their table.

'Know those chaps?' I asked, trying to make it sound casual.

'Sure. That short fellow, he's a sort of shipping agent for the government. We see him practically every day when there's one of our freighters in port. I've met his friend, too; he has some position with the harbour authority. He may be a pilot, I'm not sure.'

'What about the man who's with him?' I queried. No, they had never run into him before.

We were about to polish off a half-litre bottle of cognac when the shipping agent came over to our table and in thickly accented English invited us to join his party for a nightcap. We brought over our bottle and had a round of introductions and warm handshakes. When I was presented to Kuznov, he hesitated a moment when I told him my name, and said dubiously, 'Gabriel?'

'No, it's Greville.'

He nodded to show he understood and said, 'It sounds much better for a man.'

That was the recognition signal that had been decided on back in London.

We all sat down together and ordered another round of drinks. The harbour official and the English boys got a lively conversation going, which Kuznov and I joined. When I reached into my jacket pocket and took out a pack of Benson & Hedges, one of the young Englishmen exclaimed, 'Oh, we haven't seen anything like that for a long time.' I offered cigarettes around the table and everybody helped themselves, including the Major.

Just as I was about to take one for myself, Kuznov leaned forward with a pack of his own. 'Here, Greville, have one of these. Try one of our good Russian cigarettes.'

I took one, making appreciative noises.

'Go on,' he said. 'Keep the packet.' His searching eyes held mine as if trying to tell me something.

'Well,' I said breezily, 'you must let me offer you some of my good English cigarettes in exchange. I've got more cartons up in my room and if you'll excuse me just a moment, I'll bring them right down. Perhaps you boys would like some too? I came over well stocked-up, and my wife says I smoke too much anyway.'

The two English boys thought this was a great idea. 'We'll get you a drink while you're fetching them,' they said.

Upstairs in the privacy of my room I examined the Major's packet of Moskva-brand cigarettes with trembling fingers and tore open the foil wrapper. Inside there was a slip of flimsy yellow paper folded around a cardboard stub. Kuznov had pencilled in block capitals: 'Imperative that we meet tomorrow at the football stadium. Get in with your own ticket but use the enclosed one to join me at half-time in the seat next to me.'

Alarm bells started clanging in my head. Why was he doing this? The plan, as the Department had it worked out, made no provision for any prolonged contact between the Major and myself. That sort of thing was risky, and unnecessary to boot. London anticipated that the method to be used in handing over the gold would be a variation of an old gambit going back to the First World War, using a public lavatory as a drop. The material to be passed could be hidden in the toilet tank, and the agent on the receiving end could retrieve it at any time.

I couldn't figure it out. If some last-minute hitch had developed, the logical thing would have been for Major Kuznov to warn me off. So what did this mean? What *could* it mean? Initiative is a fine thing in the military, but in real-life intelligence work you are not encouraged to ad-lib your moves when you're out in the field. There was no other alternative: I had to trust him.

They were waiting for me down in the restaurant. I tore the paper bearing the Major's message into strips of confetti and flushed them down the toilet, then hurried down the stairs. The cigarettes were handed round the table, Kuznov gave me a quizzical glance and I managed what I hoped was an unobtrusive nod. We said our goodnights about twenty minutes later.

11

Man Overboard

Dawn broke over Odessa, mother-of-pearl streaks in a slate-grey sky, with only the barest promise of sun for later in the day. A breakfast of eggs and cheese, washed down with several cups of strong, smoky Russian tea. Feeling a good deal better with something warming my stomach, a ten-minute stroll brought me to the Intourist office on Deribasovskaya Street where I had no trouble at the front desk buying a ticket to that afternoon's football match.

It had been a long, nervous night. With my gold bar under the pillow for what I hoped would be the last time, I tossed and turned for hours, going over in my mind the implications of Kuznov's message, attempting to fathom its significance.

The two English lads: I had better make sure not to mention football in case they might want to invite themselves along. But what if they found out? I began to work out a scheme where at half-time I'd say something like, 'I'm a bit bored – think I'll give the rest of it a miss' and try to make my way to where Kuznov was sitting without being observed. Not such a good idea at that. They might agree with me and suggest that we all leave together. In that case, what? I could always stop and have a few beers with them – assuming that they sold beer and such at a Russian match – and head off towards the gents' room and disappear. I wasn't quite so worried now about being seen in Kuznov's company, if it came to that. After all, we had met socially only the night before. A perfectly natural thing to have a chat if we happened to run into each other.

At the Intourist office, I decided to take a calculated risk.

I asked the young girl who sold me my ticket if she would like to see the game with me. After my episode with Irina in Moscow, I was fairly sure what the answer would be. This girl merely smiled and thanked me politely. Sorry, she said, but she had to work. I disguised my relief as disappointment. The invitation would be reported to her superior, of course. Let them know I was far from being cagey about my visit to the stadium. Back in my hotel room, I did one more thing. I memorized the seat number on the ticket Kuznov had given me and then destroyed it.

The limousine brought me to the main gate of the stadium a few minutes before the two o'clock starting time. Thanks to Intourist, I went with a plan of the stadium. This meant that I also knew exactly where Kuznov would be sitting. He had chosen his position carefully, slightly obscured behind one of the goal posts. Not a good position to view the field, so we wouldn't be hemmed in by too many spectators. Intourist had put me in a section that was specially reserved for foreign nationals. A party of East Germans occupied most of the seats with a few scattered individuals speaking a Slavonic language I couldn't make out. They were instantly recognizable as foreigners by the fact that their clothes had a trim European cut and were much better-looking than ordinary Russian street attire.

Accustomed by now to this sartorial disparity, I had come to the game carrying my raincoat over my arm. Folded in the pocket was a peasant-style cloth cap. If a KGB man was up there somewhere scanning the crowds with binoculars, I hoped these would do for camouflage, allowing me to melt invisibly into the half-time tumult when I switched seats.

I can recall virtually nothing of the match, not even the names of the teams that were playing on the overcast April afternoon. My mind was a whirlpool of fears and last-minute misgivings. The first half drew to an end amidst sporadic cheers and applause. I waited a few minutes and let the other spectators squeeze past me, then got up and started towards the refreshment kiosk, trying not to hurry.

Gradually, clumps of people began to drift back to the seats; the second half was about to begin. I finished my second glass of vodka, paid my money and made straight for the nearest toilet. Inside, I put on my cap and the raincoat. Then I walked to the end of the stadium where I knew Kuznov had to be waiting for me. After a few minutes shuffling through the crowd, I found the proper row and recognized the Major sitting off towards the end, staring at the field with his chin in his hands. There were half-a-dozen empty seats on either side of him. When I entered the row he looked briefly up at me and glanced over his shoulder to indicate the seat on his right.

I seated myself next to Major Sergei Kuznov just as play resumed on the field. Shouts from the crowd came close to drowning out his voice, and he spoke without turning his head round, all his attention seemingly fixed on the field.

'I'm very glad to see you again, Greville. I see you've been careful about your clothes, it's a good idea, that. Tonight is going to be very important for me, the most important night of my entire life . . .' He seemed to drift away in thought. Then, abruptly, 'You have your stadium programme?'

'Yes,' I said.

'Give me the packet you have brought for me in that.' I placed the bogus cigarette pack from my pocket into the programme, folded it carefully and slipped into his dry, hard-calloused palm. Slowly, with no fumbling or hurry, in case we were being watched.

'I will now pass a sealed envelope to you in the same way.' He shot me a quick, piercing glance. 'Listen carefully. It contains the most vital information and it must be delivered to your people with all possible speed. If all goes well tonight, I will be able to give your principals a summary of its contents, but the material I'm bringing out is so important that our friends will need documentary evidence to convince the politicians.'

A roar went up from the crowd. The Major waved and cheered with his compatriots, until the noise subsided. He went on like that for the rest of the time, speaking to me in the intervals. 'Now in the event something happens to me and to the envelope, we have to count on you making it safely out of the country. So I'm going to tell you exactly what's in it. Try to remember as much of this as you can. Among other things, you're carrying a photostat of a document with Khrushchev's own signature on it. It outlines a plan to build a wall between the eastern and western zones of Berlin. For too long now, all types of professionals and skilled manual workers have been using Berlin as a bridge to freedom. They can't allow it to continue for much longer; it's hurting them.

'At first, only a three-kilometre trial wall is going to be built. This is to give them time to gauge the reaction of the Americans, British and French. The Central Committee has discussed the different kinds of retaliation they expect. They think the Americans and their allies could direct high-pressure hoses at the wall and simply wash it away before the cement's had time to dry. Or they might just as easily use remote-control bulldozers to knock it down overnight. But this is the crucial thing: if Western military forces are called in to demolish the wall, the East Germans have been given orders not to open fire. They'll send in a token force of ordinary policemen to threaten and raise an unholy fuss, but none of the Soviet occupation troops will be drawn into it.'

I wasn't sure that I could follow him entirely on this. I asked, 'What are they hoping to accomplish with this wall, then, if they seem to think they'll never be allowed to complete it?'

The Major handed me a cigarette from the packet I'd given him the night before. He lit one of his own and inhaled deeply before continuing. 'You don't know the way they think,' he said finally. 'If the Western powers prevent them from putting up that first section of the wall, they plan an exchange of protest letters and a propaganda campaign denouncing imperialist interference in the affairs of the German Democratic Republic. They'll claim the wall is only intended to shield some new administration buildings in the eastern zone from spying eyes. But if for some reason the West does not take measures to physically demolish the wall, then they are going to continue it along the whole length of the border.'

The whole idea seemed far-fetched to me. 'You mean to say they're going to just erect a wall like the Chinese emperors did?'

'People will come to accept anything as time passes: you ought to know that, Greville. Of course my country is going to look bad for a while in everybody's eyes. But in the long term, the scandal will die down and the wall will still be there.'

Still incredulous, I had to ask him again. 'These documents, you're quite sure they're genuine?'

'Yes,' he said. 'There are some less sensational matters dealt with in the rest of them, but it is important that your people have them.'

One of these snippets of information was that Kuznov had learned of the first factory in the Soviet Union to manufacture Wellington boots. To begin with, the output would be limited to one hundred pairs a month, and one of the bright central planners in the Kremlin had decided that KGB officers were to have the first priority in receiving

these boots as they came off the production line. When
Kuznov told this to my colleagues in London, our agents
throughout the Soviet Union were alerted, and as soon as
the first snowfall came that autumn, they were out in the
streets clicking away with hidden cameras at anyone
wearing these tell-tale gumboots.

It was interesting to compare these photographs with the
ones of known KGB agents in the files. Many matched, and
those that did not enabled MI6 to extend their list of known
or suspected Soviet agents.

A similar thing, Kuznov revealed, happened with the
introduction of trilby hats in the Soviet Union. In this case,
local Party officials and government functionaries had been
given the pick of the production, but the funny thing was
that nobody seemed to have noticed that in the West, these
hats were generally worn with a dip in the centre. So it was
simple to pick these chaps out of a crowd when they went
around with their comical-looking headgear.

Also included in the package Kuznov passed to me was a
list giving hundreds of names of Soviet agents from both
the KGB and the GRU currently undergoing special
training prior to being posted to embassies and commerical
delegations in European, African and Asian capitals. He
had made careful note of their cover identities and special
duties. There was no possibility of memorizing these
names, which made it imperative to get the originals back
to London at any cost.

'I'll see that these get to where they're going,' I told
Kuznov. 'But you still haven't explained how you've
worked the rest of it out. I can't have this package on me
when I take that tumble from the ship.'

'Of course not.' Kuznov nodded vigorously. 'You must
hide it in a safe place immediately after you come on board
the *Uzbekistan*. I think I can tell you where. There are
lavatories for men and women outside the entrance to the

bar. What I suggest you do is conceal the documents in one of the ventilation ducts in there. The grille comes off easily – it's only held in place with self-tapping screws. You'll find some heavy-duty adhesive tape in the package. Use that to secure the package to the inside surface of the duct. The tape is strong enough to withstand the vibrations from the engine once the ship gets underway, so you needn't worry on that account.'

'Then I'll have to embark a little earlier than I'd been planning,' I said. 'Your friends from the KGB will probably have my baggage searched when I'm out of the cabin.'

'That's possible, though I don't think at this point you'll have any trouble. As long as there's no evidence linking the package to you, I'm fairly sure you won't be in any personal danger even if something goes drastically wrong, and the package is discovered. The ship's security officer will have to radio for instructions and by that time you'll be safe in Turkey.'

'Anything else?'

'No.' The players were jogging off the field now. Major Kuznov got to his feet and looked me in the eye. 'Greville, the French say *au revoir*, let that be the word for us.' He turned and joined the spectators impatiently filing past us, melting into the crowd.

I still had hours to wait. The *Uzbekistan* was due to lift anchor at half past midnight. I went back to the hotel, packed, and had a fine meal. My two English friends didn't turn up at the restaurant that evening, but I convinced myself it was nothing to be alarmed about. At nine o'clock exactly, the Zim pulled up by the hotel, with my Intourist guide in the front passenger's seat. She accompanied me as far as the gangway, shook hands politely, and walked back to the car.

The looming bulk of the ship was lit up like a Christmas tree. Mercury-arc floodlamps focused in an ellipse of light at the spot where the passengers embarked, but the rest of the dock was poorly illuminated. A half-dozen men at the fantail end were unloading crates from a truck and placing them on a conveyor belt that led to an open cargo hatch halfway up the hull. I didn't see any passengers in the vicinity; it was still a bit early for that. Starlight glinted on the choppy surface of the water; the Black Sea never looked blacker than it did to me then.

I started up the gangway. The purser on duty at the top end, looking bored and idle, took my suitcase – I wasn't expecting that in the Soviet Union – and summoned a steward who showed me to my cabin. It was ten o'clock by my watch. More than two hours before she sailed.

Act naturally. I had to keep repeating it to myself. What would you ordinarily do? Hang up my clothes. I hung my clothes and washed my hands. The cabin windows stayed open with the curtains apart and fluttering, so the guards would know I was in my cabin and had nothing to hide.

Two hours or a little less, now. Better get rid of the packet before the ship fills up with people. Nobody met me in the corridor and the lavatory was empty when I got there. Thank God for that. I gave the four cubicles a quick glance and for no particular reason chose the second one on my right. By standing on the seat I could reach the air vent and still not be seen outside the cubicle, if anyone suddenly came in.

I had a tiny screwdriver, taken from my electric razor repair kit. The grille came loose without difficulty; it was a fairly new ship, and hadn't been long enough at sea for the fixtures to get rusty. I noticed the draught when I put my hand in the vent. It didn't seem too strong, but just to make sure I took a sheet of lavatory paper and let it dangle in the airstream. Only the gentlest tug. Good. A little cool air could only help the adhesive retain its hold.

More lavatory paper to wipe away the dust from inside

the galvanized-metal shaft. I then took the packet from my back pocket and reached in as far as I could with a five-inch strip of the Major's adhesive tape across its length. A few tugs to make sure it was securely attached. Then I waited, listening for approaching footsteps. Nothing. This part of the ship seemed deserted. I screwed the grille carefully back into place, trying not to scratch the paintwork. In case a search was made, it would have to be a damned thorough one. I balanced myself with a hand on the cistern, stepped down and wiped the sweat from my forehead.

More than anything else I wanted a drink, and wanted it badly. It's only on television you see secret agents with nerves of steel nonchalantly complete their mission, grab the girl, and shoot their way to safety. My nerves had been on edge ever since I had met the Major at the football game and now they were stretched absolutely taut. I was all too conscious that the information I was now carrying about in my head was of the very highest priority. That, along with the imminent swan dive on to the sandpile made me feel like a man with a worm coiling in his stomach.

'I've got to be sober when I make the jump,' I reminded myself. But there was still another hour until the curtain went up for the final act. In the bar, I caught sight of the purser who had greeted me earlier when I came on board. Somehow I managed to get a normal conversation going with him about the *Uzbekistan* and how he liked his job. He was thirty years old and his wife had just had a baby; I can't remember where he said he was from. Finally, he downed his beer and excused himself, saying that he had to check off the passengers who were just now starting to board. Except for the barman scrubbing glasses, I now had the place to myself.

I lingered for as long as I could over my drink, eyes glued to the clock on the wall. Assuming the merchantman weighed anchor at the scheduled time, my jump would take

place at about a quarter to twelve. At half past eleven, I left
the bar and strolled along the deck. It didn't take long to
find the spot. I saw where the bulkhead light was out of
commission and ran my hand along the railing until I came
to a section that wiggled like a loose tooth. Who had seen
to these arrangements, I did not know, nor was I in a mood
to speculate just then.

I was very conscious as the seconds ticked by that I had
to look out to sea and identify the foreign ship moving
slowly out of the harbour to synchronize my leap. The
experts in London had it worked out that I was to jump the
moment the bow of the outgoing merchantman was directly
in line with the edge of the *Uzbekistan*'s single funnel. I
heard pacing footsteps on the deck overhead. Guards?
Quite possibly. I lit a cigarette and stepped back from the
doctored railing. I concentrated on the light-speckled
silhouette of the foreign merchantman. Another few
seconds . . . there, that's it. Now do it!

I swallowed hard and launched myself over the side of
the cruise ship.

The concussion of impact shattered me into a million
pieces. I screamed as the overwhelming spasms of pain
consumed my body, and screamed again, shrilly at the top
of my lungs. No sand. Where was the sand? Damn it, I
thought fiercely, what did they do with the sand? I heard
myself whimper faintly. Shouts, running footfalls. Searchlights probed the darkness until their beams converged on
the china doll that was me, writhing and screaming as the
impassive Black Sea lapped at the pilings a few feet away.

Someone hastily threw a blanket over me. My arm
reached out to cling to the leg of his trousers. 'Don't move,
don't move,' a voice said, and I knew it was the officer I'd
been chatting with in the bar. Then he bent over and
whispered, 'Don't say you've been drinking with me,
please . . . !'

That was all I could remember. When I came round again, I was lying on a hospital table, recurrent waves of throbbing agony kept at bay by a drug-induced numbness in all my limbs. An elderly man in a white smock fastened to the back of his shirt with adhesive strips was talking to a pair of white-turbaned female colleagues. The blonde Intourist girl stood at the right of the table. She drew back in surprise when my eyes flickered open.

'Mr Veeny . . . ?' she said in a soft drawl. 'Mr Veeny. You are feeling better now, I hope.'

I tried to answer but only a sound halfway between a moan and a croak came from my throat.

'Please don't try to move,' the girl said. 'The doctor wants that you know you have broken your femur in two places. Your spine may have been twisted when you hit the ground.'

Then it started coming back to me. All I could think about was the bloody sand. What went wrong? The pile of sand that could have made it the simplest thing for me to pick myself up from the quay and complain loudly about my bruises. Probably free drinks for the rest of the cruise, profuse apologies. Now I realized the Department had slipped up somewhere. Damn them, I thought. Damn them to hell. This has spoiled everything.

'Mr Veeny, listen please. We have made X-rays. The doctor says that you will have to undergo an operation. He will place a rod in your hip of stainless steel. You will have to stay in this hospital for three or four weeks. After that, only three months on crutches.'

Dazed though I might have been, my brain functioned well enough for me to realize that the only hope of salvaging the mission lay in getting out of the Soviet Union and being quick about it. My own safety depended on it, too. I had no way of knowing if Major Kuznov had been successful in his escape. Even supposing he was, the KGB would lose no time in mounting an investigation once they realized he was gone. Sooner or later they would have to come to me and ask questions. I started blurting excuses for my urgent departure.

'My family will be terribly worried about me,' I pleaded. 'And if I stay here for three months, it will be disastrous for my business. My affairs in London need my attention. Isn't there any way you can patch me up to travel so I can have the operation done in London?'

The doctor talked this over with his two women colleagues. Then, through the blonde interpreter: 'We have already straightened your leg while you were unconscious. It is possible to put you in a plaster cast from your armpits down to your feet which will render you completely immobile. It will not be comfortable, but it serves to prevent any further dislocation of your hip or pressure on your spinal column until you are back in London.'

I nodded eagerly.

The painful business of enclosing a full-grown man in a protective mummy case took four days to complete. Alternate layers of plaster and bandages, with holes for the necessary bodily functions. Each layer had to be left overnight to dry, so the process became a kind of slow torture for me. There were a couple of times when I had to fight to keep from losing consciousness, biting my lip. Any movement in my trunk or legs was an agony. I was told that, by a miracle, my feet and ankles hadn't broken when I fell. Some miracle! At least there was the satisfaction of knowing that all those hours of training had not been entirely in vain.

I found out that I had been taken to the Seamen's Hospital in Odessa. I was crowded in a ward with eight other men, all of them very kind and pleasant, though we couldn't speak a word between us. When relatives brought gifts of cheese and smoked fish, they let me know with grunts and hand signs that I was welcome to share their bounty. I must say this touched me more poignantly than anything I had experienced in my travels or contacts with Russian officialdom. That the Russians are warm-hearted and generous as a people is one of the things we so easily lose sight of when all our dealings are limited to a cynical elité.

But the hospital itself was a disaster, violating all but the most elementary rules of hygiene. The walls were coated with a loose flaky wash that peeled off if you stared too hard at it. Beds jammed so close together that, when visitors came, they had to stand in the doorway and shout across the room. There was an X-ray machine that looked like a tin can on a clothes-pole; I can't imagine how it worked. I don't think the nurses knew about washing their hands. Not being in any hurry to die of some horrendous infection, I rejoiced that I had politely turned down their suggestion of an operation.

The third morning after my arrival, I had official visitors. I had been expecting them to turn up any time and so gave careful thought to what I was going to say, praying that everything else – Major Kuznov's getting out, the papers remaining undiscovered – had gone off according to plan.

Blue and white cap in his hand, the ship's duty officer had come along to help with the translating. He was accompanied by a stocky uniformed man from what I guessed would be the harbour police, and two grim-faced individuals in civilian clothes. I didn't need to observe how the officer and the policeman deferred to these last two to figure out where they were going to turn in their reports.

'You are feeling all right now, Mr Veeny?' the officer said. 'You gave us all quite a fright, you know. These gentlemen have come to ask you for a statement explaining how you suffered such a regrettable accident.'

My bed, with me in it, was wheeled out to the narrow

corridor and into a private room. They started in with their questioning and I had no choice but to keep to the official M16 script.

'I was walking along the deck and must have tripped over something because the next thing I can remember is waking up here in hospital. I don't know whether the railing gave way when I leaned against it or what. I couldn't see very well and I'm afraid I just wasn't paying much attention.'

They pressed for more details but I continued to act a bit dumb. 'I really can't figure out how it happened. All I know is that as I stumbled, I stretched out to grasp the rail but it didn't seem to be in place.'

The four of them discussed all this among themselves for a time, while I held my breath and waited for whatever was coming next. To my enormous but, I hope, well-disguised relief, they appeared to be more worried that I might make a legal claim against the ship and its owners than anything else. I assured them that this was the farthest thing from my mind. The accident may have been my fault. I was more than grateful for their quick attention and the excellent clinical care I was now receiving. Even the two KGB men were smiling now.

Then they brought in my suitcases. I was asked to sign a paper declaring that all my belongings were intact and had been promptly returned to me. I signed, and they excused themselves, thanking me for my co-operation. The purser gave me a knowing wink as he closed the door on the way out.

I sucked in air through my bottom teeth and my pounding heartbeat slowed a little. They had believed me.

12

Business Completed

'What happened to the documents, Greville?' The rather elderly man whom I'd met at one or two MI6 briefings hovered by my bedstead in St George's Hospital, the bottle of Scotch and carton of cigarettes he'd brought along with him lying enticingly on the side table.

Immobilized in my plaster carapace, I had been sent from Odessa to Moscow, a thirty-hour journey by train, looked after by a taciturn, middle-aged Russian nurse who gave me pain-killing injections and tablets when the jolting got to be uncomfortable. I rested for another two days in a special foreigners-only ward of the Bodkin Clinic, while the British Embassy made arrngements to have me flown out of the country. I had to change planes in Paris, which meant the additional agony of one more ambulance ride. On the British European Airways flight out of Moscow I occupied an entire row of seats, and was forced to pay triple the regular fare.

All the while I was wondering, with every good reason for anxiety, whether or not Kuznov's bid for freedom had been successful. The time factor worried me most of all. How long until the Soviet authorities realized he had gone missing? To this day, I do not know exactly how Kuznov covered his tracks; whether he had a long leave coming to him or if his high position in the GRU made the possibility of his defection unthinkable to his superiors. Whatever the smoke-screen he threw up, it had held long enough to buy me the time I needed to get safely out of the country.

The Department's emissary confirmed that Kuznov had arrived safely in Britain by now. Sixteen days had gone by since my one-point landing on the Odessa quay. When I heard that Kuznov was safe, I gave the largest sigh of relief my plaster cast would allow.

'As you can undoubtedly imagine,' the man said, 'the Major has told us that he made a suggestion to you about where to conceal the documents. Was that the cache you decided in the end to use?'

I told him that, so far as I knew, the envelope was still where I had secured it, in the lavatory air-vent. My MI6 contact could not hold back a faint sigh of disappointment.

'I suppose it couldn't be helped. We'll have to proceed under the assumption that the cruise ship is sailing round the Black Sea at this very minute with the documents tucked away in the loo, and that they stay that way until further notice. It's going to give our boys some sleepless nights figuring out how to get them back. Without those papers as proof, it won't be easy convincing the Americans that the stories Kuznov's been telling us are on the level.'

'Now you tell me something,' I said impatiently. 'What happened to the famous sandpile I was supposed to land on?'

The man gave a polite shrug. 'I haven't been told anything about that personally. I assume discreet inquiries are being made. From what I understand, you ran into a bit of bad luck.'

A few hours after his departure, I was taken to another room where attendants used a circular saw to extricate me from the mummy cast. The cast came off, and I was wheeled away to the operating theatre. When I came out from under the anaesthesia, I found myself swaddled in bandages and safety pins, with five pints of somebody else's blood swimming around in my veins and two steel rods pinning the breaks in my hip.

I stayed in hospital for another ten days. A more cheerful invalid, the nurses said, had never come their way. I was thankful to be back in England and overjoyed just to be alive. Still, it bothered me that only half the mission could be counted a success. Knowing it hadn't been my fault wasn't much of a consolation. As for what went wrong, all I could guess was that one of the Russians whom the Major had used in setting up his escape may have decided at the last minute that my falling on to sand might look like too much of a happy coincidence and therefore had it moved.

My wife had rushed to the hospital as soon as the waiting ambulance collected me at the airport. I told her as much as I could about the circumstances leading up to my accident. She also informed the companies I represented and let them know that I'd be in touch again as soon as I was halfway mobile. By the time I was given crutches to hobble about on and sent home, I knew it wouldn't be long before James would appear to hear my report. Then perhaps we would see what could be done to put things right.

A few days later, I received a message through the part-time chauffeur the Department had assigned for my use. I was driven in the back of my Humber to the barracks by Hyde Park, where we waited until a taxi let James off and he came over to join me. The driver saluted and went for a walk while we talked.

'Let's have a full report on everything that happened to you, including all the details of what the Major told you regarding the contents of that envelope,' James said, after we had greeted each other, and I had assured him the carpentry work had me well along the road to recovery.

I answered in as much detail as I could. Once again the powers of memory I'd developed as a schoolboy came in handy and I found that I could repeat the Major's conversation almost word for word. After I finished, I said, 'Can you tell me exactly what the Major had arranged for his escape?'

'One of the port authorities was a lifelong friend of our

Major Kuznov,' James explained. 'It was his intervention that enabled our man to board the cargo ship. The one big obstacle was the friend's assistant, a man known as something of a tippler. Luckily, Kuznov's friend was able to lace the assistant's vodka when they had a few drinks together before their turn of duty started.

'Next, this official took command of one of the tenders that shuttle Soviet harbour pilots on and off the ships coming in and out of the port. They rendezvoused with the Major at a deserted loading facility and gave him the all-clear signal to come on board. From there on in, it was just a matter of dropping the Major alongside the ship at the right moment, thanks to the timely diversion you were able to supply.'

'I see what you're getting at. Nothing would have been amiss, seeing the tender pull up to the merchantman.'

'That's right,' James said. 'Kuznov jumped over the side when he saw the lights go on over where you were and climbed up the rope ladder. One of the bulkhead doors had been left ajar so that he could enter the ship. He stayed hidden in the cabin that had been reserved for him until the *Uzbekistan* put into a Turkish port two days later. After that, he had freedom of the ship, as the crew would have assumed he was a passenger who boarded in Istanbul. We'd provided him with false papers and visas, so it was simple enough for him to fly directly to London from the next port of call.'

'Very neatly done,' I commented. 'Really an admirable job of organization, and I'm glad the Major's all right, but with all that careful planning what went wrong with the sand?'

James winced. 'Ah yes, Greville. Pity about that. Our information is that the sand was correctly positioned there on the very day you were supposed to make your fall. But it had been raining, as you remember, and somebody came along and placed a tarpaulin over it to shield the sand from the rain. Which, of course, meant that it did not break your fall as efficiently as loose sand would have done.

Until that moment, I hadn't known that I actually did land on a tarpaulin. It felt like concrete at the time, and concrete I assumed it was.

Little by little, over the next three months, I began to get back into something like functioning order. Four times a week in the hospital for exercises and physical therapy. During this same period I met several times with James and other officers from the Department in safe houses around the West End to consider what the next moves should be. The fact I was invited to be present at these meetings should have told me what they were leading up to, but still I was surprised when James finally put the matter to me.

'None of the plans we've had under consideration stands much of a chance of working under real-life conditions. In practical terms, it would be impossible for us to get one of our men aboard the ship with an adequate cover. A new face would be too carefully watched.' There was a pause, and he said mildly, 'Don't you think it would be natural for you to continue your interrupted business trip once you're fully fit again?'

'Wait a minute . . .' I started to protest, but James broke in. 'Hear me out on this, will you, Greville? We're absolutely sure that Kuznov's escape has not been tied to you in any way. We've had a chat with those two English friends of yours from Odessa and they say they weren't even questioned by the police. That for one thing. Obviously, the Soviet authorities haven't made any connection between the two events. We're not suggesting you should return to Odessa, that would be asking a bit much. But if you could arrange it so that you happen to be in another port when the *Uzbekistan* is scheduled to be there, it's only natural that you would want to thank the captain and the steward for coming so quickly to your aid.'

'How sure are you about all this?' I insisted.

'Absolutely sure. Our people in Moscow tell me that Soviet trade officials still regard you with the highest esteem. What's more, the friend who helped Kuznov get out is still working at the same job, so obviously there's not the slightest whiff of suspicion attached to your accident.'

I considered this for a few moments and told him I'd do it. There seemed little choice at that point. I felt personally irritated that the entire affair had been left unfinished. Logically, it appeared the thing for me to do.

Inevitably, there were complications on the home front. Relations between my wife and myself were left further strained in the aftermath of Odessa. 'What were you doing there in the first place?' she pressed. 'You had no business there.' It was no good telling her that I simply wanted to see something of the country. It was easier to pull the wool over the eyes of the Communist secret police than to deceive an intelligent wife, I was beginning to find out.

While my bones were mending, I began to make plans for my return. Putting a hesitant toe in to test the waters, I went to see Pavlov, the Soviet commercial attaché in London, who was actually the KGB's top man in Britain. He received me very cordially, laying on the iced vodka and treating me like an old friend. 'I am looking forward to assisting the British Trade Exhibition in Moscow, which I hope will be followed by the Soviet one in London and perhaps, in due time, Paris,' he said. I asked him to officially relay my thanks to the Seamen's Hospital in Odessa and the Bodkin in Moscow for their kindness in looking after me. After this encounter, I was beginning to let myself be convinced that James had been right: I was still *personna* extremely *grata* with the Soviets, and unless something quite unexpected happened, the risk involved in making a return visit to the ship wasn't nearly as great as in my nightmarish imaginings.

As soon as I was able to get about with the help of a stick, I arranged to sweep through Hungary and Czecho-slovakia to conclude some deals left hanging at the time of my accident. Officials in Budapest were very keen on some leather-processing machinery offered by one of my client companies. I'd brought them specification sheets, cata-logues, photographs and price lists, and government procedure was to study these first to make sure that no similar equipment was available from a fraternal socialist country before a purchase could be authorized. Again I reminded them that I was in a position to bring over engineers and technicians to clarify any doubts in their mind concerning the effectiveness of the machinery. None of the Soviet bloc countries could understand why they were being offered commercial and industrial know-how in this way without having to pay for it.

Shortly after my return, I applied for a visa to Bulgaria and got it. There was one last meeting with James and his colleagues, a two-day drive down to Vienna. I took a Balkan Airlines flight for the quick hop over the border to Sofia.

This time I was really frightened. Perhaps it was a delayed reaction to everything that had passed in Odessa, where things moved so quickly there hadn't been time to let the full realization of the dangers hit me deep in the gut, where the real pangs of fear are experienced. Now, there was no evading it.

Somehow, I managed to get through three days of bargaining sessions and, on a Saturday afternoon in August, travelled across the length of Bulgaria by train, a five-hour journey. The *Uzbekistan* would not be docking in Varna for another two days. I decided to wait until the last possible minute before applying for permission to go on board. Supposing the Bulgarian State Security learned of my interest, even as a matter of routine, there simply wouldn't be time for them to wire their big brothers in Moscow for a background check.

Varna is an ancient town and deservedly famous for its brilliant white-hot sun, endless stretches of warm sand and turquoise sea. At that time, you could see only a handful of steel skeletons for future hotels, foreshadowing the great tourist boom that was to come a few years later. Most of the people who came there on holiday were Bulgarian workers subsidized by their state-run trade unions, and nothing very fancy in the way of accommodation was needed for them. It was also, in 1959, the setting for many poignant reunions between husbands and wives, parents and children separated by the bitter realities of communism. The East German régime issued a limited number of visas for its citizens to come to Varna and be reunited for a few days with family members who had remained in the western zone of Germany during the occupation. More than once during my brief stay, I saw elderly couples walking hand in hand by the water, softly murmuring to each other in German, trying to make up for lifetimes forever lost. Little children hesitantly confronting fathers they knew only as a face in an old photograph.

For two days, then, I tried to behave like any other tourist, sightseeing, sunning myself, wandering into shops that sold lacework and hand-carved wooden knick-knacks, nothing of very high quality. On the morning the *Uzbekistan* was due to arrive in port, I strolled into the offices of the Balkan Line agency. 'I understand the ship to Istanbul is going to be in today,' I told the harassed-looking young clerk, and started to tell him about the events leading up to my unfortunate accident. He examined my business card, eyebrows knitting as he heard me out. This caused not a little consternation; one after another, senior clerks were summoned from the back office to listen in. Eventually a middle-aged man with a broken nose came out and put his hands on his hips while my request was explained to him. Then he turned and glared at me. In curt, not very intelligible English he told me that yes, the cruise ship in question would shortly be in port and that only passengers were allowed to board the ship; clearly, I was not a passenger and therefore could not be permitted to board the ship.

Patiently and politely I explained one more time what it was about, asking the clerk who spoke the best English to do the interpreting. For good measure, I showed him a sheaf of papers from my briefcase establishing that I was in correspondence with the Bulgarian Ministry of Foreign Trade, sporting the signatures of several of their top officials. Suddenly it was as if a little fiddling with the tuning dial had brought in the station signal loud and clear. He stared blankly at me for a few seconds and scribbled out a pass for me right then and there.

They told me in the office that the *Uzbekistan* would be tying up shortly after noon and depart for Istanbul that same evening at 6 P.M. I judged early afternoon to be a good time for me to put in my appearance, while most of the passengers would probably have disembarked to see the city. Now that I had the visitor's pass, the sole remaining hurdle was to make sure the same duty officer was on duty this trip, and locating him without losing precious time. MI6 had verified from London that he had not been dumped from the crew as a consequence of the Odessa episode, so this didn't worry me too much.

Luckily, I spotted him within five minutes of coming aboard, hurrying along the promenande deck with a clip-board in his hands. He froze when he caught sight of me and remained stock still as I approached, a blank expression on his face.

'Do you remember me?' I asked jauntily.

The thunderstruck expression didn't crack. 'You were the one that fell . . .'

'Yes,' I said, 'the one that tumbled on to the dock back in Odessa.'

'You were injured,' he stammered. 'But now you are here.' It didn't make sense to him I could see that.

'I just wanted to thank you and the other officers for looking after me,' I added quickly. 'I happened to be here on a combination business trip and holiday and when I heard the *Uzbekistan* was tied up here, I thought I would come to thank you personally for all that you did.'

'Oh . . .'

'What happened after I was in hospital? I hope there wasn't any trouble for you.'

By now he was making a quick recovery. 'There was an inquiry,' he said. 'They found the railings were not correctly fitted and the lamp had not been replaced as it should have been. After many questions, the final ruling was that it was an accident.'

'Let's go to the bar for a drink then,' and I put a hand on his shoulder to steer him in the right direction. We both ordered a beer and as he let himself be convinced that my reappearance in his life was not meant to make trouble, he loosened up a great deal. I waited to see if an opportunity to go to the lavatory presented itself.

My friend took a quick swallow of beer and said, 'Would you mind waiting just a few minutes for me? I have to go to look for somebody. I'll be back presently.' There was an American couple in the bar who overheard us speaking English, and came over to introduce themselves. We chatted for a minute of so. The woman started into an account of all the marvellous things they had seen on their Black Sea holiday.

I put my beer down on the counter. 'Excuse me,' I said,

and started off to the gents' room. Once inside, I saw that my luck was still holding. I was the only occupant. Then I realized lunch was being served at that hour and most passengers would be in or near the main dining room. I hadn't forgotten my pocket screwdriver. I quickly twisted the screws to undo the grille from its mounting. A medley of thoughts, fears and apprehension was building to a climax. Would the adhesive have been strong enough? Three months' sailing round the Black Sea meant a lot of salt air had passed through the vents of the system. The package might have worked loose and slipped down the duct, forever out of reach. Or worse. Much worse than that. What if it had clogged an air-vent and they had called in a mechanic to locate the stoppage?

The grille pulled loose. Without pausing to peer into the shaft, I reached in with my hand and felt my heart leap as my fingers brushed against the brown-paper package. Three cheers for Russian adhesive tape! I still could hardly bring myself to believe my luck as I pulled the envelope loose and stuffed it hastily in my jacket pocket.

There was adhesive still on the metal sides of the duct and though I scraped at it, it wouldn't come off. I was counting on not leaving any clues behind, but there wasn't time to be meticulous. After listening to make sure nobody had entered the lavatories, I replaced the grille and sauntered out towards the bar.

Every nerve in my body was urging me to get off the boat, make an insane dash to the nearest gangplank. A momentary irrational impulse, the culmination of all the tension mounting in me. It passed in a few seconds so I went back to the bar to finish my beer.

The American couple had vanished, and there was just a German man in there now; we tried to get a conversation going in broken English without too much success. Suddenly the glass door opened and the purser came back

into the bar, followed by a weather-beaten man in his
sixties. The new arrival wore a dark-blue uniform with
white piping.

'The captain,' said my friend. For a fraction of a second
seeing him enter with a man in uniform had startled me. He
came over to the bar with a big grizzled smile and clasped
my hand with a strong, warm grip. 'He would like to know
if you are ever going to be a passenger on the *Uzbekistan*
again after your bad accident,' the purser went on. We all
laughed.

'Someday I hope to come back,' I said, trying to put a
mask of good humour over my words. 'But next time I
won't go walking along the deck. I think it's safer here in
the bar.' That remark translated, we all laughed again.

We had another round of drinks and exchanged further
pleasantries. I waved farewell to the two officers from the
bottom of the gangplank.

The guard at the gate took my pass from me and I began
to walk hurriedly towards the centre of town, looking for a
taxi.

It had taken less than an hour from the time I went on
board and retrieved the package until now, but I still
couldn't be sure I was in the clear. How could I know if the
KGB was having me followed? All that night I slept fitfully
in my hotel room, glancing up from time to time, expecting
the door to burst open at any minute.

Much as I would have preferred to take the shortest route
out of the country, the Department had wisely overruled
me on that. 'You're on holiday, remember?' James had
said. 'People don't come rushing back from holidays. It's
better that you take your time.' So the next morning I took
a cab to the railway station, returned to Sofia, and stayed
for another night in the Bulgarian capital before making
the plane connection that brought me to Vienna after a

two-hour stopover in the transit lounge of Budapest Airport.

Incredibly, I had no trouble at all with Customs searches or the police. The Bulgarian officials stamped my passport and cancelled my visa with a gruff peremptory nod, not bothering to look in the suitcases. Major Kuznov's documents were still in my breast pocket.

As soon as I reached Vienna, I got my Humber out of the airport garage and drove to an M16-owned safe house in the Stefanplatz district. I knew one of James's people would be waiting for me there on twenty-four-hour alert.

'Hello, Greville. Trust you had a pleasant holiday.' A harmless-looking man with spectacles and a shiny bald patch, like a friar, on the top of his head greeted me with these words when my key opened the door of the flat and I hauled my luggage over the threshold.

'I suppose you could do with a drink,' he said, holding out an iced double Scotch.

I took the drink in one hand and with the other pulled the errant envelope from my pocket and offered it to him with a mock flourish.

'Ah, splendid.' He reached for the telephone then. 'Sorry I can't join you for dinner,' he said cheerfully as he dialled.

'Hello . . . yes, I've got it here.' He listened for a moment. 'He's fine.' Another long pause. 'I'm on my way,' he said, and banged the receiver down.

A split second later, he had vanished out the door. At long last, Major Kuznov's gift to British Intelligence had reached its destination. Now I could relax a little.

PART THREE
Penkovsky

13

Enter Penkovsky

Major Kuznov was somewhere safe in Britain; the documents that sweetened his welcome were doubtless now being pondered by top-level policy-makers of the NATO powers. From the Department's standpoint, the Odessa mission was just another one for the files. It could never be that way for me. My days of lifting heavy suitcases, climbing up step-ladders and bending down in the mornings to tie my shoelaces were gone for ever. Even today, if I sit in a chair for any length of time, I have to extend my right leg straight out in front of me to accommodate my pinned-together hip. The jolt to my spinal column had dislodged a couple of vertebrae in the lower back, pinching a nerve and bringing on occasional attacks of blinding pain and dizzy spells. For a time, I was deathly afraid of blackouts while driving a car. Finally, a Harley Street specialist solved this one for me by prescribing special shoes with an extra quarter-inch built into one heel, relieving pressure on the nerve.

I suppose you could say my marriage was an indirect casualty of the Odessa affair, too. Like my body, it had been put through the mangle but came out limping and serviceable. There was a period of angry questions at first, then coolness and silence. 'Why didn't you come back sooner this time?' Sheila demanded to know. 'Why did you have to take the car?' I said something about having to haul a lot of heavy catalogues around with me, but I could see she wasn't believing a word of it. It was obvious by now that I had built a wall around a substantial part of my life from which Sheila was excluded. Most hurtful of all to her was the awareness that whatever it was I had got myself involved with, I had done so willingly, and had no apparent regrets at the outcome.

I stayed on in Vienna for about a week after handing over Major Kuznov's package, unwinding in the company of an old friend, Kurt, and the lovely Viennese girls he seemed to have the knack of producing for the occasion. We dined out in the city's best-known cellar restaurants, went to night-clubs and in the afternoons I'd go for long, leisurely walks with one of the girls Kurt had introduced me to.

This cooling-off period had been expressly indicated by the Department. They knew from long experience about the mixed feeling of tension and elation that overwhelm an agent on completion of a mission, a potentially dangerous mental state of giddy anticlimax. It's virtually an occupational hazard in the spy business. You have nobody in whom to confide. The tension has been building up in you like pressure in a steam boiler. You have this perversely impulsive desire to go shouting state secrets from the rooftops or nudge the person sitting next to you on the bus and say, 'Psst, I'm a spy!' Well, it isn't quite as bad as all that, but I think the meaning is clear. And this is why it is after the mission is over and finished with that the inexcusable, often fatal slip is made.

Knowing this, and as a way of thanking me for my services, James made me a present of the keys to the Stefanplatz apartment. 'Keep these,' he said, 'and in the future you can use the place whenever you're in town. If we need it for something, we'll check with you first.' During the next three years, I used it as a personal hideaway and operations centre for my business trips into Eastern Europe. There was one thing I was scrupulous about doing: if it happened that I had a girl with me to finish off a pleasant evening, I was careful to take her to the nearby

Stefanstrasse Hotel. That way, MI6 would know that I could be discreet.

I took my time driving up the Rhine Valley, and when I reached London I was feeling much better except for the confrontation with Sheila I knew was brewing. A day or two after I got back, James and I got together for lunch at the Shangri-La Chinese Restaurant opposite the Brompton Oratory, a place we had used once or twice before. They had a little alcove off to one side that was ideal for MI6's purposes, because you could dine, well out of earshot of the other tables.

During the meal I gave him a quick summary of what had taken place in Varna. He congratulated me on the success of my mission, emphasizing how important the smuggled documents had proved to be. 'They support evidence coming in from other sources, so at least we've been able to alert our American friends as to what's developing in Berlin.'

'What's on next for me, then?' I asked blandly.

'For the time being, nothing. We want you to continue your legitimate sales operations in the Soviet bloc countries without having to worry about doing us any special favours on the side. Keep your nose clean and pointed in the right direction: where the profits are. If, for example, you should happen to be approached by someone over there who says he wants to defect or pass information to us, don't get involved. Tell him you're a businessman, and make it obvious that he's put you on the spot.'

James prodded with his chopsticks at a prawn on his plate. 'You'd be surprised at how many tourists and such do get approached on the street and cornered. Just in case you come across a situation like that, pass the word to us and we'll attend to it. The important thing is that your reputation be completely untarnished.'

Now it was my turn to smile. 'Because you're going to

ask me to do another errand for you later on, isn't that what you mean?'

'There's always that possibility,' James conceded.

About a week after this meeting, James got back to me on the telephone. 'You'd be free this evening to stop by at Coleherne Court? Come over around ten or so. I've got somebody who'll be there who says he'd like to have a word with you.'

When I got there James let me in, took my raincoat and said mischievously, 'Follow me.' In the sitting room, Major Sergei Kuznov, looking very dapper and almost unrecognizable in a smart Savile Row suit, launched himself from an armchair, bellowing 'Greville!' in a bull-roarer voice.

'I take it you've met before,' James teased. Kuznov threw his arms around me and gave me a bone-cracking Russian bear-hug.

'I'm sorry to hear you broke your hip in the fall,' the Major added. 'I hope you're feeling better now.'

'I'm fine. I trust you are keeping well, too?'

Kuznov laughed. 'Your friends have been taking very good care of me, yes. I shall be going to America presently, did they tell you that? The Americans have found a job for me at the Soviet desk in the Pentagon and will be coming to fetch me in another couple of weeks. But tell me, I hope you enjoyed Odessa while you were there.'

'Much better than Kiev. I thought it was a little on the quiet side, though.'

The Major gave another roar. 'Ah, it's a pity, a real pity, you know. We might have been able to show you some true Russian hospitality at the Seamen's Club. Though not that last trip,' he added quickly. 'The Club is constantly kept under surveillance because the sailors do a lot of their black-market deals there.'

'I can't say I noticed many pretty girls, either.'

'No,' Kuznov said, 'you wouldn't have.' A sly, rakish note in his voice made me wonder if the Department had already introduced him to some nice British girls with security clearances.

'Have my friends been looking after all your needs?' I probed.

'In every way, Greville. The GRU could learn a thing or two from your people – *our* people, now.' He grinned a little sheepishly and I figured my guess had been close enough to the mark.

I was glad to see the Major in good spirits at the beginning of his new life in the West. James brought over drinks for the two of us and remarked, 'It's a pity, as you know, that we can't give Greville any sort of public award for what he's done and I'm sure you in particular, Major Kuznov, must understand how grateful we all feel.' Kuznov nodded emphatically.

Later, in fact, I did have occasion to ask a favour of James and he was as good as his word. I wanted my son to go to a first-class public school. Did he know of anyone who could provide the necessary recommendation for Andrew?

'I'll take care of it immediately,' was the answer. Ten days after that, James was on the phone saying, 'That matter we were discussing the other day – I've got everything arranged at this end. Perhaps we'd better meet up again at Coleherne Court.' When I got there, James and his associate Roger introduced me to Colonel Brian Montgomery, the Field Marshal's younger brother. 'Colonel Montgomery's an old friend,' Roger said. 'His brother is an ex-pupil and governor of St Paul's School in Hammersmith. The Field Marshal says he'll be delighted to meet you and talk it over. I'm sure he'll be prepared to sponsor your son.'

(As it turned out, however, Andrew was not able to take advantage of the opportunity the Department had arranged for him. Just as he would have been ready to enter school, the KGB arrested me in Budapest and I became headline news. To avoid being hounded by the Press, his mother decided that it would be better if he were sent to a boarding-school in the country, and MI6 made the arrangements. But at the time I first brought the matter up with James, St Paul's seemed a wonderful chance for my son to continue his education).

I asked Monty's brother if there would be any objection to my wife coming along. There had been something I remembered seeing in the papers about Field Marshal Montgomery feeling uncomfortable in the company of women following his wife's tragic death.

'No, not at all,' the Colonel said. 'It's perfectly all right. That was just one of the stories the newspapers print. No problem at all.'

Before the week was out, I received a handwritten note on heavy, cream-wove paper, a personal invitation signed with a formal flourish, 'Field Marshal Montgomery of El Alamein'. Monty wrote to let me know that he was staying at his country home and would be pleased to see us if we didn't mind the drive out there.

I'd read somewhere that the great man was a stickler for punctuality, so I made sure our arrival was timed to the exact minute. Montgomery was waiting for us by the gateposts, dressed in an old green sweater and corduroy trousers. 'Drive on and park at the far end of the drive, over on the left,' he said, as he unlatched the gate himself and waved us through. 'You'll see the house just beyond.'

The Field Marshal was a delightful host. He took Andrew and myself round the back of the converted mill to show us the caravans he used as his field HQ in the North African campaign. Inside, we leafed through the scrapbook of yellowed press-cuttings and photographs of Rommel. He let us inspect the celebrated fly-swatter he used to carry with him in the desert and said, 'Some mad American offered me ten thousand dollars for that, can you imagine?' To which I replied that if he ever felt like starting up a business to supply Americans with fly-swatters, I'd be pleased to line up distributors. He grinned and said he'd keep it in mind. 'He always used to stand just there,' Monty remarked a few minutes later, indicating the door to the caravan. 'Always in the damn way, with that wretched cigar of his.'

'Who used to stand there, sir?' asked Andrew.

'Churchill. Couldn't stand the damn smoke.'

We then went to see the budgerigars and other cage-birds he was breeding on one of the terraces. 'By the way,' he said. 'I suppose you could do with a drink, Wynne. You know I don't, but please help yourself from the cabinet.' Then we went to meet the housekeeper and two young boys who were proctors at the school. He'd thoughtfully invited them along to keep Andrew company and tell him something of public-school life. There were tea and cakes set out for us, and Montgomery insisted on doing the serving himself.

In the comfortable sitting room there was a large painting of the Victory Parade, showing Monty along with Attlee, Morrison, Bevan and other political leaders of the time. 'Recognize any of that lot?' he grunted. 'Tell you something, I'm about the only one who's left. All the rest are dead, you know.'

I remember that from there we got into a heated discussion of the Common Market. Monty argued against it on the grounds that it was absurd to hope to see so many countries set aside their petty squabbling and work together for the good of all. I realized that as former Commander-in-Chief of NATO, he was doubtless speaking from unhappy personal experience. My own view was that Britain was in no position to stay out of the Community, and gave the reasons for my disagreement. Monty questioned me shrewdly on my international trading background, and closed the subject with a slow-motion shake of his distinguished grey head. 'I suppose you have a point,' he chuckled. 'But thank heaven at my age they're not going to ask me to keep the peace with that lot.'

I remembered all the stories about the ferocious Field Marshal who swallowed subalterns for his breakfast, and it occured to me then that this legendary crustiness of manner was probably a cover for the man's deep-rooted personal shyness. He seemed pleased to have somebody around to ease his loneliness and hold his own in a bit of a wrangle. It was a pleasant afternoon's visit with a man I'd always admired, and I was grateful to the Department for having made the introduction for me.

I should make it clear that this kindness and a few other small favours (such as the keys to the Vienna flat) were the Department's way of saying 'Thanks!' to me. Of course, James made sure that my hospital bills were paid and took care of other expenses while I was on assignment for them, but that was the extent of it. I never asked to be paid for the work that I did on their behalf.

This, I know, will raise a few eyebrows. But it happens to be the literal truth. For one thing, there was no reason why I should have come to them for money. Setting my sights on the East European market had been one of the shrewdest business moves of my career. Now that the Department had me temporarily on the shelf, I redoubled my legitimate business activities, flying to Leipzig, Budapest and Potsdam to attend trade fairs and have talks with officials in an atmosphere more relaxed and worry-free than was usually the case in a drab government office.

Once I'd got the knack of doing business within the

framework of an economic system where increased output and fulfilment of the almighty plan were the stark priorities, I never had any problems dealing with government deputies who did the buying for state-run industries. Khrushchev's policy of 'peaceful coexistence', and the openings that resulted from it, were a businessman's dream.

Accordingly, for a period of about a year, I busied myself on behalf of my companies without directly involving myself in any sort of intelligence work. Occasionally, I'd have a drink with James and he'd ask me about my trips to Prague, Moscow, or Budapest, any changes of personnel in the ministries, and what were my general impressions of the mood of the capital, things of that sort.

There was, however, one incident rich in irony. It started with a phone call from a man named Kulikov, one of the Russian officials at the Highgate mission. He always seemed to have difficulty following when I talked business with his better-informed comrades, so I had put him down already as one of Pavlov's straight security boys. I knew the Soviet practice was very different from our own in the matter of cover. Spying is a big industry in Russia (by one reckoning, giving employment to around 330,000 people) and their low-level operatives receive a very thorough training in intelligence-gathering techniques. But the Soviet spymasters regard an agent's cover as secondary to the training, with often sloppy results. The British thinking is that whereas a genuine plumber or carpenter can be trained to be an agent, you don't ask one of your spies to bone up on some books from the library and try to pass himself off as a carpenter. It just doesn't work that way.

This Kulikov asked if we could meet after dark, some place away from his office. Curious, and willing enough to follow his instructions, I found him sitting on a bench in the little park on the Chelsea Embankment where the statue of Thomas Carlyle gazes in stony splendour across the

Thames. The evening was drizzly, the park deserted, the yellow lamplight a perfect atmospheric touch. Kulikov huddled in a belted raincoat with the collar turned up. He was fidgety and extremely nervous. I was given to understand that he was prepared to see that I would be suitably rewarded if I might care to obtain certain kinds of technical information for them. Surely, as a worldly and experienced businessman, I was aware that information often changes hands . . .

I cut him off in my stiffest tone of voice, hoping that it would convey just the right note of indignation. No, I said, I would most definitely not be prepared to do anything of the sort. Kulikov backed off immediately. He hoped I would not misconstrue anything he had said. I smiled serenely and watched him scuttle away down the colonnade of shadowy trees and vanish in the darkness.

'Pavlov again,' commented James, when he heard about this encounter. 'Moscow must be on his tail to step up recruitment. You handled it just right. I'll bet our Russian friend simply withered in the face of all that British rectitude.'

'He was absolutely smothered with it.'

'Good for you, Greville. Stay incorruptible and keep on doing your bit to help the British balance of payments.'

Early in November 1960, James and I arranged over the telephone to meet briefly for drinks. I came, not expecting anything much out of the ordinary, and after polite inquiries about my family and business, James said, 'Ever hear of an organization in Moscow called the State Committee on Scientific and Technical Research?'

'As a matter of fact, yes. I understand it's headed by a man called Gvishiani.' His name had come up more than once in trade discussions. A key Kremlin figure, Gvishiani was the one who had final say in determining long-range goals for Soviet industry. He was, in fact, the son-in-law of future Premier Alexei Kosygin.

'That's the one. You might want to see about getting together with some of their people. Among other functions, they have a department that's been put in charge of monitoring contacts between Soviet scientists and technicians and visiting delegations from the West.'

I hadn't realized that until now. My pet idea had always been to talk the Soviets round to authorizing two-way consultations between their experts and ours. If properly qualified people were called in at the beginning stages and consulted as to which products best met their needs, I thought it would be a good way of by-passing the bureaucratic tangle in pushing some deals through. Thus far, the officials I'd spoken to were politely interested in the idea, but nothing had been done.

Now, for just a moment I had the idea that James was trying to be helpful. Apparently I hadn't submitted my proposals on a high enough level or managed to find the right door to knock on. But his next words quickly dispelled that illusion.

'We'd be very interested if you could develop relations with them.'

There it was again! The hint dropped, another assignment in the offing. What would it be, this time? I was eager to find out.

I told James that I would write directly to the committee, requesting an appointment.

'Do that,' he said. 'Make it firmly worded and sound urgent. We'll meet again after you've been to see them.'

About the middle of November, I had my answer in the form of a telephone call from Pavlov, asking me to stop by his office in Kensington Park Gardens and fill out a visa form. The committee had contacted him to expedite communications. I had an appointment with them in Moscow on the first day of December.

The Scientific and Technical Committee was housed in a well-guarded, somewhat run-down building at Number 11 Gorky Street, just a few minutes' walk from Red Square. I was conducted to a conference room on the third floor and taken in hand by a stocky, heavy-jowled man in a suit that badly needed pressing. 'I am Bodenikov,' he said. Six of his comrades came forward to be presented. Then we all sat at the table and I explained my proposal for an exchange of specialists. I laid particular emphasis on the fact that the British were more than willing to make a detailed technical presentation to their Soviet opposite numbers, to familiarize them with current research and new developments in their various fields of specialization.

'How soon might all this take place?' asked Bodenikov, clearly sceptical.

I replied: 'A matter of weeks – before the year is out, in any case.' Here I was really putting my neck on the block. There had not been time for me to discuss my idea with any of the firms who were expected to send over their specialists; news that the Russians had been promised a visit would come as a total surprise.

Two days later, I had my answer. Returning to Gorky Street, I was taken in to meet the top man, Gvishiani. With him was a square-jawed, scowling man named Levin, deputy head of the committee.

Gvishiani spoke fluent English. 'Your idea for a delegation, Mr Wynne, I think it a splendid one. When your colleagues come to Moscow, I hope to be able to welcome them personally on behalf of the Council of Ministers. Comrade Levin's department will make all the arrangements.'

I noticed that Gvishiani was wearing a light-coloured suit of raw Italian silk and sported a gold Rolex on his left wrist.

That gave me a fair idea of how high in the world of Soviet officialdom I had climbed.

Levin and Bodenikov, together with three or four smaller fish from the committee, took me out to lunch at the National Hotel. As we discussed a provisional itinerary, one of the committee men at the far end of the table inquired about the slide and film equipment required for the lectures. Something in his deep, rich voice led me to lean forward to get a better look at the speaker. He sat ramrod stiff in his chair, deep-set eyes flicking from face to face as he followed the conversation attentively, but he seldom spoke himself unless he had something to contribute that was directly to the point. Unlike Levin and his underlings, he was neatly, immaculately dressed, and, for a Russian, extremely well groomed. A military man, clearly, I thought to myself. Mentally reviewing the list of names I was bringing back to James, I remembered that he had been introduced to me with his rank. Colonel Penkovsky, that was it.

I rushed back to London and hastily telephoned the directors of the firms I represented, arranging for an emergency meeting to decide on the make-up of the delegation. They took the news very well, I must say. A little stunned at first, but they quickly saw that this could be a definite opportunity for them to boost their export sales.

When I saw James at the Kensington safe house he had two associates with him.

'Tell us about the Committee, Greville. Everything you can.'

I told them. They were full of questions. Whom did I talk to? Who seemed to be in charge? They put some photographs on the table and I began to turn them over. 'There's Levin, yes. I didn't run into this other chap. No idea who he is. Yes, this one – you wouldn't forget a face like that. Here's Penkovsky—'

'Wait. Who did you say?'

'This is Colonel Penkovsky.'

James quickly snatched the photograph from the table and pressed it into my hand. 'Yes, Penkovsky. That's your target, Greville. We think he may be trying to come over to us.

14

Too Clever

By anyone's reckoning, Oleg Penkovsky should have been one of the most self-satisfied and instinctively loyal members of the Soviet establishment: a complacent career man and hard-nosed Party member. Talented and energetic, he occupied a choice position not far from the top of the Communist power pyramid. He had made the long upward climb aided only by sheer dedication, personal courage, and – as is virtually a requirement in 'classless' Soviet society – by having the right connections. As a young officer in the disastrous war with Finland and later, commanding an artillery unit in the Ukraine that helped break the relentless advance of the Nazi *Panzer* divisions, he had been wounded in action and decorated four times for bravery. He also distinguished himself during the Soviet-Japanese war. They made him a full colonel at the age of thirty – one of the youngest ever in the Red Army. Cementing his ties to the military high command, he married the daughter of a top general who subsequently was put in charge of the Soviet Union's rocketry and ballistic missile development programme.

Russia's ruling élite knows how to make use of men like Penkovsky. Party bosses and generals scoop them up for their key staff positions, the bright, hard-working specialists who keep the machinery of state oiled and running. The system has built-in rewards for the dedicated ones. Penkovsky was given a coveted posting as Senior Deputy to General Serov, head of the GRU, the Military Intelligence Directorate of the Red Army. A year before I met him, in 1959, he was cleared for advanced training at the Dzerzhinski Artillery Academy prior to his appointment on the recently formed Committee. What could have induced such a man to turn against the powerful and privileged élite that had welcomed him to its ranks?

Penkovsky acted entirely on his own. He had nothing to gain and everything to lose. There was never any question of self-interest. The people I worked for in London did not resort to bribery, blackmail or low tricks; indeed, they never even *asked* him to spy for the West in so many words.

And this is what has thrown so many commentators off the scent. A man like Penkovsky had no reason to be disloyal, the argument runs. What they fail to see is that he had no reason to think of it in terms of disloyalty to his country, for most Russians have no difficulty in drawing the line that separates themselves from the régime in power. The bosses and the bossed. Any so-called expert who wants to scoff at that notion, in my view, has a pathetically limited understanding of the Russian character.

Penkovsky was a soldier and a patriot. In Russia, you have to take these words at their face value. An idealist by nature, he joined the Party when he was a young private soldier. His faith in Party infallibility was shaken as he advanced in its ranks and saw the corruption, in-fighting and cynicism that surrounded him, and was probably crushed underfoot in the aftermath of Khrushchev's revelations of the Stalin Terror. But the idealism remained. In the simplest possible terms, he loved his country. In conversations with me, the Russian people were never far from his thoughts. 'My poor countrymen,' he said. 'So good and decent, and so easily misled.' Granted, he was far from the first Party loyalist to realize that the Revolution had been betrayed, but there was more to it than that.

He was a soldier on three different fronts and had witnessed the devastations of war first hand. But then he knew what he was fighting for. Now, as a senior military officer, he heard the rumbling from the Kremlin and feared that the recklessness and stupidity of the Soviet leadership under Khrushchev, if it went on unchecked, was almost certainly going to bring about a nuclear war.

The game was called 'brinkmanship'. It is easy to look back on those years now and see the East–West confrontation in terms of political moves on the chessboard of global strategy and Cold War manoeuvring. How quickly we have forgotten what a big business there was in fall-out shelters, how each day's headlines screamed of 'crisis', 'escalation'. The Berlin Crisis, the Cuban Missile Crisis – no, Penkovsky was hardly the only man alive who was convinced that the world had reached the flashpoint.

He was convinced of it because he saw the machinations of Khrushchev and his cronies from up close. It quite simply terrified him. Loyal Communist or disillusioned idealist, he was, to the last, a great patriot. He had to do something to tip the scales. He was in a position to do exactly that. He did it.

So much for the question of motive. If you take into account also that freedom and frivolity were essential to his psychological make-up, that he wholeheartedly admired our decadent Western way of life, this in no way contradicts the foregoing. Nor does the fact that personal resentment may have played a part in triggering his decision to pass information to us; it was not in itself enough of a motivation. From the way he told the story to me, I could tell, however, that a run-in with the KGB had been like a slap in the face to him from the régime he served so long and so loyally.

After his tour of duty in Ankara, Penkovsky was being considered for a posting as senior military attaché at the Soviet Embassy in New Delhi. Until that point, his rise in the service had been without blemish. At some point, the KGB did a routine background check and uncovered a

counter-revolutionary skeleton in the closet. The father he
never set eyes on had been one of the leaders of the White
Russian faction in the bloody civil war that followed
Lenin's takeover. Moreover, his mother, still living, was
found to be a deeply religious woman and regular church-
goer. Thus doubly suspect through no fault of his own,
Penkovsky's name was quietly dropped from the short-list.
Any further promotion in the service and a foreign posting
were out of the question now, and his travel abroad would
be restricted.

None of this was known to British Intelligence in
November 1960. True, Penkovsky had first come to our
attention five years earlier in Ankara, when somebody
pointed out that his (by Soviet standards) 'anti-social'
behaviour made him a man worth watching. No overtures
were made to him by any Western intelligence service. The
almost comic truth is that he fell into our lap only after
twice having attempted to make contact with us – and was
turned down each time!

The first of these was when a group of Canadians
representing their country's pulp and paper milling
industry came to Moscow for talks with the Committee.
With his security background, languages and personal
presence, it was natural for Levin, as head of the Foreign
Relations section, to delegate him as chief liaison to
Western visitors. Penkovsky was their official security
watchdog. He was also told to keep a sharp eye out for
foreign scientists who might be induced or pressured into
giving information to the Soviets.

Penkovsky approached one of the younger executives
and asked him to take an envelope out of the country. The
young Canadian, terrified, stammered a flat refusal. But as
soon as he returned home he reported the incident to
Ottawa and in due course word was passed to MI6.

Next Penkovsky decided to appeal to the United States.

On the evening of a big reception at the American Club (the Americans have a separate building for their social activities in a Moscow suburb) he waited outside in the parking lot. Two young American students came by. Penkovsky stepped out from behind a tree and asked them to take the envelope inside and hand it over to the US military attaché. The student couple hesitated, but Penkovsky just thrust the envelope into their hands and walked away, paying no heed to their protests.

The American official who examined the envelope was not much impressed by its contents. 'Alex' had a letter inside giving some personal details about himself, and requesting a secret rendezvous. Several places, dates and times for making contact were suggested. The attaché dismissed it out of hand as a clumsy provocation, and this time the British were not informed.

Nevertheless, on the basis of the run-in with the Canadian, London was prepared to take a limited risk. One of their trained agents would have to go to Moscow to be on hand if and when the attempt was repeated. It had to be someone already equipped with a solid cover and, furthermore, one that would serve as a pretext for meeting Penkovsky in the course of his official duties. In other words, I was the man.

James was very precise that I must wait and be patient. 'We can't have you compromise yourself in any way. Stay close to our boy, but don't let on that you're expecting anything to happen.' Those were my orders.

I flew to Moscow five days ahead of the British delegation. Cables had gone back and forth between London and Moscow; and from these I gathered that Penkovsky had been put in charge at the Moscow end. Since he was nominally Levin's deputy and spoke English more fluently than his chief, it was only reasonable to expect that we'd be seeing a lot of each other.

The guards at the front entranceway had the ear-flaps on their caps down when I presented myself at Number 11 Gorky Street for last-minute consultations with the committee. Penkovsky was present at these. Though Levin did most of the talking, it was obvious that Penkovsky was shouldering most of the detailed work. When he spoke at the green-baize-covered table, his manner was crisp and formal.

On 8 December 1960, I went to the airport with Colonel Penkovsky and two Committee members to greet the British delegates who were due to arrive on the 5 P.M. flight. This was when the other side to the man's character began to reveal itself.

A heavy thunderstorm closing in on Moscow resulted in a two-hour initial delay. Pulling rank on the control tower officials, Penkovsky wrested from them an admission that the flight might have to be diverted to another airfield. He slapped his forehead with the heel of his hand and gave me my first and most all-encompassing lesson in Russian profanity.

'On behalf of the Committee and the Council of Ministers of the USSR, Mr Wynne, I am pleased to invite you to have a beer – on the house, if that is the correct expression, yes? I know I could do with one at this point.'

I laughed at this and said, 'I'll teach you another expression. It's short and it goes like this: You're on, mate!'

Our friendship was off to a much more promising start than the official visit of my twelve British businessmen.

Penkovsky and I had another hour in which to chat while Ulyanyov, the Deputy Head of Protocol, was dispatched to the other airport. He asked me about my family, about life in England and I saw that there was something warm and genuine behind the studied politeness.

A voice over the loudspeakers summoned him away. 'They've landed at the other field,' he reported, and we made a mad dash back to Moscow, only to find to our further consternation that the bus had still not dropped them at their hotel. What now? Two hours passed. Penkovsky and I sat and talked; he could see I was getting snappish. At long last, their winter greatcoats all bespattered with mud and grey Moscow slush, the dozen disappearing directors came trudging wearily up to the lobby entrance of the Leninskaya Hotel, fit but tired. Their bus had broken down somewhere out in the suburbs and, unwilling to be parted from their luggage, they had to get out and push it the rest of the way to their destination.

The British businessmen quickly recovered their aplomb, fortunately, We began with three days of sightseeing, to be followed by another three days of conferences. Penkovsky was at pains to see that everybody had a good time as he escorted us on a tour of Moscow's tourist attractions, competent and affable. We posed together for photos on the steps of the Bolshoi Theatre and later made the obligatory visit to the red-granite Lenin Mausoleum (at that time, Stalin's mummy still lay side by side with the waxy remains of the founder of the Soviet state). I should imagine the directors were more impressed by our expedition to the sprawling, 500-acre Permanent Exhibition of Soviet Industry and Technology. Only when we were being taken round the Kremlin Museum did Penkovsky give any hint that there might be other things on his mind, when he abruptly tugged my sleeve and asked, 'Feel like stepping outside with me a minute? I need some fresh air.'

I went with him as he walked towards the fortress walls of the Kremlin, hands buried in the pockets of his greatcoat, as the wind churned and swirled the powder-like motes of snow from the drifts. I've always had the feeling that at that moment he really wanted to break down the last barrier of suspicion, took me aside with that idea in mind, but his nerve failed him. We trudged in silence through the snow, puffing on cigarettes, each lost in thought.

The talks seemed to be going down very well with the audience of senior Russian specialists from factories and technical institutes all over the Soviet Union. The Committee should have every reason to be pleased, I thought to myself. The twelve British experts each gave a lecture on new manufacturing and processing techniques in his field of specialization. The Russians heard about developments in rotary machinery, industrial refrigeration, tanning equipment, bottle-washing plants and other industrial research, responding with questions that went on for an hour or longer.

After each presentation, we were taken into another room where our hosts had laid out enormous cold buffets of pickled vegetables, smoked fish, thin-sliced black bread with iced pots of caviar. The Russians like to alternate nibbles with tumbler after tumbler of vodka. We tossed the fiery liquid to the back of our throats, Russian-style, to the accompaniment of endless toasts to the glorious future of Anglo-Soviet trade.

There were many times when Penkovsky and I found ourselves plausibly alone during that week. Though I could not make any direct approaches to him, I did all I could to make sure we talked as much as possible about personal things. It came out that we were the same age, and both had been raised in villages where mining was a way of life. An exchange of snapshots brought to light that my son and his daughter had been born within a few months of each other.

As we talked, it was obvious that Penkovsky was under some kind of stress. Little by little I found myself becoming convinced of his sincerity. More than once, when we were together at the head of the group, I'd notice these questioning sidelong glances at me while my attention was directed elsewhere. As if he were trying to make up his mind about me. Hoping but not daring to believe.

Our last evening in Moscow was set aside for a night at the Bolshoi. The performance as usual was quite spectacular and the curtain-calls a bit lengthy. While I clapped enthusiastically, Penkovsky said, 'I think your people will find their way back to the hotel without difficulty. We could have a beer if you like.'

I was elated, could feel my blood tingling with excitement. This could be it, I thought. We found a café nearby, brushed the snow from our coats and went inside.

Penkovsky stretched his legs out in front of him. 'Well, Greville – you don't mind if we drop the surnames, do you? I'd say it's been a fair success, wouldn't you?'

I nodded. 'And I believe you answer to "Oleg", with your father's name coming after that. Or is that only for the more formal occasions? I've never quite understood how it works.'

He scowled and took a sip of beer. Then he said something very strange. 'Oleg – that is for my mother. You can call me "Alex" – yes, do that, it sounds much better, I think.'

'So do I. Alex is a perfectly good English name.'

Maybe a psychiatrist would know what to make of this. I suppose you could see it as his way of asserting a new identity, a symbol of the rift in his mind about the person he was and the person he so desperately wanted to be. Oleg to the Russians. Alex to the British. Two different names, two different lives.

We talked about the forthcoming visit of a return delegation of Russian specialists to London, agreed on as part of the deal with the Committee, but as yet unscheduled. I said, 'When your people come over, I'd be delighted to show you around the town. Have you ever been to London before?'

Strong emotion played on his face and a few seconds passed before he answered, in an odd, distant tone of voice.

'No, I've never been there. I've heard about it—' then he seemed to check himself. 'It doesn't necessarily mean that I would be allowed to go with them.'

I was puzzled, for I did not know about the black mark in his dossier. 'Surely, after all that hard work, Levin wouldn't begrudge you that. Ask him, Alex.'

'No,' he said. 'It would be much better if the suggestion came from you.'

Then, abruptly, Alex's eyes were focused on something going on over my shoulder. Now they darted quickly from table to table. He propped his arm on the table and tugged at the corners of his mouth, seeming to stifle a yawn, but the hand remained in front of his face. 'I'll see you back to your hotel,' he said, and already had his chair pushed back from the table.

Had he seen something that made him think we were being watched? I really don't know. Alex pumped my hand and wished me goodnight in the lobby. The look on his face was trying to tell me something.

Back in London I was absolutely crestfallen when I reported to James. It had been such a close thing. Perhaps another agent would have better luck.

James looked down at the table and folded his hands. 'You needn't blame yourself, Greville. If anyone's to be faulted, I daresay I'm the one. We may have miscalculated this thing badly.'

'Wait,' I countered. 'Are you trying to tell me that Penkovsky is a Soviet plant?'

'No, no, it's not that.' Then the truth came out. MI6 had gone behind my back and inserted another of their own agents in my delegation. 'Not that we don't rely on your judgement. It just happened that we had such an agent available, one, in fact, who shares a similar background. We thought a back-up man would be handy.'

I let out a long, low breath. If my lips had been pursed, it would have been a whistle. I mentioned a name.

'Quite. He's been with us since – well, going back to before the war. He was in Moscow for a time on a military mission.'

Now many things began to make sense for me. When I was rounding up delegates, a certain northern-based firm had introduced him to me as their representative. But what was it . . . yes, there was something. The lecture he gave was about grinding and crushing machinery. One of the Committee men had remarked to me privately that the Soviets had found his lecture disappointing, the old boy didn't seem to be much of an expert. Mentally I had classified this frail, grandfatherly type as an obsolete fixture of the executive boardroom. The sort of company man who follows the progress of a business from its balance sheets, not really understanding the day-to-day operations end at all.

For one in my life, I was aggressive with James. 'All right, then. What went wrong?'

A preliminary sigh, then: 'You could say it went a little too smoothly for our man. Penkovsky did make the approach, thinking that he would understand. Told him it was vital to the security interests of Britain, and so on. Practically pleaded with him to take a package out of the country.'

Sullenly, I said, 'I suppose your chap didn't believe him. Too much of a good thing, et cetera.'

'More or less, yes. He pretended to be panic-stricken at the idea of such knavery. We instructed him to proceed according to his own evaluation of the situation.'

Now I had to swallow back my anger. 'You were both dead wrong!' Then I could see it wasn't going to solve anything, so, with difficulty, I continued in a level voice,

'He couldn't have been alone with Penkovsky for more than ten minutes at a time. How would he know what the man's about?'

James let this outburst pass. 'I thought I'd already made that clear. We were being too clever for our own good. You obviously have a much more informed knowledge of Penkovsky's character. If there's any way this operation can be salvaged, we'll give your friend his chance.'

That chance did not come until some months later, when I returned to Moscow during the first week of April 1961, to meet again with the Committee and work out an itinerary for the Soviet delegation I'd arranged to tour British industrial centres.

After the session was finished, I walked with Alex up the hill to Red Square. The wind was howling in my ears and I had to rub shoulders with him to make myself heard. 'Look, Alex. I'm none too happy about this list of names. We must get that settled first. You know these aren't the qualified people I asked for. They're minor officials and functionaries.'

Alex, who was slightly taller than me, had to lower his head. 'Does it really matter all that much?'

'It most certainly does. My companies are expecting experts. Unless we can settle this matter between us, I'll have to bring it up before the Committee.'

Suddenly his hand was clutching the sleeve of my coat. 'You must not do that,' he hissed. 'They would cancel the visit, cancel it entirely.'

Then I saw my opening and decided to play my ace card. With a great show of testiness, I said that I didn't see it as being any great loss.

'But, Greville! You don't understand. They've given me permission to go. It is I who must go to London. Not for pleasure. I . . . I have things to bring with me. Papers.

Important papers. Your government must have them.' He was very agitated, anticipating another rebuff.

'You're sure about this?' I asked quietly. We stood face to face, almost in the middle of Red Square.

Alex's head jerked mutely up and down. 'You know important people . . . Not political people, not the police.'

I made up my mind right then and there that I would have to trust him. 'I know the people you mean,' I said. 'They are friends of mind.'

Now his eyes widened in disbelief. I just nodded and repeated, 'They are friends of mine,' unwilling to compromise myself further than that, but Alex took my meaning perfectly and, from that moment on, the bond between us was sealed.

Anxiously, Alex went on talking. 'Then you must take these documents with you. But I must have your promise. It's vital, you understand? I want you to give them only to a man you can rely on absolutely. Your chief of section, he is under M16, is that not so? You trust him?'

'We worked together during the war.'

He thought about this for a moment, then sighed. 'That is acceptable. But I want you to understand that I will deal only with you and your immediate superior. When I come to England, the branch of your Secret Service that is called MI5 cannot be informed of my activities. They must not know that I am the source of this information.'

'Why, Alex, why?'

We walked a few paces more and sat wearily on one of the public benches behind the entrance to the Metro station. Alex fished up a packet of cigarettes from the interior of his heavy woollen coat, but spoke before he lit it. 'I am with the GRU. It is understood in my bureau that our friends – the KGB – have placed one of their agents at the very highest level of MI5. So they must have no knowledge of who I am and what I am doing.'

I was absolutely stunned by this. 'Are you certain, Alex? Who is this man?'

'Ah, Greville,' he replied, inhaling deeply from his cigarette. 'That is not only the highest secret, it is a KGB secret.'

'But you know about it!'

'Oh, yes. Our service monitors all the incoming radio traffic to Moscow.'

I told Alex I would inform my chief back in London and get his personal guarantee that MI5 would not be brought in on it, if he came to London.

That night Alex handed me a fat buff envelope stuffed with official-looking documents and photostats, none of which, of course, I could make out. He unclipped the papers, and flipped through them with his thumb. 'Rocket installations. Their exact locations given here. Minutes of the plenary meetings of the Central Committee. It would make your blood run cold, Greville. Look, there's a letter from Khrushchev. Wait until your friends get a look at what's in that.'

'My God, Alex. How is it you've got access to this stuff in the first place?'

'Very simple. I have to give a lecture twice a year to officer cadets being trained for the GRU on military and policy matters. I have a clearance to go down into the vaults. Nobody questions me. They lock me in and I rummage around.'

I did not want to upset Alex by saying anything, but I was now faced with a serious problem. He had assumed, quite naturally, that I was flying from Moscow to London. In point of fact, I had to stop for a few days in Budapest where I was expected by the Hungarian Ministry of Foreign Trade. So when Alex left, I shoved the envelope in my pocket, put on my coat and had the clerk at the front desk ring for a taxi. Ten minutes later, I got out at the British Embassy.

If the two Russian policemen on duty by the gate took any notice of my arrival, there was nothing out of the ordinary in that. Many English-speaking Moscow residents used the club in the Embassy compound as their local watering-hole, so the guards were used to people coming and going at odd hours.

James had briefed me on what had to be done in cases such as this. For obvious reasons I cannot name the official I was told to contact nor hint at his position (he has since been posted elsewhere but remains active in the service). I found him playing bridge at the club.

'Can I have a word with you privately?'

'Well, I don't know—' but before he could go on I whispered an innocent sentence that was the Department's recognition signal.

'You!' It utterly flabbergasted him. We had known each other on a casual basis dating from my earliest visits to Moscow.

'Let's go outside,' I said to him.

Beyond the reach of the probe microphones we all knew riddled our embassy buildings, we walked briskly around the grounds, oblivious to the numbing cold, and I told him what it was all about. 'You've got to take it off my hands and see that it gets back to London. I can't carry that around with me in Budapest.'

He didn't seem too happy about the complication that had just landed in his lap, but he took the envelope and muttered, 'Very well. It'll go out tomorrow.'

I thought that left me in the clear but I couldn't have been more mistaken. The next morning, Alex turned up in the Committee limousine. 'Levin told me to make sure you don't miss your flight,' he said.

Alex didn't say very much on the way to the airport, but

looked extremely tired. When the chauffeur went ahead to carry my luggage into the terminal, Alex sauntered behind. 'Greville,' he whispered. 'Go to the check-in counter now. I'll wait for you in the men's room.' Nervously, a bit stunned, I did as he asked and washed my hands at the sink until the last Russian left the lavatory and Alex emerged from the cubicle. From his breast pocket he took a white, unmarked business envelope and pressed it into my hand.

'Alex . . .' I began.

'Look Greville, it seems to me that our friends will want to have this. In the other package there is nothing that will identify me as the source of the documents. That way it's safer. I have written something here to explain who I am and why I want to do this thing. There are photographs, a copy of my Party card. My GRU identity papers. Give it to them so that they understand.'

What other choice was there? I wasn't about to beg off now, try and make him see that it wasn't safe for me to go to Hungary, carrying this on me. That might have brought crashing down the precarious scaffolding of trust that was the only thing keeping Alex from falling into the abyss. The risk of that happening was still too great, so I took the envelope from him without saying a word.

All Soviet airports are filled with armed security men and plain-clothes KGB agents. You see them lolling behind every pillar, young-faced guards in grey uniforms with the tell-tale blue epaulettes and collar tabs. On that cold, blustery morning, there were, as usual, two of them out on the tarmac guarding the plane. As I approached, I saw them walk up the gangway, rubbing their hands, and stop just in front of the curtained-off cockpit. They gave me only the briefest of glances as I squeezed past them and into the passenger cabin. I walked down the aisle towards the aft section and put my coat down on a seat in one of the last rows. Where to cache the envelope? A quick look for'ard showed that the guards were not looking my way. I cast my eyes around and hastily slipped the envelope between some brown, lint-speckled lap blankets on the overhead rack, then moved a few seats up the aisle and chose an empty row for myself.

The worst should have been over, but it wasn't – not yet. According to my watch, we were running ten minutes late for take-off. A routine delay? Through the plexiglass window, I saw a jeep come rolling up to the aircraft and three uniformed officials jump out. They were coming up the gangway. I unfolded my copy of the English-language *Moscow Times* and pretended not to notice any of this. Out of the corner of my eye, I waited for them to enter the cabin. There was some sort of discussion going on up there with the crew members. Twenty minutes went by. Twenty more, and the officials went back down the gangway and the jeep sped away in the direction of the terminal.

I took out a handkerchief and mopped the beads of sweat that had collected at my temples. As the plane taxied into position, I willed myself to forget about the envelope and let my mind roll back to my last sight of Alex, standing there in the cold and the heavy wet snow, waving farewell to me. His parting words echoed over and over again: 'In a few weeks, Greville, only a few short weeks, we shall have a drink together in London.

15

Presidential Visit

Alex made two trips to England in 1961, each time bringing with him priceless information concerning the Soviet Union's political, economic and military capabilities.

The first time, he came in April at the head of the Soviet delegation of engineers and specialists for whom I'd arranged some visits to British factories. I met Alex at Heathrow and was only able to greet him formally in the presence of so many others, but as soon as we were alone in his hotel room, he almost danced for joy and nearly squeezed the life out of me with a hug from his powerful arms.

'It's wonderful, Greville! I always dreamed that it would be this way.'

Lowering my voice, I said, 'Look – my chief wants you to know straight off that we've kept the matter to ourselves. It's being handled just as you insisted. MI5 will never be told about your activities. Our people will see to that.'

Alex nodded. 'Then it is all right, when I hear it from you. I feel you would not lie to me.'

'Of course not,' I said. 'We're in this thing together.'

James had shown no visible reaction when I'd passed along Alex's extraordinary request, merely promised that I'd have an answer from him as soon as possible. On the morning I went to greet Alex at the airport, he just said, 'Tell your friend not to worry. Everything's arranged the way he wants it.'

What action, if any, may have been taken at that time to investigate the possibility of there being a highly placed double-agent in our sister service, I am in no position to say. I have, to be sure, followed recently (1981) reports in the British press that tend to bear out just such an allegation. In view of the unquestioned veracity of the rest of the information Alex provided, I should think James's people would have taken the matter very seriously indeed and started to poke into corners. If there was some connection between the man Alex feared, but could not name, and the individual who has lately been accused of being the MI5 'mole' – who was, in fact, the acting director at the time Alex pointed an accusing finger – all I can say is that I would not be in the least surprised.

The Russians were all staying at a hotel in the neighbourhood of Marble Arch. In a nearby block of flats, a team of specialists from MI6 had quietly set up their elaborate operations HQ. They took over an entire floor of the building, installed a telex and telephone lines to Washington, and assembled a staff of interpreters, stenographers and military weapons specialists, as British Intelligence cleared the decks for Alex's sake. Senior intelligence officials were to preside at the friendly but exhaustive debriefing sessions.

As was almost inevitable in view of the strategic implications of Alex's revelations, representatives from the American military command and CIA were on hand. Henceforth the running of Alex was to be a combined Anglo-American project. James later told me that all expenses were split down the middle, although our overseas cousins more than once tried offering unlimited sums of money if we would let them have complete control of Britain's prize intelligence catch. Naturally, the offer was refused.

The procedure was for Alex to slip away in the middle of the night, while his comrades were fast asleep, and present himself for hours of intense questioning. The delegation would be in England for almost four weeks, and there was a lot of pumping to be done in the meantime. By day, of course, Alex had to attend to his official duties as head of the delegation. Any other man would have been quickly demolished by such a routine, but Alex's amazing vitality kept him going for the whole period, more often than not getting only three hours' sleep at night, yet never once did I see him looking drained or even flagged out by it all.

At the beginning, Alex was understandably on his guard. When he turned up for his midnight rendezvous on his first night in London, he had been greeted warmly and assured of his welcome – but this was from people he didn't know, had never seen before in his life. 'I want to have Greville Wynne here,' he insisted obstinately, and it was not until I had been roused out of bed at my home in Chelsea, rushed over and given him my personal assurance that he was in the best of hands, that he relaxed a little.

Apart from the sheer mental strain, there was also a question of conscience. Convinced as he was that only direct action of this sort would provide a check to the reckless policies of nuclear sabre-rattling the Kremlin was pursuing, it was nonetheless hard for a dedicated soldier to walk into the arms of his country's arch-enemies without some misgivings. Fortunately, the officers in charge sensed what was wrong and knew exactly what had to be done.

When Alex returned to the operations base a few nights after his arrival in London, the door was opened for him, and as he stepped into the room a tall man who had been standing quietly inside smoking a cigarette with his back to the door turned round with a huge grin on his face and said something to Alex in Russian.

Alex just stood there frozen to the spot, absolutely petrified, his mouth open wide and unable to get a word out.

For the man who came up to him now and flung his arms round Alex's shoulders was a dead man.

They'd known each other in Russia. He was a general in Alex's service. And he had been reported dead in a car crash, years ago. Now, talking rapidly in Russian, he took Alex by the arm like a little child and led him into the next room. There were twenty others like him, all former top Soviet officials, a number of them, I gather, who had been acquaintances of Alex or well-known personalities in the Soviet military. They had been flown in from the US and assembled from all over Britain. They came to tell Alex that he was among friends.

I happened to be present when this meeting took place because Major Sergei Kuznov was one of the twenty Russian defectors who had come that evening. Not even James, for all his security-consciousness, could have turned down Kuznov's request to see me again.

Kuznov had put on some weight since I last saw him and was wearing an American suit in a pattern I thought a bit on the flashy side, so when he told me that all was going well for him at his new job in Washington, I could readily believe it. He seemed hearty and relaxed, and was full of stories about Washington night-life.

For me, it was a very moving experience. I've mentioned the constant sense of frustration a spy always experiences because he never is told enough to know if the results were worth the game. Now, here I was with my hand being pumped in gratitude by a fellow human being who was enjoying the gift of freedom thanks in large part to something I had done. In addition, it will be remembered that this was one assignment where I have been privy to the secret information I was smuggling, and recognized its importance. So it was a good feeling, seeing Kuznov after two years and bringing all this to mind.

After that evening, the log-jam of honest doubts had been swept away in Alex's mind and he was ready to co-operate with us to the hilt. The outpouring of inside

Kremlin gossip, extensive details of Red Army orders of battle and the Soviet defence programme including the top-secret locations of huge industrial complexes where production was exclusively devoted to supplying the military. Most valuable of all, perhaps, was what he could tell us about the Soviet Union's ICBM (Intercontinental Ballistic Missile) programme and location of hidden rocket sites, by virtue of the fact that Marshal Varentsov, in charge of rocketry development, was Alex's father-in-law.

I was not present at any of these sessions, but heard about them afterwards from Alex himself. 'They think I am an engineer,' he complained, 'they keep asking me for technical details.' During the daytime he and I were together almost constantly, either travelling with the delegation as we went round to visit factories in Leeds, Manchester, Wolverhampton, Sheffield, and other industrial centres. With his Soviet colleagues for an audience, Alex gave one of the best acting performances of his life. Ironically, it was my old friend Pavlov at the embassy who provided the excuse for us to spend some time together in the evenings. Despite the failure of Kulikov's overtures, Pavlov must have had the idea that there was something rather shady about Greville Wynne but, luckily for us, he erred on the side of the angels. He told Alex that it might be a good idea to stick close to me to see if I might be bribed to obtain a badly wanted computer part manufactured by one of my companies. The two of us had a good giggle, I'll tell you, when Alex told me what was up. Through James's good offices, I was given an obsolete model of the item in question which I duly passed on to Alex, and a few days later he returned with £50 for me in greasy banknotes, courtesy of Comrade Pavlov.

True to my promise in Moscow (and with the enthusiastic approval of James's people) I took Alex around London to see the Brompton Oratory, the Houses of Parliament so that he could see for himself what British democracy was all about. When I was with him, it was Alex's turn to play the interrogator's part, as he heaped on the questions. Why this, Greville? Why that? not letting up for a minute. Wandering along Oxford Street, he'd be drawn to a window display and stand there for the longest time just staring. Later I took him to Harrod's where I remember him picking up something from the gadget counter to examine it carefully.

'What *is* this for?' he queried.

'It's a thing for slicing eggs. Here, you put a hard-boiled egg on it like this, lower the top part and you've got it all sliced at once.'

He held it in his hand and turned it over, not quite able to take it in. Utterly stupefied, he went on: 'And do workers in your country make many things like this? Why do you need a mechanical device when a knife will do? Has your wife got one in her kitchen?'

'Yes, of course! Why shouldn't she? Look at what it costs. Workers make them and other workers buy them and that way everyone stays happy.'

After that bit of capitalist indoctrination, I accompanied Alex on a number of shopping expeditions in London. That, too, was a part of his official duties. His bosses back in Moscow craved French perfume, silk stockings, electric shavers and other consumer items that were not to be had from the bleak, barren shelves and gaping shop-windows of Moscow. Alex had to stop and marvel at the crates and bins stacked outside a Soho greengrocer's. A pineapple was something he had literally never seen before. What impressed him most of all, I think, was the ease with which ordinary people went about their business and lived their lives without having first to seek official permission to do so.

On a Friday when we were supposed to be touring a

factory, I rang up some friends in Brighton to make a date for lunch and invited Alex to come along. In Victoria Station, we watched the queues forming at the ticket windows. Alex made a joke about this. 'People waiting in a queue – Britain too is on the path to socialism, I see. But here the people advance so fast!'

'Why shouldn't they? It's nothing very complicated, buying a train ticket.'

Once again Alex was momentarily at a loss for words. 'You mean they do not demand to see your identity documents and travel permits? Don't the authorities want to know where people are?'

'It's none of their bloody business,' I answered. I could see he was still incredulous, so I gave him some money and said, 'Try it yourself. See that queue over there? Walk up to the clerk and buy us tickets to Brighton. Go on, nothing's going to happen.'

I looked on, grinning, while the transaction was carried out. When Alex came back, I began to say something by way of a joke, but caught myself when I saw the utter self-absorption on his face. He was holding the ticket between thumb and forefinger as if it were the most precious thing in the world to him.

At the end of each day, Alex had to make a full report to Pavlov on his activities. Where had he been? Who had he talked to? When the delegation visited factories in Manchester, Sheffield and Wolverhampton, Alex was present as their official spokesman. We instructed him to give Pavlov exactly what he wanted, descriptions of machinery and facilities, all the official literature he could collect. It was important that Alex prove himself an exceptionally able and observant and utterly reliable contact man to his bosses. With any luck, they would send him back. All of which meant that the demands on Alex's physical stamina would have been just about unbearable for any other man.

The nightly interrogations continued until Alex had to return with the delegation on 6 May. On the last day of that same month, I went to Moscow again for follow-up talks with a Committee and to hear their evaluation. I saw a good deal of Alex during this time: both at the Committee offices and socially (with the Committee's blessing) when our work was done – which was when our real 'work' began. I had come to Moscow with more rolls of unexposed film, and he gave me the films he had made use of since his return, photographing documents in the secret vaults of the GRU buildings on Znamensky Street. 'It seems to me that I'd better go with you to the airport,' he said. 'If there are any problems, my credentials will get you through all right.' (Likewise, when I entered Britain with secret materials, all I had to do was ring the number of a special line at MI6 central administration.) Just before leaving Moscow, I had it confirmed that Alex was going to be in London again in July for the Soviet Trade Exhibition at Earls Court.

Again, I was delegated by James to look after my friend, given money to see that he was taken wherever he wanted to go and saw whatever he wanted to see. It was little enough we could do to show our gratitude, and certainly far from representing 'payment' for his services. What good would money have done him in Russia? When Alex arrived on 18 July, he was beaming with excitement. He would be staying for three full weeks this time, and neither his official nor his unofficial duties were to be as gruelling as last time. Mostly, he was supposed to escort General Serov's wife around London. (If I remember correctly, the British had made it clear that Serov himself, the man who brutally crushed the Hungarian Revolution of 1956, would not be welcome.) For its part, MI6 saw no reason to put Alex through another ordeal of sleepless nights. As the new films were submitted for analysis, it would be enough for him to just make himself available to clarify certain items.

The Coleherne Court safe house would do nicely for that purpose.

So altogether it was a leisurely, more enjoyable routine. There was time for Alex and me to visit some personal friends of mine (I introduced him as a visiting Yugoslav businessman), do a bit of pub-crawling – he was delighted by the informal cheerfulness he found there and the open way people chatted over a pint – time for afternoon drives out in the country. Questions all the time. British life and British institutions held an endless fascination for him. Nothing in his Soviet education had prepared him for anything like this. He wanted to know about employment exchanges, life assurance schemes and, above all, building societies – these last completely mystified him. He was also impressed by the popularity of the Royal Family, but seemed unable to grasp their function in a constitutional monarchy. 'You can often see the Queen herself mixing in the crowds at a polo match, with just a few plain-clothes detectives in attendance,' I told him. As soon as he heard that, Alex would give me no peace until he had witnessed it for himself. So the following weekend, we found ourselves in Windsor Great Park, and Alex got the chance to see Her Majesty standing just a few yards away, dressed in casual country clothes, leaning against a Land Rover with a couple of corgis in the back. I could barely restrain him from attempting to rush up and speak to her. 'In the Soviet Union, a head of state would never move about so freely!' he exclaimed. 'I must talk with her, Greville. She ought to know what I am doing for the cause of peace. I'm sure she will speak to me.' It was only with difficulty I held him off, trying to make him understand that she could not under any circumstances be involved with what we were doing, it just didn't work that way.

That same evening, in Coleherne Court, Alex would not stop talking about the day's events and his desire to meet the Queen of England. Partly, I'm sure, it was his constant need of being reassured that his actions were the right ones. Nothing we could say was enough to dissuade him; the more we insisted, the more indignant he became. 'If the work I am doing is so important, I am sure she would want to receive me,' he went on repeating.

Everyone who was present that evening glanced uneasily at each other as the scene got increasingly tense. Finally, one of the CIA men sitting in on the session cleared his throat and said, 'Well look, Alex, I know our President isn't quite the same as the Queen, but how would you like to meet him instead?'

'Only on the condition that Greville comes with me,' Alex loyally replied. Twenty-four hours later, the two of us were on our way to the United States – just like that.

In retrospect, it does seem incredible that this operation could have been carried out under the nose of the Soviet security agents who were prowling round the Soviet exhibition. I have a theory about this. Possibly we were able to get away with it only because James had taken measures to see that the MI5 leak was isolated from our activities. The Russians would sit back and let their mole do their work for them, since the behaviour of Soviet citizens in London would ordinarily be an MI5 affair. Or is that being too far-fetched? In any case, Alex's duties were light. The risk was a worthwhile one.

Alex and I travelled by separate cars to an American air-base, each accompanied by a CIA agent. We did not meet up until we boarded the military jetliner that was to fly us to a US air force base not too far from Washington. On arriving there, we were again whisked off in separate unmarked cars that brought us to the capital. I was given glasses and a trilby to wear, and cars were changed en route to further confound Soviet agents who might have the base under observation.

We arrived at the White House within five minutes of each other. A very important-looking senior aide took our coats and asked if we'd like to have a drink and a tidy-up before meeting the President. We waited for about five minutes with our escorts, before being shown into an adjoining room by a third CIA agent who had joined Alex's car at the base.

President Kennedy was waiting for us in the company of three other men whose names were never disclosed to me. As soon as he saw us enter, he came over to us with his youthful energetic stride, smiling and with his hand outstretched, and told me, 'I've heard about the work you've done for us. I'd just like to add my personal thanks, and the thanks of the United States.' Then he turned to Alex and, drawing him gently to one side with a hand on his arm, I heard him say, 'Oleg Penkovsky, I want to assure you, from what I know about the situation within the Soviet Union, that I am very aware of all that you've done to help the cause of peace in the world, not only for the West, but for the sake of your own people as well.' The President's sincerity and warmth as he said these words were unmistakable. He continued: 'If only it were possible to tell everyone of the efforts you have made, the name of Oleg Penkovsky would be acclaimed throughout the world. You know very well that we wish no harm to the Russian people, that we are concerned solely for peace on earth.'

I could hear no more of the conversation as President Kennedy had drawn Alex out of earshot of the rest of us. Obviously, he was determined to speak to him personally. Later Alex told me that the President confirmed the accuracy of the information he had been able to obtain about the Soviet missile system. As a result of Alex's efforts, he said, the United States was prepared to deal with any situation that might arise. Throughout these remarks, I could see that the President kept his hand on Alex's arm and that the latter was visibly moved. His eyes were moist, and for once he was at a loss for words. I, too, was touched by the President's obvious sincerity.

As they talked, I noticed that there was no American flag in the room or national emblems of any kind. I assumed this was done to avoid putting too much emphasis on purely national interests, and later my CIA escort confirmed this impression for me. It was tastefully done up with an antique desk, mirrors, a thick wine-red carpet, and an early landscape on the wall showing a Mississippi riverboat scene. We all remained standing throughout the reception, which only lasted half an hour. Refreshments were offered. I sipped a lager and Alex, too overcome by the experience, drank nothing at all. President Kennedy spent almost the entire time with him.

When we left the White House, some of Alex's exuberance returned to him. 'Nobody knows me here,' he exclaimed. 'Let's go somewhere and celebrate. We'll be perfectly safe in Washington.'

I had to explain to him that it just wasn't on. 'If we leave immediately, it will mean that you'll have been away for eighteen hours by the time we get back there. The chances that you'll already have been missed are considerable. If we are to continue successfully with your work, it's vital that we return straightaway.'

'Yes. Of course you're right,' he replied. 'The work is what matters.'

16

Cherchez La Femme

On the plane that brought us back to London, Alex was strangely quiet. I thought it might be perhaps because he was still a little overawed, and therefore made little attempt to engage him in conversation. After the plane touched down at Northolt, we bade farewell to our CIA escorts and hurried back to Alex's hotel in Wright's Lane, just off Kensington High Street. My friend was still in an uncommunicative mood, and with some prodding I managed to persuade him to tell me what it was.

'Greville, I didn't want to say anything because I know how upset it will make you, but while I was in the lobby room of the White House after the President left, the three CIA men who were with me tried to talk me into giving up my links with you and the British. They wanted me to agree to work exclusively for them. I was convinced we were all working together – and now this happens. How is it possible?'

Alex was right; I was extremely annoyed, but I tried not to let it show. By their foolish ill-timed duplicity, the CIA had threatened to wreck the whole atmosphere of trust and respect the visit to Kennedy was supposed to encourage. I was frankly appalled, but did my best to make light of it.

'Oh, is that all that's been worrying you?' I laughed. 'They were just teasing you to see if you were the man we told them you were. It was just a test of your integrity. Thank you for coming through it so well. I knew you would.' The whole thing had been arranged in advance, I told him. But Alex did not seem entirely convinced by my improvised excuses. 'Why did they do it?' he repeated in bewilderment.

As soon as I left the hotel I rang James and told him what had happened, in a state of some indignation. Later I heard that the three American agents were immediately withdrawn from their London postings and, I devoutly hope, consigned to the file-room for the rest of their working lives. My understanding is that the whole London station of the CIA was given a thorough shaking-up as a result of the strong representations that James and his colleagues made to the United States Government, who made the fullest apologies for their actions.

The problem now was that, having met the President of the United States, Alex was more determined than ever to be received by the Queen.

Wanting to avoid ruffled feelings, the Intelligence chiefs made an alternative proposal. As a token of their good faith, he could, if he wished, be immediately appointed to the rank of colonel in the British Army. The CIA, never to be outdone, made a similar offer. Alex was so pleased when it was suggested that the next briefing be held in full military dress, that he gave his eager assent. That session, in fact, was entirely taken up by a reception in his honour to celebrate his simultaneous appointment in the armed forces of the two nations. Photographs to commemorate the occasion were made of Alex first in his British uniform, then in his American one. These pictures, tragically, were later to provide damning evidence against Alex at his trial when the KGB found them in a secret drawer of his desk in his Moscow flat. It is indicative of how much they must have meant to him that he kept these with him despite the appalling risk.

All of the combined MI6/CIA operations team wore their full dress uniforms that evening, and I was promoted to lieutenant-colonel for the occasion (though I finished up at the end of the Second World War as a major). However strange such a performance may seem, psychologically it was a great success, for Alex visibly grew more confident when he was in uniform, surrounded by professional military men. This was the world he knew and understood and in which he felt at ease.

Drinks were brought in, congratulations offered all round. In his enthusiasm, he asked what would happen if he stayed on in England and was told that he would be provided with a lump sum of money to enable him to buy a suitable house for himself, and given a position at full colonel's salary in the Soviet section of British Military Intelligence. The Americans quickly chipped in that they were sure they could equal or better the offer, if Alex ever felt he might like to settle there.

'What do you think, Alex?' I asked him. 'If you did take up residence over here, what would you consider doing?'

He looked pensively at the glass of Scotch in his hand and it was a few seconds before he answered. 'I've been thinking a good deal about that these last few days. Really I have. And do you know? If such a thing were possible, I see myself doing something very different. What I'd like to do, really, is own a small hotel or restaurant in some little resort town by the sea. Does that surprise you? I expect I'd be very happy just meeting new people and having a quiet sort of life.'

A few days later, however, Alex was in another of his difficult moods. The Queen. He had to go to see the Queen. James rang me up and said, 'We need you over here. Our friend is playing it tight as a clam. Keeps saying, "I will only talk if Greville Wynne is present".'

'Good Lord! What is it this time?'

'We brought some people to see him. Trouble is, their

names and positions don't signify very much to him. So far as he can make out, they're just new, strange faces.'

I hurried off to Coleherne Court. James was waiting for me in the hall. 'Look,' he said. 'When you go in there you're going to see someone whom you'll recognize immediately. Pretend that you and he are old friends, and greet the Americans who are in the room that same way. You don't know them, but it should help in reassuring our friend.'

The man who had come to meet Alex was none other than Lord Mountbatten. 'Oh, hello, Wynne,' he said, when I entered. 'Glad you could be with us.'

'Hello, Greville,' echoed some American voices.

Alex was there, looking puzzled and ill at ease, but as soon as I joined the group his face lit up and he began to come out of his mood. Mountbatten invited him to visit his country home. I did not accompany Alex on this occasion though, to be sure, I heard all about it the next time we met. 'The thing that impressed me most,' he said, 'were the swans on the river in the middle of that beautiful estate. Birds like that wouldn't have a chance of surviving in my country, they'd be killed and eaten by Party bosses.'

Another time, when we were out for a drive in Surrey, he was full of questions. The number of single-family suburban homes we passed to him was just a staggering sight. How was it that so many people could afford to own houses? I tried to give him an idea of what a mortgage was, how banks and building societies worked, but wasn't sure if I was getting through to him.

'Does that mean you have a mortgage on your home?' he wanted to know.

I said, yes, most people in Britain could go to a bank or a building society to get money.

Then a thought struck him. 'Greville – tell me, did Lord

Mountbatten have to go to a building society when he
bought his house?'

Peals of laughter just roared from my throat until I
thought I'd have to pull over and wait for it to pass. 'Ask
him, Alex,' I chortled. 'The next time you see him, you ask
him that and he'll tell you!' Alex just looked at me with
mute incomprehension at all this sudden hilarity. Seeing
that, I quickly added, 'But don't tell him I told you to do
so. His sense of humour may not stretch that far.'

During the time Alex was providing vital information to
my chiefs at the Coleherne Court safe house, I only got to
hear bits and pieces of what it was all about. The
information was largely economic, I believe. But the facts
and figures were for ears other than mine.

There was one important exception. Just days after Alex
returned with his delegation to Moscow, newspapers all
over the world blared in headline type that the East
German Government had erected a barbed-wire barricade
cutting the city of Berlin in half, and within a matter of
weeks, concrete for the six-foot bastions of the Berlin Wall
had already hardened – permanently. The world may have
been taken by surprise, but the British and the Americans
had been given two years' warning of the Soviet plan,
thanks to the documents I had smuggled out for Major
Kuznov. When Alex came to London he brought with him
proof that the Kremlin was ready to implement it and even
named the day – 12 August 1961.

Kuznov had made it more than clear that the Soviets
regarded the Berlin Wall as a provocation that could not be
pushed beyond a certain limit. If forceful action were taken
against them, they would have to back down. Now Alex
was able to confirm that the Kremlin had not changed their
thinking during the intervening two years.

Alex had insisted on knowing what action was going to
be taken. He wanted to be sure that the information he gave

us would be used against the Soviet aggression. To their credit, James and his people told the truth. The answer was – no retaliation, none whatsoever. Why were we allowing the Russians to do this?

Between Alex and James I was able to piece together the story. Britain was strongly in favour of taking whatever measures were necessary to keep the Berlin Wall from going up. On this, however, they had been cynically overruled by the Americans. It was decided that Western interests would best be served if we stood back and allowed the wall to be built. The number of skilled refugees in recent years had been multiplying beyond the West German economy's capacity for absorbing them, the Americans maintained. More importantly, they wanted the Berlin Wall to serve as a lasting monument to the Communist system of government. In the eyes of the world, dramatic proof that a country under their domination became a cage to its citizens.

When Penkovsky was informed of this, he was absolutely furious. 'They're acting like fools,' he told me, clenching and unclenching his powerful fists. 'Why can't they understand the Kremlin respects only power . . . it's the only thing they understand!'

I do know that as a result of this, Alex for a time threatened to break with the Americans and refuse to co-operate with us unless we did likewise. Eventually, he let himself be convinced that perhaps it had to be this way, that the existence of the Berlin Wall was a more effective answer to all the millions of lies of the Soviet propagandists than anything the West could contrive.

Personally I was saddened by the whole sorry affair. When I saw President Kennedy on television giving his famous 'I am a Berliner' speech, I could see the point the Americans were trying to make. But when I thought of the dangers that both Major Kuznov and myself had been through to get that information into the hands of the governments concerned, and then not to be acted on for the sake of totalling up a few Cold War propaganda points – no, it wasn't a very satisfying feeling at all.

Before Alex left for Moscow on 7 August, he had been briefed in the use of a long-range radio transmitter and coding techniques so that he could continue sending out information as it happened. It was hoped that he would not have to use these too often. As long as his Soviet bosses saw that he was a useful and competent liaison for contacts with the Western business community, there was every reason to expect that his official duties would provide him with the opportunity for making person-to-person contact, contact with me, whenever possible.

Later that same month, I flew from Amsterdam to Moscow, with two huge suitcases loaded with material for Alex. He was at the airport to guide me through Customs, for I had brought with me a radio receiver and paintings whose frames were filled with more film and operating procedure typed on wafer-thin paper.

After this material had been handed over, we did not see too much of each other this visit. Levin received me in Gorky Street and was full of enthusiasm when we talked of the Soviet Trade Fair that was to be mounted in Paris in September. I was given an unsolicited invitation to attend. Nothing could have been better, for the chances were that Alex's presence would be required to smooth-talk French industrialists. After all, hadn't he done such an outstanding job with that British fellow, Wynne? Of course, I couldn't put it to them as a direct question, nor was Alex himself sure of the posting, but when I returned to London, preparations were made accordingly.

Having Alex travel to the West was a stroke of unexpected good luck for James and his people; the value of the information he gave us tripled when Alex was there and available for cross-questioning. When this was not possible, I would continue to act as courier whenever there was a good reason for me to be in Moscow.

Alex did eventually turn up in Paris, but not until 20 September. I had been waiting for him there for three weeks, since before the Trade Fair officially opened. My instructions were to meet him at the airport and once again act as a combination of go-between and nanny, letting him know when it was safe to make contact with our agents. The arrangements was similar to the one used in London; MI6 had installed themselves on the top floor of a house in one of the most distinguished Paris neighbourhoods. A team of specialists was flown over to supervise at the briefings.

Alex had come with dozens more rolls of film in his suitcase, but from the moment he was waved through the French Customs of Le Bourget, I sensed a potentially dangerous change of mood. He always was high-spirited and full of life and, as far as he was concerned, Paris was heaven and he'd just been handed the keys. Now I thought I detected an edge of recklessness in his words, as he went on and on about what a great time we were going to have, what a fantastic opportunity it would be for him. Just you wait, and didn't he have it coming to him.

Everywhere we went those first days, the Eiffel Tower, the Louvre, leisurely rambles by the Seine, the thronging street markets, I watched with mounting alarm as Alex's eyes darted from one female face to another with only too evident appreciation. Girls! Well dressed, nicely groomed, smiling and flirtatious. Dark-eyed, chattering French girls, American co-eds with long, straight dusty-blonde hair, West German tourists with meaty legs and pinkish cheeks, each one received his loving scrutiny and appraisal and I could see that we were going to have a problem on our hands unless something was done.

In conversations with me going back to our encounters in Moscow, Alex had been frank and forthcoming about his womanizing. That, too, was part of the burden of secrets that had to be shared with the one man in the world he trusted. In Moscow, there had been an endless series of casual affairs: here a Zhenya, there a Masha, Evgenia who worked in a factory, secretaries, shop assistants, librarians – he had a stable of lovelies. 'They're the only escape valve I have,' he admitted. 'I couldn't live without girls.'

All too well I understood my friend's dilemma. Partly, I suppose, it was just one manifestation of his incredible vitality. But there's another factor to be taken into account too. Alex cared deeply for his wife, I gathered, and loved his young daughter beyond any doubt, but she knew him only as an officer in the Red Army; his GRU work was secret. When a man has his life divided into two sealed compartments, what else is available to him for solace? Every man can understand the hunger of physical separation. What, then, if the distance is not something that can be measured in miles, but in years of having lived as a stranger to the person with whom you promised to share your life?

In speaking of Alex and his infidelities, I have to acknowledge my own. In Helsinki, there had been a girl named Mariette, a secretary. Then, in Budapest, a very pretty girl, Helen Serespysn, assigned to the Ministry as my translator. We'd go off for weekends together at the resort area of Lake Balaton and dine splendidly on the fresh-water fish they served there. We both liked dancing. With Helen as my guide, I spent many enjoyable hours in the night-spots of Budapest, and it is largely thanks to her that I began to see a little of the easy-going penchant for good times, good food and good living which characterizes the Hungarian people and has never been extinguished in the decades of Soviet domination. Even in Moscow, under the watchful eyes of the KGB, I kept company with one of the girls working as a secretary in the Canadian embassy. But compared to Alex, I was a shining example of a dutiful husband.

Women had a way of falling for Alex, that I knew already. In London, I'd introduced him ('my friend from Yugoslavia') to a girl who was doing part-time secretarial work for me. His grip was like a wrestler's, she told me afterwards. But what a charming man! You could tell he was a real gentleman, she added. Still, I hadn't quite foreseen the headaches this was to cause me, once Alex got to Paris.

'The girls smile at me,' he announced. 'You never see that happen in Moscow.'

'I'm glad. Just don't forget about security.'

Very soon I realized that keeping the short reins on Alex where the ladies were concerned could turn into a problem for the Department. Preventive measures were called for. Emergency measures. I had to get through to James on the phone.

'Help,' I said. 'I need help.'

'What's the matter?'

'Look, it's getting impossible. I can't control him much longer. The minute I let him out of my sight he's going to end up in some *boudoir* somewhere. He is extremely restless.'

There was a sigh at the other end of the line. 'We'll have to do something about that, then, won't we?'

Shortly after lunch I received a message at my hotel saying that the cargo was being shipped with the utmost urgency, and gave me the flight number. 'You'll recognize one of the four.'

'You can relax now, Alex,' I told him. 'The girl situation is being attended to. They're on their way now, four of them.'

'Oh! What are they like? How old are they?'

'Never mind, you'll like them. We only supply the best, you ought to know that by now.'

I drove out to Orly Airport to pick up the Special Branch ladies. 'What's the victim like?' was the first thing they wanted to know.

'Our VIP?' I said. 'Very distinguished, very charming. I have him all spruced up for you.'

I took the four girls straight to the safe house. The Department had taken over a suite of rooms on the floor, so there was no reason for them to be put up elsewhere. I told the tall, leggy blonde of the group to knock on the door opposite and introduce herself.

I stationed myself around the corner to listen. I heard the rapping on the door, a shuffling noise as of a chair being pulled away from the table. Then came the sound of the girl's voice, simultaneous with the door creaking open. 'I am your present from the Department.'

The girls stayed at the flat for the whole time Penkovsky was in Paris. That evening Penkovsky and I, together with the Department watchdog who was on duty to make sure the house was not under observation, took the four girls out to dinner and afterwards to the Lido. In the following days, I'd sometimes invite them out for a drink, or on a shopping spree when they were not needed on 'duty'.

It's worth mentioning, perhaps, that these girls were not only strikingly attractive, but they hadn't been swept up from the back streets of Soho by any means. The accents, their bearing throughout was of trained security agents. And they accepted this as a part of their duties with a graciousness I found both surprising and pleasant.

But it wasn't enough to contain Alex. He seemed to have this need to go off on his own and pursue a lovely face glimpsed on the street. When I walked with him along the boulevards of Paris, he would let his eye be caught by a girl in a short skirt, and say, 'You won't be needing me for the next few hours, Greville, will you? You shouldn't work too hard, it isn't good for you.'

I shook my head firmly. 'No. Out of the question. Come on, Alex, you *know* better.'

Another time, it had been arranged that he and I would meet in a restaurant in the Avenue Friedland. When I got there I found that the restaurant was closed and there was no sign of Alex. What I'd been trained to do in such cases was not to hang about. If the contact is not made at the scheduled time, the agent must go away for a few minutes, then try again. I did just that. Five minutes later, I had another look. I walked around the block a few times – it was raining buckets that day, so I had to take my time dodging under shop awnings – and fully twenty minutes had gone past when, finally, I spotted him.

He was standing in the doorway of a small chemist's shop, half a block down the street from the restaurant where we were originally supposed to meet. There were two girls with him, and he had an arm around each one.

'There's Greville!' he shouted.

I walked quickly over and said, wearily, 'All right, Alex. They've got to go.'

He wasn't happy about that, not happy at all. Vainly he protested, but I would not budge. The two ladies watched us while Alex bellowed at me and I quietly went on insisting. No, Alex. It's just not on, Alex. Let's go now, Alex. Finally I pulled some francs from my pocket and gave each of his companions a wad, motioning and trying to shoo them away. At first they refused, until I took them by the arm and pushed them away while they gave their opinion of me in a shrill French. Perhaps it was just as well I couldn't understand it.

Alex's indignation gave way to sullenness after that. I don't think he quite realized that he had picked up two tarts. All of my explanations would not satisfy him. He could get all the girls he wanted, if you please, and my meddling was not appreciated. I took him and the girls from MI6 to the Moulin Rouge again that evening, he was still sulking.

I mention this incident only because it gives some idea of the strain he was under during those weeks in Paris. Any other man would have broken, I should think. What we were putting him through, no matter how we tried to sugar-coat the pill with day trips to Fontainebleau, afternoons in the Louvre, champagne corks popping at the Moulin Rouge, the burden was too much for him.

And yet he knew he was free to come over to us at any time he wished. Alex had done more than enough. Arranging his disappearance in Paris would have presented not the slightest difficulty. The British and Americans had been sincere with their offer of citizenship, physical and financial security, and he knew that if they accepted him as a senior military officer, a very reasonable sort of life was his for the asking. Why go back?

It was Alex's decision to make. London had instructed me not to influence him in any way, and I didn't. I could see, however, that thoughts of his family weighed heavily on his mind. It would be unpleasant for them, very unpleasant.

There was another cause for moodiness in that Alex knew he was going to have to face the long Russian winter without me. It was most unlikely that my business affairs would provide me with an excuse for returning to Moscow in the near future. Other arrangements would have to be made.

I flew off to Yugoslavia for a week while Alex carried on with his double duties in Paris, returning just a few days before the Soviets were scheduled to pack their bags. James told me later that Alex continued to co-operate fully during my absence, and managed to attend the rounds of factory visits and embassy cocktail parties. But, he said, you could tell the old light-heartedness was missing. Alex was the boat and I was the anchor. He was used to working with me, his trust in me was total. It was a kind of dependency relationship that often happens in the spying business, paralleling, to some extent, the way I regarded James. There has to be one man you can trust, one man who knows what you know.

I was the middle link between James and Alex and now the chain was going to be broken, rather than endanger my cover. All the free-flowing champagne, all the girls, all the wonderful sights of Paris that we indulged ourselves with in Alex's remaining days in Paris were not enough to keep his mind from the gloomy, apprehensive certainty that we might not ever have the chance to see each other again. I felt it, too.

17

Arrested

Nobody knows exactly when or exactly why the KGB first became suspicious of Colonel Oleg Penkovsky and cautiously, ever so cautiously at first, so as not to risk playing the fool in the eyes of their rival Intelligence service, began to shadow his movements, summon his Moscow friends to their Dzerzhinski Street HQ to answer 'routine' inquiries, and build up a dossier on him.

Almost certainly it began as a consequence of Alex's fast-rising star in Soviet trade circles. Levin was terribly pleased with the work he'd done in London and Paris, Pavlov had sent glowing reports praising Alex's minor espionage coups in obtaining inside information about British industrial processes. For 1962, Alex was being considered for an important post in the Soviet delegation to the Seattle World's Fair and to a Book Fair held in Cyprus. When London got word of this, they had their agents in both countries rent flats well in advance under innocuous cover-identities, just in case we would get a chance of make use of them.

Before leaving Paris, Alex had been briefed on the procedures that would keep the information flowing through the pipeline when I could not be in Moscow to act as a go-between. We gave him the names and telephone numbers of about a dozen members of the British and American diplomatic staff, and he had been introduced to the attractive wife of the commercial attaché at our Moscow embassy, who happened to be in Paris on holiday then, and agreed to co-operate in the elaborate plan.

As a result of the confession that Alex's interrogators

wrung out of him, the names of these British and American diplomats came out at the Moscow trial of May 1963, and this was followed by the Russians ordering their immediate expulsion. The Foreign Office made its usual noises when this happened: 'How absurd. Utterly without foundation. We absolutely deny all knowledge of this affair,' etc.

Official denials of this sort must always be taken at their 'official' value, but it certainly seems ridiculous to try to keep up the hollow pretence that British Intelligence does not use agents with diplomatic cover. We do it, the Americans do it, the Russians are past masters at it, and everybody knows that's part of the game.

At first, all seemed to be going smoothly. Direct contacts were always preferable, so in a matter of weeks after his return to Moscow in October 1961, Alex had started to rendezvous with one of our agents at the Balkan Restaurant on Sadovnicheskaya Prospekt. The following month, November, Alex and his family were given a long holiday in the Caucasus. His wife was then expecting their second child.

When he returned, the embassy wife mentioned earlier became his new contact. He was present at an official reception where the two of them were ostensibly 'introduced' and, in weeks to come, meetings were arranged while that lady was strolling with her children in Gorky Park. It came out at the trial that, on at least one occasion, film was passed in a box of sweets handed to one of the children, causing as much of a sensation in the Moscow courtroom as it did when the news hit the British press.

In January 1962 there was the first incident. Alex came a bit early to the rendezvous and noticed a small car parked in the vicinity. There were two men in the car. Alex did not stay for a closer look at them. The following week, when he turned up, the car was nowhere to be seen. But the week after that, he thought he spotted the same sinister vehicle cruising slowly up and down the main road that gave access to the rendezvous point.

Now, there was no choice but to implement the plan that called for material to change hands at the dead-drops, 'letterboxes' as they're called. When Alex had film for us, he rang the number of an American embassy aide, but said nothing when the phone was answered at the other end. As a further precaution, the agent who took the call would have to look for a mark chalked on a lamp-post at some distance from his home. That was the all-safe signal. Hours later, a different agent would be dispatched to the pick-up point – there were several that they used in rotation: a steam radiator in a suburban apartment block, a headstone in a Moscow graveyard. The letterbox system is not a popular one with spies because it doubles your chances of being observed, when the material is brought to the cache and again when it is recovered.

By that time, London had made its decision. Alex had to get out. Several plans were suggested and, for one or another reason, had to be discarded, including one that called for a rendezvous with one of our submarines. In the end, MI6 came up with a scheme that seemed to us then the least risky alternative. It called for the construction of a mobile exhibition caravan designed to tour the circuit of European trade fairs. I would take charge of the project, line up companies to rent display space where a selection of heavy industrial equipment could be transported, at considerable savings, from one city to another.

All that spring I was busy drawing up the plans and supervising construction. I designed it so that the two units together were sixty-five feet long from end to end and, when fully mounted, were divided into four sections that could each hold up to two tons of equipment. In addition to that, there was a built-in kitchen just behind the driver's cab, a fitted bar in the conference room, toilet facilities, even space for a Mini Minor for transporting people to and from the exhibition.

The company directors who booked the caravans were all extremely pleased, they thought it a great idea for attacting new export business. But that was not the purpose. The only reason that justified the £35,000 that it cost to have these vehicles built to my specifications was a concealed space just behind the driver's compartment of the towing van, a space just long enough and wide enough for a tall man to lie down and be hidden.

We were prepared to go to any lengths to get Penkovsky safely out of the Soviet Union.

But building the caravans took time, far too much time. One delay followed another: lack of parts, union restrictions. Soon it was obvious that the vehicles would not be ready until mid-autumn. And that was infuriating, because the Soviets had scheduled a trade fair to be held in Leningrad in late September. We had been aiming for an earlier delivery date, in the hope of making it to Leningrad. Now it looked out of the question.

There still remained one, no, two chances to get him out. The mobile exhibition caravans ought to be ready by October. That would still give us time to be in Bucharest at mid-month for the first British trade exhibition held in Romania. And after that, I was counting on obtaining official permission from the Hungarian government to mount a private exhibition in Budapest. Budapest would have been the better choice because it was no more than a two-hour drive from there to the Austrian border.

Accordingly, the means had to be found to see to it that Alex could make it across the Soviet frontier to whichever of the two satellite capitals was playing host to the exhibition when he made his break. The department put its experts to work and produced a set of beautiful forgeries of the array of documents that every Soviet citizen is required to carry with him to prove identity: an institutional work pass, residence permit, and, of course, a passport. This documentation was smuggled into Russia and would be ready for him when he needed it.

In July I went to Moscow for three days to go before the Committee and explain my proposals for eventually bringing the caravans to the Soviet Union. Alex was there to greet me at the airport, but it was a changed Alex, a man whose powerful frame sagged from haggardness, exhaustion and nerves. We went directly to my room at the skyscraper Ukraine Hotel, exchanged films and discussed our preparations for effecting his escape from the Soviet Union. At Alex's suggestion, we turned on the radio and let the water run noisily from the taps to foil any bugging device.

It was a wise precaution, but all in vain. Later, in Lubyanka, the KGB played a tape of this conversation. They had some device that washed out the background noise we were so careful to provide. For Alex was right, and the KGB had the two of us under surveillance. Still, they dared not make a move until they were absolutely sure, until they caught him red-handed with the evidence.

On the last evening of my stay in Moscow we were supposed to meet at the Peking Restaurant for dinner. I waited there for him, saw him walk by the entrance without looking at me and followed him a good distance behind, to an alleyway. 'You're being followed. You must get out quickly! Six o'clock tomorrow morning at the airport.'

I followed his instructions to the letter. When Alex got to the airport, he took me aside and said, 'You've got to go on the first plane that goes to the West. What time does your flight leave?'

It was scheduled for noon. 'That's no good,' he said. 'I'll use my credentials and get your ticket changed.'

He did exactly that; and I managed to get aboard a flight

to Copenhagen that left shortly after nine.

In London, the risks were carefully weighed. How much did the KGB know? Our margin of safety depended on that. If it was all part of a routine investigation connected with Alex obtaining permission to go to Seattle or Cyprus, then, most likely, we were in the clear. If, on the other hand, he was definitely suspected of spying for the West, they could be simply giving him enough rope so that he could identify his Moscow contacts. Either line of conjecture meant that Alex conceivably might be arrested at any time.

In late September, the caravans had been road-tested and were ready for their maiden voyage. A professional driver took them down to Vienna, where I was waiting. Then the caravans went to Bucharest, and I set off for Budapest. The Hungarian government granted me permission to set up my caravans as from the last week in October. It all seemed business as usual, but I didn't like the way things were developing. A feeling that I was being watched. A new interpreter was assigned to me, and there was something about him I didn't care for at all.

I was glad when I returned to Vienna and made contact with MI6. In Moscow, Alex was still passing information to us. The word from London was go ahead. Proceed to Budapest and wait for our signal.

My thoughts, naturally enough, were entirely given over to the dangers of the mission, the timing, to keeping up my cover. It wasn't until I arrived in Bucharest to rendezvous with my caravan and catch the last days of the Romanian trade fair that I discovered that people there – as, indeed, people all over the world – were gravely preoccupied with the fast-breaking confrontation between Kennedy and Khrushchev that was showing every sign of getting dangerously out of hand.

October 1962: the Cuban missile crisis.

The short-wave radio in the caravan gave me the details. For the past week, American reconnaissance flights had brought back definite evidence that Russian freighters were docking in Cuban ports and unloading supplies and equipment for rocket-launching installations. The USSR was putting offensive land-based missiles only ninety miles from the United States border.

My mind raced back in time to an overcast afternoon three years earlier, when I'd been pretending to watch a football match and listening to the man sitting next to me telling me about matters that even inside the Kremlin were talked about in whispers.

Major Kuznov told me the whole story then, and later, when his package of documents was recovered, it was confirmed in every particular. It was then and there, and thanks entirely to Kuznov's resourcefulness, that the Americans were given advance warning of the Russian plan to station their short- and medium-range missiles on the Caribbean island where Castro had come to power just three months earlier, and still had not declared himself a Communist and ally of the Soviets. The grey men in the Kremlin were making their plans as far back as that.

But the truly startling piece of news was Kuznov's explanation of *why* Khrushchev and his friends were willing to make such an obviously provocative move against the United States. Kuznov claimed that the Kremlin saw it as a matter of strategic necessity because without a base for their rockets that was within easy striking range of North America, the entire Soviet ICBM system was, for all practical purposes, an empty threat.

The problem, he said, was not the rockets themselves, not the warheads, but in the long-range guidance systems needed to direct the rockets to their targets. Apparently they were having serious difficulties with the mico-thin wire and miniature circuitry at the heart of the system. Nothing the Russians could come up with could guarantee them any reasonable degree of accuracy. In the course of testing, there had been serious accidents where hundreds of soldiers and technicians had died when their rockets exploded on the launch pad or wobbled out of control after take-off.

Thus, in 1959, the Russians already had their eyes hungrily on Cuba.

The Americans, to their credit, have acknowledged that the information Alex gave them enabled President Kennedy to strengthen his hand in the crisis and avoid a war that nobody wanted.

What has not been said is how he did it. He did it by providing unquestionable proof that the Soviet position in a nuclear exchange was virtually a hopeless one.

Again, it was the guidance systems. By sending missiles to Cuba requiring only short-range gear, Khrushchev had left his own country in no condition to withstand an American attack. He had, in fact, denuded his country's land-based nuclear umbrella to send those rockets to Cuba. The idea was to bluff the West into thinking they could supply Cuba with unlimited quantities of operational missiles and still have enough left over to defend themselves.

Kennedy had no other choice but to make sure Khrushchev realized that the Americans had the proof in their hands. He read excerpts from the official minutes of the Central Committee meetings at which the Soviet Premier admitted his country's vulnerability in his own words. In doing so, he signed my friend Alex's death warrant. He had as much as admitted that he had a highly placed agent supplying him with the most vital secret information.

After that, it was simply a matter of rounding up everyone who conceivably could have had access to the documents in question. On 22 October 1962, Alex was arrested in Moscow. That was the day that President

Kennedy made his famous speech announcing a naval 'quarantine' of Cuba to take effect immediately.

The KGB interrogators were efficient and thorough with Alex. Eleven days later, I was picked up in Budapest where I had gone, knowing nothing of Alex's arrest, to wait for the final rendezvous and escape.

Many times I've thought about Alex, broken down under the merciless interrogation, jeered at and reviled by his countrymen as a traitor and degenerate, if he ever knew how much he had accomplished. Khrushchev's irresponsibility was self-evident now to the Kremlin colleagues who a short time afterwards were to engineer his downfall. The Russian people he loved had been saved from a war in which the only thing certain was that they were bound to be the losers. I wonder if they will ever know how much they owe him.

PART FOUR

Homecoming

18

Echo from Odessa

'How wonderful it is to be home again!'

Those were my first words to the thronging reporters who swarmed and buzzed like wasps round the RAF plane that brought me from Germany to England. We landed at Northolt shortly after noon. The familiar English sky was grey and overcast, the air unpleasantly chilly. I still had trouble making myself believe that it wasn't all just a dream.

'Mr Wynne! Over here!' A barrage of exploding flash-bulbs caught me unawares and it felt as if my eyes were being seared in their sockets with a red-hot poker. For the first time I realized what those endless days of prison gloom and vitamin starvation had done to my eyesight.

Military police cleared a path for me at the foot of the gangway. I blinked away the painful black spots and took the steps one at a time. A half-dozen or so youngish men in shadow-striped suits and gleaming black Oxfords came forward to escort me to the VIP lounge.

'Would you like a chair?' somebody asked.

'No. No, thank you. I prefer to stand.' Then, to the hordes of Fleet Street's finest, 'Can we have the pictures now and get it over and done with? Please, it's bothering my eyes.' All but a few inconsiderate nitwits complied.

Roger had remained on board the plane until the reporters bore me off; he now paused briefly outside the reception room but did not come in. Seeing that I was all right, he quietly slipped away. The smartly dressed Whitehall welcoming committee would see me the rest of the way home.

My eye was suddenly caught by a tall, lanky man in his

forties who seemed to be directing the operation. My God, I thought, where have I seen this chap before? Then I remembered. He was a long-time customer at my Chelsea local, the 'Cross Keys'. I would always see him in the pub in the days when I used to make a habit of stopping in before dinner for a pint and a chat with the regulars.

Now, here he was looking terribly spruced-up and official, and when he saw the ridge of my nose wrinkled in bewilderment, he gave me a sly, knowing look, as if to say, 'Well, Wynne; now you know.' I was just stunned. For a few brief moments I could think of nothing else, as the realization hit home. All these years – my own people were having me watched.

Yes, surely it's the same one. I remembered that he always used to be in the pub when I went there at weekends for lunch. Memory pictured him sitting at a corner table with a fair-haired woman who could have been his wife or girlfriend. She often had a French poodle sitting at her feet. I don't recall that they ever did much mixing with the regulars, but then, I hadn't any reason to pay attention to the couple. Now I saw clearly that they were two trained agents sent by James to keep a watchful eye on me and make sure I was not misbehaving or developing a drinking problem.

The reporters were hushed, waiting for me to begin the press conference. They must have noticed the peculiar expression on my face and attributed it to mental strain and confusion. The truth, if they had only known it, would have provided them with a very different sort of sensational copy. Shock gave way to professional petulance. James had damn well better have a good explanation for this, I thought angrily.

A torrent of questions from the newspapermen distracted me from any further thoughts on this, however. Most of the queries were asinine and trivial. Did I make any toys for my son in prison? What books did I read? Mr Wynne, can you tell us how you're feeling right now?

'I feel just about the way I look. Judge for yourselves, gentlemen.'

One of them asked if I knew about Gordon Lonsdale, the Russian agent the British had to exchange to get me back. I had to be cagey here so I told them, 'Lonsdale? Who is Lonsdale? Oh yes . . . there was something about a trial. No, no one ever told me that I was being exchanged for this Lonsdale. They just told me I was being moved.'

Which is almost, but not quite, the whole truth. Indeed, I knew exactly who the man who insisted on calling himself Gordon Lonsdale was. For a very good reason. Konon Molody (his real name) had been arrested in January 1961, putting paid to a five-year career in which he ran one of the most successful spy networks in Britain. Two underlings who worked at the Admiralty Underwater Research Station at Portland naval base had fed him secret plans and data. Lonsdale, his two agents and another couple who acted as radio operators for the team were put on trial in March 1961, and Lonsdale received a twenty-five-year prison term.

That was just a few weeks before I returned to Moscow to make my second attempt to get through to Penkovsky. And it was then that James told me that Lonsdale would be my 'insurance policy' (as he put it) if I ever ran into any trouble over there. The Russians were keen to have him back. This was a year before the Americans exchanged their prize catch, Colonel Rudolf Abel, for downed U-2 pilot Francis Gary Powers, setting the precedent for future exchanges. But at the same time it was made clear to me that it would take time for the policy to mature. As long as five years, they said; in any case until the secrets that Lonsdale carried around in his head were out of date. As it turned out, I was not exchanged until Lonsdale had served three years of his sentence, by which time the value of any information he might have given his Russian masters was virtually nil.

All throughout my captivity, I remembered the promise

James had made. Willing myself to survive, I kept on telling myself that they dare not let me die. All their efforts to break me down, both physically and psychologically, were attempts at putting pressure on the British Government. This was why they granted my wife a visa, a cynical way of letting Whitehall know that my health had deteriorated. She saw me in March; a month later I was freed at the East German border.

The reporters stepped up their questioning. More bloody-minded, irrelevant nonsense. Did I learn to speak Russian. Did I miss a sex life?

'Of course,' I replied. 'But I'll do my best to make up for it now.'

One reporter wanted to know why I pleaded guilty at my trial in Moscow. I dodged it, of course, saying that I did not wish to talk about those matters now. 'Things have happened so swiftly. I need time to gather myself together.'

With that, the conference ended. After I put a brief phone call through to my wife to let her know I was on my way home (the Department had informed her of my imminent release twenty-four hours earlier), the men from Whitehall led me off to a grey Rover.

There were crowds of the curious, policemen, TV cameramen, half the population of London, it seemed, choking the street in front of my house. People rushed up to the car; I felt like a triumphant pop star. Photographers leaned out from the top-storey windows and peered from behind the chimney-tops of the neighbours' homes. There were cheers as I got out of the car and bobbies pushed back the crowd so that I could stumble to my own front gate. I appreciated the cheering and managed a wave and a beaming smile.

Sheila was standing in the front garden. As I threaded my way through, she came running up to give me a welcoming embrace; it was a very emotional moment for both of us.

My son Andrew stood by the door, looking understandably perplexed at this gaunt stranger with the deep-lined face and stubble of grey hair. It didn't look much like the father he remembered, the father he'd last seen two years ago. Then we all posed for a picture and went inside.

The first few days after my return are not too clear in memory; I was still dazed by the shock of my release and the excitement. Friends and neighbours with the very best of intentions kept turning up at all hours to bid me welcome. Ian, the landlord of the 'Cross Keys', arrived that same afternoon with a case of champagne but I wisely decided to sleep through the festivities.

Not everyone was glad to see me, though. Our cat, a big black-and-white Tom named Whisky, took one look at me when I came through the door and scampered away in terror. We'd always got on well when I was at home but, for about a week thereafter, he didn't want to have anything to do with me.

The press, meanwhile, intensified their siege. My wife or I would answer the door in the evenings and be greeted by the glare of TV floodlights. 'Mrs Wynne . . . Could you please establish . . . ?' Or 'Just one picture.' This went on night and day without respite.

The day after my release I had a visit from two Harley Street doctors. It was given out to the newspapers that these were my family doctor and his assistant, whereas actually it was the Department who arranged for them to give me a thorough going-over. It wasn't much of an examination, but I was told to take things very easy for a while yet.

Take it easy! The phone was constantly ringing; it took the Post Office a few days to change the number for us. The newspaper people continued to pitch their tents on my doorstep, and if Sheila tried to go out to do some simple shopping, they would pounce and badger her with more of their inane 'human interest' questions. Worse for me, I was eating and drinking not wisely but too well, trying to make up for all those hungry months in Lubyanka and Vladimir. Smoking, too. I was going through three packs a day, lighting one cigarette right after another. Not surprisingly, on the fourth day after I returned home, I suffered a total nervous collapse.

I was sitting in an armchair in the lounge when it happened, and I cannot recall any extraordinary sensations associated with the experience. Apparently my wife lost no time summoning the two MI6 physicians. I was injected with a sedative and taken away by ambulance to the Gordon Hospital in Vauxhall Bridge Road.

I, however, knew nothing of this. The only part I can remember is waking up in hospital surrounded by white-coated doctors and nurses who asked me how I felt. 'What the hell has been happening to me?' I demanded.

'You're all right now,' was all I got for a reply. I certainly didn't feel it. My body was completely drained of strength and I couldn't get my eyes to focus. My left arm was pitted like a drug addict's and my thighs and bottom felt good and tender.

'What have you been doing to me?' I whispered. They told me that I had been kept under sedation for twelve days, awakened from time to time for feeding, and then given injections to knock me out again. I could recollect nothing of the semi-lucid intervals.

Next morning they let me sit up in bed and gradually the dizziness and nausea ebbed. After two days of tablets and injections, they allowed me to have a go at standing on my feet. I tottered a bit at first, but by the fourth day I was able to walk around pretty well and read for short periods.

When the doctors saw I was able to sit up in a chair, they told me that I might as well do my sitting at home. Three nurses working shifts looked after me round the clock and monitored my progress. Soon I was able to take short walks in the garden and felt my strength return to me. Two fingers of Vat 69 in the evening, self-prescribed, probably helped as much as anything to speed my recovery.

The official verdict was that my breakdown was in part due to the delayed-reaction shock that followed my release from the Russian prison as well as being simply the effect of too much rich food and drink on a system that had not been prepared for anything so substantial as home-made steak-and-kidney pies.

I had to go from one Harley Street doctor to another in the days that followed to get a final balance sheet on my health. Nothing could be done to put right the damage from lack of vitamins and general malnutrition. I had nearly all my teeth extracted and an eye specialist fitted me for spectacles – I'd never had to use them before. Additionally, one side of my face had collapsed when I'd been struck by my KGB interrogator; a bit of plastic surgery was necessary to fix that. I'd lost a lot of hair, too.

The final physical reaction to Lubyanka was a hernia. Eating had pushed the top of my intestine through my bowel. The remedy for that was a long diet, and I underwent treatment at a health farm until it eventually eased off.

By then I was feeling almost fit again, and did not mind a bit when I got word from the Department, setting up a meeting. Two months or more had gone by since I'd been sprung from Lubyanka, and during all this time I'd had only second-hand contacts with the Department. People are surprised that I wasn't immediately hauled off for a debriefing or instructed how to handle the growing publicity. James and Roger had confidence in me. I went to Hyde Park by taxi, got out and crossed the bridge over the Serpentine, walked to the other end of the park where James was waiting in a taxi. We drove round the outer circle once or twice, then signalled the driver to pull over.

'Now look,' James began as we strolled down the path, 'you need a holiday. You still look pretty bloody awful. Where do you want to go?'

'Up the Amazon,' I replied, trying to make a joke.

'All right. I'll fix it.' He started to walk away.

'Hold up a minute! I don't think my wife will want to go up the bloody Amazon and I'm not sure I do either.'

'Look,' James said firmly, 'just go somewhere and build yourself up. I don't like to see you looking like this. Give me a ring when you've decided where you want to go, eh?'

I went to Cook's and came home loaded with brochures. The French had a ship called the *Antilles* that made a six-week cruise to Trinidad, Martinique, Guadeloupe and Barbados. That sounded just about ideal.

I was also anxious for Sheila to get away for a time. Ever since the KGB picked me up in Budapest, it had not been pleasant for her. James came directly to explain the situation. That was when she first learned the truth about my double life. The Department did what it could to ease her through the ordeal, looking after family expenses while I remained in gaol, and arranging for several women to act as live-in companion and run interference with the reporters. Three times she came to Moscow and, every week, there had been a letter and various packages of food and warm clothing – none of which, of course, the Soviets let me have. Sheila had been wonderfully loyal, acted with great dignity and affection, and I knew these last couple of weeks had been a terrible strain for her too.

While we waited for the sailing date, there was one other matter that occupied my attention. The only way I could see of getting the newspapers off my back was to make a deal with one of them and let the others know it was an exclusive. Several offers had come in – the sensational papers bidding high against each other – but I finally decided to go with the *Sunday Telegraph*, as I felt confident they'd be more likely to stick to the facts.

So it was a tremendous relief when at long last we were able to get away for our holiday. Even then, the reporters would not let us wriggle off the hook. A friendly purser warned us when we came on board that Chapman Pincher and Walter Terry had booked as far as Vigo, so we had to lock ourselves in our cabin until we were shot of those two.

I had been hoping that a long sea voyage with plenty of sun and quiet would be just the thing for me. There was plenty for me to think about. I still had no clear idea of what I was going to do with myself, what sort of future plans I should start thinking about. Alas, the sun-drenched Caribbean, with its palm trees, exotic birds and rioting colours, proved too much a distraction for such weighty considerations as these. But I daresay it did me a lot of good. After spending a few weeks in Barbados, we flew to Bermuda, a place I'd always wanted to have a look at. An American couple offered the use of their magnificent beach house, servants and all. While we were in Hamilton, a Royal Navy frigate called in port and the captain invited us to come aboard for a dazzling reception. I was beginning to see that being a celebrity had its good side.

Sheila and I were both happily relaxing in Bermuda when one day a completely unexpected phone call shook us from our interlude of lethargy and luxury. The voice, American and unidentified, began by saying, 'I think you might have met some mutual friends of ours at an address in London on Coleherne Court.'

'Ah . . . Yes, I'm with you.'

'Well, Mr Wynne, we were wondering if you might care to extend your holiday by a few days and pay us a visit in New York.'

'I've already got passage back to England for my wife and myself.'

'No problem at all. You can transfer your ticket to New York and sail home on the *Queen Elizabeth*. At our expense, you understand.'

Who could say no to an offer like that? Telling Sheila that there might be some business prospects in the offing, we flew up to New York for a few days at the behest of the

CIA and, between rounds of sightseeing and shopping, I met several times with America's espionage and counter-intelligence experts.

There were three of them working in a team, and they said they were very interested in my future plans. If they could do anything to help, I had only to ask. 'Right now I'm still convalescing,' I told them, 'but possibly later on I might consider setting up a sales promotion agency for companies in Canada, or South America.'

'Then take your time. We'd be only too happy to supply you with introductions here and there.'

I promised I wouldn't forget. The following day, when we met by the Metropolitan Museum of Art, we walked a few blocks to a very posh and exclusive hotel where I was taken upstairs to a lavishly decorated suite of rooms. A voice I immediately recognized said, 'It's Greville!'

Major Sergei Kuznov bounded over to welcome me. We talked for quite a while over drinks, about my imprisonment, about Alex, and half a hundred other things. In New York, Kuznov was in his element – or perhaps I should say the former Kuznov, for hardly a trace now remained of the Soviet major whose fate had brushed with mine in that far away port city on the Black Sea. He had grown into his new identity – the English he spoke was fluent and peppered with American slang.

Also, while I was in New York, I sat down and leafed through a heavy album filled with photographs of suspected Soviet agents, in the event I came across any of them.

We had pleasant sailing back to Southampton on the *Queen Elizabeth*; the papers trumpeted 'Wynne arrives tanned and fit'. I had put on weight and was beginning to feel something like my old self again. I was eager to get back to work. But what work is there for a cover-blown spy in this world of ours? Soon enough, I would find out for myself.

19

The CIA Entertains

Making a new start in life at the age of forty-five is by no means a negligible undertaking, even under the best of circumstances; for a somewhat shopworn secret agent, the process was a doubly complicated and painful one.

To begin with, I was hoping that I could rebuild my agency work in some other part of the world, once all the fuss died down a bit. That was naïve of me, I'll grant you. It was rather like asking a mother to bring her child to Dr Jekyll's surgery for a check-up, immunization shot and lollipop. Although the boundary line between my spying and my business career had always been clear in my own mind, other people, of course, perceived things in a different way.

After a few lunch dates with some of my contacts, it was made clear, with polite noises, that no firm in Britain would possibly consider taking me on as their representative. Confidentiality would always be suspect in everyone's mind. What's this fellow Wynne really up to this time? To make it worse, the Soviet Government, in an act of phenomenally petty vindictiveness, ordered a boycott of all the companies I'd previously had dealings with. That was their way of putting a fright into other businessmen who might be induced to do similar favours for their country.

On top of that, the newspapers would not let off fanning the flames of public notoriety. Every time I'd go out for a walk young boys would trail after me yelping, 'Spy, spy, spy!' attracting the stares of passers-by in the street. There were threatening letters. A certain lorry-driver wrote once a week: 'I know where you live and the pubs you go to, and

I'll mow you down in the street next time I see you.' (All such hate mail was forwarded to MI6 and investigated.) On the other hand, I did not mind so much the autograph hunters and well-meaning people who'd approach me in restaurants and pubs, shake my hand and offer to stand me a drink. It showed that there were decent, fair-minded countrymen of mine who had given some thought to my experiences and appreciated that there were people willing enough to do something (as one chap put it) 'to show those bloody Commies we mean business'.

My term of imprisonment had not cured me of my love of travel, new faces and new experiences. I happened to mention this to James one day and added that I was beginning to miss my former gypsy-like existence.

'Well,' he observed, 'your name came up recently when I was talking to our American cousins. They say you're welcome to go there any time and they'd be only too pleased to show you around, let you meet all their tycoons.'

'I think I just might take them up on that.'

'Also,' James continued, 'it might be worthwhile to think about it – about starting up business over there. My understanding is that if you should decide to settle in the States, our friends are prepared to help you.'

At the very least, it promised a welcome change of scene; so I immediately said yes to the proposal. Sheila was invited to join me, but after our Caribbean cruise of six months ago, she had had her fill of travelling. As always, her desire was for the simple home life. She always was a quieter, less outgoing person than me. Most definitely she was not keen on leaving home just now and leaving our son at his boarding-school, so I decided to go over on my own.

The red-carpet treatment began even before I left London. At the US Embassy, I was allowed to jump the queue to deal with the formalities of a visa. I booked a first-class stateroom on the *Leonardo da Vinci* and flew to Genoa to meet her.

The crossing was uneventful, no reporters on my tail this time. Nearing New York, I had a radio telegram from a CIA man, 'Al', whom I'd met on my previous visit. 'Greetings: will visit you on board', it said, and that's exactly what he did. As the boat steamed into the mouth of the Hudson River, past the Statue of Liberty and the spectacular Manhattan skyline, a pilot boat chugged up alongside the liner and there was Al on the deck, waving to me. He and another CIA chap climbed up the ladder. He introduced his friend to me as Rodney, and the two of them had only to flash a card to get me through Immigration and Customs as soon as we tied up.

From there I was taken by car to the towering and exceedingly posh New York Hilton. Al and Rodney accompanied me to my room on the thirtieth floor to make sure I was comfortably settled in. Everything was laid out for me: Scotch and ice, an itinerary of business appointments, and a cheque-book. A more than ample sum of dollars had been deposited in an account opened under my name, and I was told just to ask if I needed more.

Rodney then started to show me how to work the air-conditioning, but it appeared there was something wrong with this particular unit. 'You stay here and fix it,' Al said to his colleague. 'We'll go down to the bar, it's far too hot in here.' Twenty minutes later, Rodney joined us and announced, 'It's working now.'

I had to raise my glass to my lips to cover a superior smirk. Good God, I thought, don't they know I'm an old hand at this sort of thing? As soon as I was alone, I took a careful look at the air-conditioner but decided not to bother taking it apart. The bug they'd obviously planted could be elsewhere in the room. I just went down to the lobby and asked if I could have a room on the lower floor. I wonder what my two CIA babysitters thought when they heard strange voices coming out of their earphones. If they really wanted to be stuffy about it and bug my room while I was out, there wasn't much I could do to prevent it but, just to be on the cautious side, I dismantled my telephone every morning in case there had been a listening device planted there during my absence.

Later than evening I joined Al in the lobby. He suggested a steak dinner at a celebrated Broadway restaurant. All the time we were together, Al categorically refused to touch a drop of drink. Does the straitlaced CIA have a rule about no drinking while on duty? I did not want to embarrass him by asking. He just sat there and looked at me whenever there was a bottle of wine on the table as if he would have loved to join me, but daren't so much as take a sniff. Rodney, on the other hand, was a different sort of personality, a lot more relaxed and enjoyable to be with. Al was a man doing his job – doing it too well, I reflected, hiring cars, seeing to travel arrangements and making himself useful, whereas I would have much preferred to be left to my own devices. Still, I have to allow that New York is far from the safest of cities to wander about in, and it would have been terrible from their point of view if Greville Wynne, having stood up to the worst that the Soviet police state could throw at him, were to be found bleeding to death on some Manhattan sidewalk, the victim of a mugger.

Early the next morning began the rounds of visits that were to be my introduction to American industry. The very American adage about 'starting at the top' was nowhere better proved than by my first stop, the Wall Street offices of a very well-known banker whose name it is perhaps better not to mention. That gentleman gave me two hours of his time, answering my questions and explaining the inner workings of American finance.

Nothing had quite prepared me for an encounter like this. The interview was held in an 'office' so large that two London buses could have been parked side by side without bruising the panelled walls. These were all covered with paintings by modern masters. A thick carpet spread over acres of floor space, at one end of which the banker had his desk and an electronic control board for routing telephone calls that came in from all over the world. While we talked, he accepted just two calls, one convening a meeting of the World Bank, another to order the demolition of a building on Paris's Champs Elysées. At the end of this extraordinary conversation, he invited me to his penthouse suite facing Central Park for cocktails and dinner afterwards with various other guests.

While I was in New York, I was given constant reminders by Al and Rodney about the dangers of wandering around the streets after dark. From the way they described it, it did sound a pretty ghastly business. But I was more intrigued than frightened. 'If it's as bad as all that, I'd like to have a look for myself. Interesting to see how it operates. You two are the experts, I take it.'

'Well, I don't know . . .' began Al.

Rodney just laughed. 'You're certainly an odd sort of tourist. What's the matter, the Empire State Building isn't good enough for you?'

But I stuck to my request and they talked it over between themselves, wondering whether Washington would have to be advised, until Rodney said, 'The hell with it. I'll go over to Queens with Greville and look in a couple of places. If it so happens that there's some action on tonight, then that's fine.'

I never did get a clear idea of exactly where it was that Rodney took me. Surprisingly, the bar itself was not the squalid dump that imagination had pictured it. It was quiet inside, and the furnishings made some pretence of smartness. The same could not be said of the patrons. Men and women alike, they seemed a fairly unsavoury lot. We sat in a booth upholstered in plastic. 'Now you watch this fellow who's just come in,' Rodney said, taking a pull at his beer. 'Here's the way it's done. Look at his hand between his forefinger and thumb.' I looked. When the curly-haired customer rubbed his chin, I could see a red square and a green cross inked on the web of his hand. 'That means he's got two different drugs for sale, heroin and cocaine,' Rodney observed. A few minutes later an unpleasant-looking type in a dirty, fleece-lined corduroy jacket slid on to the adjacent stool. Some conversation passed between them. The prospective buyer touched the red square to indicate the nature of his purchase, and counted off on his fingers to signal the quantity or the price of the desired goods. I couldn't be sure which it was. The drug merchant went off to the toilet while the other man hung back another minute or so before following him to complete the transaction.

It was all so very familiar. Contact in a public place. Using a lavatory to exchange illicit materials because it guaranteed privacy and easy access. For the first time it struck me to what an uncanny extent the two worlds overlapped, the spy's and the criminal's.

Al and Rodney took another two days to show me what I wanted to see of New York, then it was time to be off and get down to the real purpose of my American visit: meeting other businessmen and manufacturers. The list of companies I wanted to call on was itself a representative cross-section of my interests: chemicals, plastics, machine tools and electrical engineering; I still wasn't quite sure what I wanted to get into but was confident in my ability to smell out an opportunity.

First stop was Detroit, where I went to see a company that had developed a highly advanced and completely automated system for producing machine tools to exact specifications. The engineer in me was fascinated by all that ingenuity. We visited other machine-tool factories in the Detroit area and took the Greyhound bus to Chicago because I wanted to see as much of the country as I could squeeze in while I was there. We stayed in that city two weeks, making the rounds of manufacturers who specialized in engineering components, switchgear, and heavy electrical equipment. Ever vigilant and seldom letting me far from their sight, the CIA provided me with a Playboy Club key to make the most of my free evenings.

We then travelled on to the West Coast via the celebrated Sante Fe railway. For three days, the train winds along at a comfortable speed through the spectacular scenery of the American Southwest, each twist of the line enabling passengers – most of whom seemed to be elderly ladies – to catch the panoramic views from shifting perspectives. At the Grand Canyon, one coach was shunted on to a siding for those travellers who wanted an extra day's sightseeing. It was a very civilized trip, the food was reasonable and the service quite good. My only grumble was that one or two of the states we passed through still practised some form of prohibition.

I cannot say I was much impressed with what I saw of Los Angeles. Built on one level, the city is architecturally rather tatty; one- or two-storey imitation-Spanish stucco buildings stretched for miles along the tangle of urban freeways, lit up by garish neon signs advertising hamburgers and used-car lots. San Francisco was much more to my taste, an extraordinarily beautiful and easy-going city, one of the most attractive in the world, I'd say.

We flew on to Seattle, another pleasant city and manufacturing centre. Here, as elsewhere, I was impressed by the extraordinarily hospitable American way of doing business. The directors of the firms I visited almost all invited me to their homes for dinner or a drink. I stayed in Seattle for close on a·month, thinking seriously that if I did want to relocate myself and set up a concern in the US, Seattle might not be such a bad place to do it. A very melancholy occasion for me was when the CIA took me round one evening to see the apartment they had rented a year in advance to be used as a safe house for Alex if and when he came to the World's Fair.

On my way back to New York, a thoroughly satiated sightseer, I stayed a few days in Washington to meet with senior CIA officials so that they could hear directly from me everything that had happened during the Penkovsky assignment and its aftermath. Most of the facts they already knew, but they spent a week picking my brain for the minute details. It was while I was in Washington that I was informed that President Johnson had expressed a wish to meet me. Unfortunately, the President was in Texas at the moment and feeling unwell. 'If you don't mind staying on for a week or so longer . . .' Al said.

'Not at all. It's a great honour.'

'Then that's fine. Just take things easy, why don't you. Where would you like to go?'

Miami, I said on sudden impulse – much to my subsequent regret. The CIA gave me first-class air-tickets, plenty of pocket money and told me to behave myself. What a hideous place Miami turned out to be! Gigantic air-conditioned boxes for hotels, all crawling with the most detestable children I've ever had the misfortune to see in any country of the world. Screeching and bawling, the little terrors infested the parks and beaches and the corridors of the hotels. Their middle-class mothers, hair done up in curlers, made no effort to keep them under control. Four days of Miami was more than enough for me. Without letting Al and Rodney know of my change of plans, I flew back to New York and booked myself into a more modest hotel. When they caught up with me just three days later, the CIA were furious, but when I explained how I needed some time on my own, Al had to relent. 'I can't force you to take sound advice,' he said ominously. The next day he was back with a tear-gas weapon that you wore concealed up your sleeve. 'If the pollution and the traffic don't finish you off,' he grunted, 'maybe this will give you some protection from the muggers at least.' Thankfully, I did not run into any muggers. Yet the next time I met my two guardian angels from the CIA, they seemed to be unusually well-informed about my nocturnal social life. So they put a tail on me after all!

At my request, the CIA arranged for Melvin McKinnon to come up from Philadelphia for a reunion. In my previous book, *The Man from Moscow*, I wrote about him under the name of 'Kelly' – he was the young (I think no more than twenty-three), frail American who for a short time shared my prison cell in Vladimir. The Russians had caught him taking pictures where he shouldn't have and slapped an eight-year sentence on him. He had to serve two and a half years of his terms until the Russians released him, afraid that he was going to die. Certainly he was in terrible shape when they put us together in Vladimir, coughing and spitting up blood. The Soviets later sent him to a hard-labour camp in the fever-ridden swamps of the south, and he'd nearly died there. I'd asked about him on my previous trip to New York and was told that he was then undergoing open-heart surgery.

Now the CIA installed McKinnon and his fiancée in the New York Hilton, and we had dinner together, talking over these not very pleasant memories we shared. My former cell-mate was healthy and in good spirits. It was obvious the CIA was taking care of him medically and financially. Since we dared not speak of such things in Vladimir, it was only now that he confirmed that he had been no more of an innocent victim than I was. The CIA had recruited him as a student at the University of West Berlin. Prompted as much by a sense of adventure as by patriotism, he agreed to go to Russia as a tourist and take the pictures. It was now clear to him that the CIA had used him as a diversion to cover another agent who was operating in the vicinity. No, he said, he bore the CIA no ill-will on that account. His deep Christian faith remained unshaken by his experiences.

By this time I had been in America for three and a half months, and was anxious to get back to London to see how work on my house was coming along. Accordingly, I told my CIA liaison that I hoped the President would still wish to see me after he had recovered completely, but preferred to be off. Perhaps something could be arranged in the future? Al and Rodney nodded their understanding. I sailed back to England on board the *New Amsterdam*, still uncertain of what to do with myself in the future.

20

The 'Concordski' Affair

A cover-blown spy is decidedly a liability for any intelligence service. Apart from the direct damage sustained by the organization when an agent is exposed and the operation compromised, it is the long-term effect of publicity at home and a propaganda jamboree on the other side that worry the spy chiefs, but only to the extent that the facts which come to light reveal an accurate picture of their methods and resources. The value of any single piece of information depends on the other fellow not knowing that you possess it.

Thus, for their protection as well as mine, MI6 had woven an ingenious fabric of half-truths to shroud the Penkovsky case in mystery and, insofar as my life depended on it, throw the KGB off the scent if I were caught. As a result of this, when I was released from prison and returned to England, the press and public all had a jolly time trying to unravel the threads. I did nothing to enlighten them – at first, that is.

The story the Soviets gave out to the world when Alex and I went on trial before the Supreme Court of the USSR in May 1963 had in large part been scripted months in advance by James and his colleagues. The impression it was designed to convey was of a somewhat naïve businessman who had been gulled at first and subsequently pressured into working for British Intelligence against his will. In his own testimony, Alex protected me: one more debt I shall never be able to repay him now. He told his interrogators that he had practically bullied me into taking that first package of secret documents out of Moscow under a threat of breaking off business contacts if I refused. I stood in the dock and related how I had been put in touch with MI6 through an imaginary security officer at one of my companies. I said that I had been given false assurances that the nature of the contacts I was asked to maintain with Alex were a matter of secret trade negotiations – nothing whatsoever to do with the dirty business of espionage. Later, as the trusting, albeit rather thick-witted, Greville Wynne of the scenario had begun to get suspicious, the ungentlemanly types from the Foreign Office had threatened to take measures ensuring that his business would be ruined if he did not co-operate.

How much of this the Russians believed, I can't really say. Whatever they thought privately, it suited their purposes if the story was left to stand. The reason for that was that all along they were hoping to use me as bait in the proposed exchange for Gordon Lonsdale. It made them look very good indeed if the world thought they were sacrificing an inept pawn for a powerful KGB spymaster. In other words, it was good domestic public relations for them if, by minimizing my own importance, it appeared that they had got the better of the deal.

As a result of this tactic, the Soviet prosecutor demanded only an eight-year sentence for me. Alex was condemned to death. Five days after the final rap of the gavel, Tass announced that Alex's execution had been carried out in secret. The arch-traitor Penkovsky, whose love of loose living had led him to sell out the Soviet motherland, had received his just due.

Inevitably, the stratagem that saved my life gave rise to speculation and wild conjecture. Had Wynne's confession been the result of 'brainwashing'? How much of it was true? Was Penkovsky really executed? Or had the British fallen victim to an extravagant conspiracy? Some maintained that Penkovsky, as an intelligence agent (the Soviets had not admitted that) tricked Wynne (the guileless businessman) into compromising himself to obtain worthless information so as to have a scapegoat for a show trial to whip up domestic frenzy against the West.

For two years I kept quiet and let the 'experts' have the field to themselves. The reason why I did this was simple: Alex was still alive. Kept under constant armed guard, brutalized, but alive, in a nameless village hidden in the swamplands of the south, one of the uncharted islets of the Gulag. Killing him outright was not in keeping with the policy of the practical-minded Kremlin bosses. They wanted him alive for further interrogation, to assess the damage he had done. As the seriousness of what he had disclosed to the West became apparent, the heads began to roll. Marshal Varentsov, the head of their rocketry programme, was dismissed, and Serov, chief of the GRU, packed off into obscurity. In 1964, came the ousting of Khrushchev.

The following year, MI6 received proof from one of its agents in the Soviet Union that no further harm could come to Alex as a result of the truth being made public. He had succeeded in his final act of defiance against the régime he detested: he took his own life.

It was then that I asked for and received permission to write a book about my involvement with Oleg Penkovsky. The Americans had already come out with *The Penkovsky Papers*, based on documents that Alex had smuggled to the West (I am certain these were authentic, by the way) and, at the Department's suggestion, I agreed to write a preface to the book.

I felt that it was about time that we did some blowing of our own trumpet and that if anyone was going to write a book about the Penkovsky affair, it ought to be me.

In December 1967, when *The Man from Moscow* was published, the cat was out of the bag and I was back in the headlines. 'Greville Wynne comes up as a secret agent.' It's true, I had resented all the remarks that chided the government for having agreed to exchange a valuable Russian spy for a hapless businessman. That part of the record I was glad to have set straight. It was dismaying, however, to find that not everyone was prepared to believe that Alex had been a genuine defector.

One result of the world-wide publicity *The Man from Moscow* received was, curiously, that I was able to make myself useful to the Department again on a semi-official basis. Now that it was abundantly clear that I did have a long-standing working relationship with British Intelligence, it was convenient for me to act as their representative in making contacts with friendly Intelligence services. At the Department's request, I have travelled to West Germany, Switzerland, France, and other European countries to meet with their agents, when certain types of information had to be exchanged. I can only say that part of this work was connected with the spy-hunts that came about as a result of information Alex had given us.

Ironically, because the Soviets did such a splendid job of publicizing my name and features in their propaganda circus, I have been approached by more than one East European defector in the years following my release. After all, defection is not an easy matter. Here I must keep the details vague. But as I travelled through Europe, I would be approached by individuals who asked, 'I understand certain friends of yours may be able to help me with my problem.' My standard reply would be something along the lines of 'Yes, well, ring this number at 2 P.M. and ask to speak to Edward.' Or I might be asked to take a package.

In March 1969, I was living in Malta when a call came through from MI6, asking me to return to London to make myself available for a special assignment.

My life had undergone many changes by then. Realizing that I was unlikely to improve as a husband, Sheila and I had agreed to a divorce. I was travelling around Europe, as I had been doing for some time, with my secretary, translator and girlfriend. I had joined a consortium of

international financiers as anchor-man for a development
scheme calling for the construction of a high-rise shopping
centre and office-block complex in the Maltese capital. My
secretary came back with me to London and we stayed for
several weeks. Two visits to a safe house in a northern
suburb of London were necessary to explain the outlines of
the mission to me.

A former aide of James's was in charge of the operation.
'We want you to be at Heathrow on a certain day to make
contact with one of our agents – well, in any event, a man
who's been very useful to us. He's an East German who's
been working both sides of the fence.'

'Why does it have to be me?' I asked.

'Oh, you know him,' replied James's colleague. 'More to
the point, he knows you. In fact, you were the one who put
us on to him a few years back. Recognize the picture?'

I looked hard at it for a few seconds and then I placed
him. A tall, cadaverously thin fellow – an East German
who was in charge of promotion at the Leipzig Trade Fair.
That would have been about 1959 or 1960, in the interim
between the Kuznov and Penkovsky assignments. My
orders then were to play it safe and look after my business
interests, and under no circumstances to do anything to risk
my cover.

The East German made his approach as I was finishing a
cup of coffee in a restaurant near the exhibition area.
Without warning, he sat down next to me with his elbow on
the table and a conspiratorial squint. 'Ah . . . Mr Wynne. I
must ask you for your help regarding a certain matter. It is
most delicate. You have been to the German Democratic
Republic before, I understand. I thought, well, as an
experienced traveller in the Socialist countries, surely you
must know of people in Britain . . . special people, you
understand . . .'

I hadn't been sure what he was leading up to, but decided

to cut him off before he got there. 'Look here,' I said curtly, 'I'm not sure that I get your meaning but it's best if you just drop it. I'm here on business. Please don't approach me again.'

'Oh . . . I *am* sorry,' he muttered and had to collect himself before he went on his way. But a little later I managed to find a photograph in which he appeared among the publicity shots taken at the fair and passed it on to James. I had never thought to ask what action was taken, and the whole affair slipped from my mind.

The young man from MI6 said, 'He's a double, of course.'

'But you're using him.'

'Quite. We need you to meet him at the airport and give him a certain small canister, with our compliments. His regular contact is unavailable and he refuses to deal with a stranger. But he remembers you and knows you've been working for us. He's agreed to the transfer only on condition that you represent us.'

One of the other men at the briefing picked up a note-pad and made a rough sketch of the international departure lounge at Heathrow airport. 'We've booked you two tickets on a flight to Malta leaving at almost the same time our boy gets on a plane to East Berlin. You'll have to be there a little early to intercept him on his way to the gate. There's a bar over here. That's where you station yourself. He comes, maybe has a drink, and walks away with our little souvenir.'

Following instructions, I turned up the day before the rendezvous was to take place for a meeting with James in Hyde Park. We went for a drive in the Bentley, pulled over in a shady spot, and James handed me the canister. It was about the size and shape of an ordinary spool of Kodak film. 'Here's the routine,' he said. 'You are to wait there at the bar. He'll make the approach. He is going to squeeze up next to you and order a drink and all you have to do is slip him the canister. You've seen what he looks like, and he's been shown an up-to-date picture of you and your wife. So there's no reason for you to have to speak with him.'

'It sounds simple enough. He's a double agent, you say?'

'Always has been, but we're getting a lot more than we give. He demands big money for his services, but it's well worth it, you know.'

At 4 P.M. the next day, my secretary and I were in the lounge at Heathrow Airport. Our flight to Malta was due to leave at 5.05. It was a Sunday, and the main terminal was filled with travellers, so it made sense when I suggested we go through passport control straightaway and have a coffee by ourselves, apart from the crush. After about a quarter of an hour, I spotted my contact. He was carrying a khaki overcoat over one arm, a newspaper and an old-fashioned black satchel case. One quick look round, and he started walking towards my end of the bar. Then all at once he stopped, gazing briefly in my direction, spun on his heels and glanced back at me once again. Hastily, he searched around the lounge for an empty table, and found one as far away as he could get from where we were sitting.

What's the matter? Has he spotted someone watching him – or me? That was all I could think. I hunched over my drink, trying to puzzle it out and decide what to do next. My instructions were to wait, and as I waited I grew increasingly worried.

A metallic voice over the loudspeaker system announced that the Polish (Lot) Airlines flight to East Berlin and Warsaw was ready for boarding. I saw my contact get up and walk to the queue that started to form at the final checkpoint. Abruptly I turned to my secretary and said, 'Let's go over to the departure bay now. It doesn't matter if we're early, we'll be able to get some decent seats for a change.' I threw some coins on the bar and got up, hurrying as fast as I dared after the elusive East German.

He slowed down a bit as I caught up with him, his sallow face frozen in a mask. 'What's the matter?' I hissed.

'The woman,' he said, and glanced over his shoulder at my poor secretary, who was struggling with our travelling cases and wondering what in the world was going on.

'She's my girlfriend. It's all right.'

'Oh, I knew it wasn't your wife. In the photograph I saw, you were with a different woman.'

As he spoke, his fingers fumbled with the snap-catch on his satchel, and I nudged over close to him, bumping shoulders and muttering, 'Excuse me.' The little canister of film that I fished from my pocket dropped into the satchel. 'That's done it,' the East German said. 'Now our Russian friends are going to have a surprise when they test their supersonic passenger jetliner. Pleasant flight, Mr Wynne.' Immediately he veered off, and with my secretary now joining me, I showed my passport at the final checkpoint and proceeded to the departure gate where, forty-five minutes later, our BEA Trident took off on schedule for Malta.

Four days after the airport encounter we were settled into our flat at Msida, overlooking the yacht harbour of Valletta. We had gone out for dinner and drinks and it was late in the evening by the time we returned. 'The telephone's ringing inside,' my secretary said, as she fumbled with her key in the door. I picked up the receiver and a voice said, 'Greville? You know who this is. All hell will shortly be let loose in London. The papers are coming out with a story that you've defected to the East. Headline news. Thought I'd better warn you.'

'Go on,' I said, lowering my voice.

'A constable by the checkpoint at Heathrow saw you going through just when the flight to Berlin and Warsaw was boarding. He was a new chap and made out an official report stating that you were among the passengers on that flight. A senior detective at the airport countersigned it, without checking. Brennard's, the news agency, got wind of it and phoned the news to every paper in Fleet Street.

'You'll have to handle the situation as best you can, I'm afraid,' James said before ringing off.

Within the hour, the phone resumed its incessant jangling. Mattresses and eiderdowns over the infernal thing didn't help much to muffle the noise. Then the banging at the door started. 'We'll sit it out,' I said to my secretary. 'After a while, they'll give up and go home.' My annoyance had hardened into stubbornness. Perhaps it was not very clever of me, but I did not think it was wise to face the reporters until I had a chance to see what was in the press reports. If there was anything to connect me with that East German, I'd have to get a story ready. The ringing and banging continued throughout the night.

At eight o'clock the next morning, I put on my dressing-gown and flung open the door. 'Mr Wynne!' they exclaimed – a handful of reporters had kept the siege up all night.

'I'm not saying anything until I've had a chance to see the newspapers. They won't be in until three, as you very well know. Come back at half past and I'll have a statement for you.'

'But Mr Wynne . . .' they began, and I had to slam the door in their faces. That afternoon, when I had a chance to scan the headlines – 'Wynne Sensation', 'British Spy's Mystery Trip Behind Iron Curtain' – I summoned the reporters in and showed them the stamp in my passport proving that I had entered Malta on the date in question. I let them know that I was extremely angry about this, as it might jeopardize my business dealings with Malta which at that moment had reached a delicate stage.

The news was wired out from Malta, and it took a few days more for the dust to settle. Scotland Yard held an inquiry to determine why the young constable who started the whole mess did not check my ticket, as he should have done, to see where I was going. The East German Foreign Ministry rather huffily announced that 'Mr Wynne is *persona non grata* in Communist countries for obvious reasons', as if the matter was ever in doubt. Eventually, all the newspapers printed formal retractions of the story and I had an apology from the news agency who originally circulated the story.

And there, for the public, the matter ended. As well it should have. But I wanted to find out more. The next time I came to London I rang the old number and asked James to meet me in the bar of the Ritz Hotel.

'Anything the matter?' he wanted to know.

'No – nothing like that. I just thought we might have a chat.'

When I came to the bar, James was sitting off in a corner with a glass of Scotch. 'Mind telling me what I can do for you this time?' he inquired mildly.

'Buy me a drink, for one thing. And then fill me in on what your boys have done to the poor Russians and their supersonic plane.'

There was no change of expression, I'll give him credit for that. 'Really, Greville, it's you who should do the explaining,' he said.

'Well, that scene at the airport. When I dropped the canister the other fellow dropped a hint.'

'I see.'

'Naughty of him, wasn't it? But what's done is done. I'm hoping you can give me the whole story. Might as well, you know.'

James conceded the point. It all began years before, he recounted, when the Russians pulled off something of an intelligence coup by bribing a British engineer to photograph the complete plans and specification for our country's prestige airliner, the VC-10. The Soviets built what amounted to a near-exact replica of the plane. If I'm not mistaken, it's still in service today over there. Apparently my old acquaintance from East Germany had been the courier who managed to get the VC-10 plans out of Britain.

Eventually British Intelligence unravelled the story and traced the leak back to the British Aircraft Corporation. In the late 1960s, when we got together with the French to develop a supersonic passenger aircraft, the same East German national was approached by our people and persuaded (or threatened or bribed, probably a combination of both, from what I gather) to act as a double, under their control. Likewise, the engineer who sold the VC-10 plans was allowed to continue his work at the British Aircraft Corporation. It was a typical move by our people. Rather than arrest a spy, who anyway will be replaced by another one – the 'devil you know versus the devil you don't know' hypothesis – it is standard practice to 'turn' him, either knowingly or unknowingly, against the other side by feeding him misleading information.

Thus, thanks to some quick thinking the Concorde carbon-copy Tupolev Tu-144 has proved a tremendous headache to the Russians. The East German agent was paid a very substantial amount of money and almost-but-not-quite-genuine plans were exchanged for the real item. It is particularly unfortunate that we could not have known that Russian stupidity was to cause the death of fifteen innocent people when the 'Concordski' made its maiden flight in public at the Paris Air Show.

I don't think that British Intelligence can be held responsible for the tragedy. In their mad rush to beat the West in the race to develop a supersonic passenger aircraft, the Soviet engineers had not bothered to test the plane adequately. There had been some directive from on high telling them that they had to get the plane in the air in time for the Paris Air show on 3 June 1973.

I was there and I saw it happen. I was one of the 30,000 people in the crowd who watched, fascinated, as the real Concorde – ours – made a graceful demonstration flight. Certainly I was not expecting the horrifying sight that followed as the needle-nosed Soviet plane tried to imitate the Concorde's manoeuvre and pulled into a steep climb. All at once there was a gasp from the crowd as the Concordski plunged uncontrollably into a vertical dive. Plummeting inexorably down on the village of Goussainville, the aircraft exploded in a ball of red-orange flame, the wings shearing off and spewing red-hot debris.

The Russians blamed the disaster on pilot error. I can't see how anyone could have been convinced of that. After years of further testing, it finally had to be withdrawn from service, I've read. It seems the airframe is no good. The Concordski could manage only the lightest loads and rattled so noisily that passengers in the cabin had to shout to make themselves understood.

Except for the Paris tragedy which could not have been foreseen by anyone, it would have been a just and costly lesson to the Russians. After all, it is not as if we sabotaged *their* plane. As long as they continue to spend money on pilfered plans rather than finance research and development programmes for their industry, it may even happen again. For those who traffic in other nations' secrets, the rule has always been: let the buyer beware.

If this were a work of fiction, I should have been careful to provide a swell of excitement at the end, for the reader's benefit. I am sorry that reality has not been so obliging. Bringing my story up to date required only a brief mention of places and people. In 1970, I was married for the second time. For two years I stayed on in Malta working on the property-development scheme mentioned earlier. In the end, however, it had to be abandoned. Since that time, I have been involved with developments in Gibraltar, Cyprus, Spain and the Canary Islands, and on the Mediterranean island of Majorca where I have found plenty to keep me occupied and reasonably prosperous in several types of business ventures. Recently my time has been devoted to the development of a commercial rose-growing enterprise, producing cut flowers for export. James, now approaching eighty, is retired and farming in Sussex. From time to time, he sits in on discussions at MI6 headquarters where his wealth of experience and expertise is still valued by the younger generation of spy-chiefs who are now running the show.

Admittedly, it is not terribly likely, but I sometimes wonder if someday I will pick up the phone and hear his voice again. Let's have a drink together, Greville. When are you free for lunch? In a way, it might be pleasant; that tingling of the blood knowing that something's come up. No; those days are past for me, I'm afraid. Not that I feel particularly regretful. As far as spying is concerned, I think I have more than earned my retirement.